Amish-Country Cookbook

Volume III

More Favorite recipes gathered by
Das Dutchman Essenhaus

Edited by Bob and Sue Miller, Anita Sekora
Artwork by Harriet Miller

Bethel Publishing, Elkhart, IN

Bethel Publishing Company
1819 South Main Street
Elkhart, in 46516

Printed in the United States of America

ISBN 0-934998-49-3

Beginnings

Das Dutchman Essenhaus, Amish Country Kitchen, is located in Middlebury, Indiana. It is a family restaurant, offering a varied menu and a unique atmosphere, not only to local patrons, but also to visitors from other states and many foreign countries. The large restaurant seats 600 diners and on a busy day serves 6,000 meals.

The Owners, Bob and Sue Miller, grew up near Sugarcreek, a small settlement in the heart of Ohio Amish country, where Christian living and good home cooking were everyday experiences. They, along with their five children, moved to Middlebury and purchased the tiny Curve Inn restaurant where they continued this tradition. After a little remodeling and the hiring of 25 ambitious employees, they opened in 1971 as Das Dutchman Essenhaus.

Because of the Miller's belief in good service, good measure and good food, the business prospered, making frequent additions necessary. After one year of business, the **bakery** received a much-needed addition to meet the growing demand for pies. Increasing popularity with visitors and tour groups led to the 1975 **barn addition**, two floors of large family dining rooms accommodating groups from two to 300. Here guests enjoy delicious down-home meals in a lofty, barn-like setting of heavy oak beams, antiques and country decor.

Over the years that followed, there has been steady growth, including two more additions to the bakery. In 1984, an adjacent farm was acquired. Some of its buildings were removed and others renovated. A three-story chicken barn became a **gift shop**; a Quonset-style farm implement shed is now a **clothing store**; and a corn crib and dairy barn were transformed into a **craft store**, **book loft** and **candy kitchen**. Two antique log cabins, dismantled and reassembled at Essenhaus, provide housing for a **handweaving operation**. Other recent additions are a **silo observation tower**, an **outlet store** and a **homemade noodle operation**.

Essenhaus Country Inn was built to resemble an Amish farmhouse, complete with windmill and pond, and opened for occupancy in 1986. These accommodations were recently enlarged by the renovation of a nearby Amish home into **Dawdy Haus Inn**.

In 1993, trails and a heavy-timbered **covered bridge** were added to accommodate carriage and buggy rides.

Many guests, after enjoying their unforgettable experience at Essenhaus, ask about the unique recipes prepared in the Essenhaus kitchens. The Millers responded with a cookbook filled with their own original recipes, as well as others gathered from their employees. Many of these recipes had never been published previously. After the phenomenal acceptance of the first edition, the Millers provided a second, and now a third, edition of the **Amish Country Cookbook**.

The desire of the Millers and all of their employees, now numbering as high as 350 at peak season, is to provide quality products and service and to make every guest feel "at home in Amish country."

Contents

EQUIVALENCY CHART

1 pound flour	4 cups
3 cups cornmeal	1 pound
1 medium lemon	3 tablespoons juice
1 medium apple, chopped	1 cup
1 medium orange	1/3 cup juice
1 pound unshelled walnuts	1 1/2 to 1 3/4 cups shelled
2 cups sugar	1 pound
3 1/2 cups powdered sugar	1 pound
2 1/2 cups brown sugar	1 pound
7 ounces spaghetti	4 cups cooked
4 ounces uncooked noodles (1 1/2 - 2 cups)	2-3 cups cooked
4 ounces uncooked macaroni (1-1 1/4 cups)	2 1/4 cups cooked
6 cups cooked macaroni	8-ounce package
7 cups cooked noodles	8-ounce package
28 saltine crackers	1 cup fine crumbs
2 tablespoons fat	1 ounce
2 2/3 cups coconut	1 1/2-pound carton
16 marshmallows	1/4 pound
14 square graham crackers	1 cup fine crumbs
22 vanilla wafers	1 cup fine crumbs
1 1/2 slices bread	1 cup soft crumbs
8-10 egg whites	1 cup
10-12 egg yolks	1 cup
1 egg	4 tablespoons liquid
1 cup chopped nuts	1/4 pound
3 1/2 cups almonds	1 pound
3 cups walnuts (broken	1 pound
3 1/4 cup seeded raisins	15-ounce package
3 cups seedless raisins	15-ounce package
2 1/3 cups rice	1 pound
5 cups grated American cheese	1 pound
2 2/3 cups cubed American cheese	1 pound
6 2/3 tablespoons cream cheese	3-ounce package
Grated peel of lemon	1 tablespoon
Grated peel of orange	2 tablespoons
1 medium banana, mashed.	1/3 cup
1 pound carrots	4 medium or 6 small; 3 cups shredded; 2 1/2 cups diced
5 cups ground coffee	1 pound
1 cup whipping cream	2 cups whipped
1 cup evaporated milk	3 cups whipped

SUBSTITUTIONS

1 T. cornstarch (for thickening)	2 T. flour or 2 tsp. quick-cooking tapioca
1 tsp. baking powder	1/4 tsp. baking soda + 1/2 tsp. cream of tartar
1 c. powdered sugar	1 c. granulated sugar + 1 tsp. cornstarch (Whirl in blender or processor until powdered)
1/2 c. brown sugar	2 T. molasses in 1/2 c. granulated sugar
1 c. sour milk	1 T. lemon juice or vinegar + sweet milk to make (let stand 5 min.)
1 c. whole milk	1/2 c. evaporated milk + 1/2 c. water or 1 c. reconstituted non-fat dry milk + 1 T. butter or 1/3 c. dry milk + 1 c. water
3/4 c. cracker crumbs	1 c. bread crumbs
1 sq. (1 oz.) chocolate	3 or 4 T. cocoa + 1 T butter or margarine
1 T. fresh herbs	1 tsp. dried herbs
1 small fresh onion	1 T. instant minced onion, rehydrated
1 tsp. dry mustard	1 T. prepared mustard
1 c. tomato juice	1/2 c. tomato sauce + 1/2 c. water
1 c. catsup or chili sauce	1 c. tomato sauce + 1/2c. sugar and 2 T vinegar(for use in cooking)
3 medium bananas	1 c. mashed bananas
10 miniature marshmallows	1 large marshmallow

Brown and White Sugars: Usually may be used interchangeably, measure for measure. Brown sugar must be firmly packed.

MISCELLANEOUS HOUSEHOLD HINTS

MICROWAVE HINTS

1. Place an open box of hardened brown sugar in the microwave with 1 cup hot water. Microwave at high for 1 1/2 to 2 minutes for 1/2 pound or 2 to 3 minutes for 1 pound.

2. Soften one 8-ounce package of cream cheese by microwaving at 30 % power for 2 to 2 1/2 minutes. One 3-ounce package of cream cheese will soften in 1 1/2 to 2 minutes.

3. Thaw whipped topping...a 4 1/2 ounce carton will thaw in 1 minute on the defrost setting. Whipped topping should be slightly firm in the center but it will blend well when stirred. Do not overthaw!

4. Soften Jello that has set up too hard—perhaps you were to chill it until slightly thickened and forgot it. Heat on a low setting for a very short time.

5. To make dry bread crumbs, cut 6 slices bread into 1/2-inch cubes. Microwave in 3-quart casserole 6-7 minutes, or until dry, stirring after 3 minutes. Crush in blender.

6. Refresh stale potato chips, crackers or other snacks of such type by putting a plateful in the microwave oven for about 30-45 seconds. Let stand for 1 minute to crisp. Cereals can also be crisped.

7. Nuts will be easier to shell if you place 2 cups of nuts in a 1-quart casserole with 1 cup of water. Cook for 4 to 5 minutes and the nutmeats will slip out whole after cracking the shell.

8. For stamp collectors: place a few drops of water on stamp to be removed from envelope. Heat in the microwave for 20 seconds and the stamp will come right off.

9. Shaping meatloaf into a ring eliminates undercooked center. A glass set in the center of a dish can serve as the mold.

10. Heat left-over custard and use it as frosting for a cake.

11. Toast coconut in the microwave. Watch closely as it browns quickly once it begins to brown. Spread 1/2 cup coconut in a pie plate and cook for 3-4 minutes, stirring every 30 seconds after 2 minutes.

TERMS AND DEFINITIONS

Baste: To pour or spoon pan drippings, marinade, or cooking juices over meats while cooking to prevent drying out and to add flavor.

Bone: To remove the bones from meat, poultry, or fish, to "debone".

Cream: To soften a fat, especially butter, by beating it at room temperature. Butter and flour or butter and sugar are often creamed together, to make a smooth, soft paste.

Cube: To cut into cubes 1/2 inch on a side or larger.

Cut In: To combine solid fats and dry ingredients, especially shortening and flour, by chopping with two knives or with a pastry blender.

Dice: To cut into cubes less than 1/2 inch in size.

Dredge: To coat lightly with flour, cornmeal, etc.

Drippings: Juices and browned particles that collect in the bottom of the pan in which meat or poultry has been roasted; used to enrich and flavor sauces and gravies.

Fillet: To debone meat or fish. A fillet is the resulting tenderloin of beef or piece of fish without bones.

Fold: To incorporate a delicate substance, such as whipped cream or beaten egg whites, into another substance without releasing air bubbles. A spatula is used to gently bring part of the mixture from the bottom of the bowl to the top; the process is repeated, while slowly rotating the bowl, until the ingredients are thoroughly blended.

Fry: To cook food in hot oil or fat, usually over direct heat. The food is not stirred, but is simply cooked on one or both sides. Deep-fat fry. To cook food by immersing it completely in heated fat. Stir-fry. A Chinese method of preparing meat or vegetables by cooking very rapidly in a frying pan or wok over high heat, stirring constantly.

Glaze: To cover with a glossy coating, either a concentrated stock for meats or a melted and somewhat diluted jelly for fruit deserts.

Marinade: Usually a strong flavored liquid, cooked or uncooked, used to make meats tastier and more tender, typically made of wine, olive oil, or a combination of the two, and seasoned with carrots, onions, bay leaf, and other herbs and spices. Other popular marinades are based on soy sauce or lemon juice. A dry marinade is a combination of herbs and spices rubbed into meat, which is then allowed to stand before cooking. To marinate is to let food stand in marinade, either at room temperature or (for a longer time) in the refrigerator, before cooking. Most recipes specify the length of time to marinate; recipes vary from 1/2 hour to overnight to a couple of days.

Poach: To cook very gently in hot liquid kept just below the boiling point.

Puree: To mash foods until perfectly smooth by hand, by rubbing through a sieve or food mill, or by whirling in a blender or food processor.

Saute: To cook and/or brown food in a small quantity of very hot fat, stirring or turning frequently.

Scald: To heat just below the boiling point, when tiny bubbles appear at the edge of the saucepan.

Score: To cut shallow slits or lines in meat or fish, usually in a diamond pattern. As well as being decorative, scoring allows seasonings to penetrate more easily. Score the fat edge of steaks to be broiled, to keep them from curling.

Sear: To brown and seal the surface of meat quickly, in a very hot oven or in a frying pan, over high heat.

Simmer: To cook in liquid just below the boiling point. the surface of the liquid should be barely moving, broken from time to time by slowly rising bubbles.

Steep: To let food stand in (hot) liquid to extract or to enhance flavor, like tea in hot water or poached fruits in sugar syrup.

Toss: To combine ingredients gently with a lifting motion.

Snacks, Dips, Appetizers & Beverages

SEASONING GUIDE

Get acquainted with spices and herbs. Add in small amounts, 1/4 teaspoon for each 4 servings. Taste before adding more. Crush dried herbs or snip fresh herbs before using. If substituting fresh for dried, use 3 time more fresh herbs.

APPETIZERS, SOUPS

Cranberry Juice: Add cinnamon, allspice, and/or cloves. Serve hot or chilled.

Fruit Cocktail: Try adding mint or rosemary.

Stuffed Celery: Mix caraway seed with cream cheese; fill celery. Dash with paprika.

Tomato Juice Cocktail: Add 1/4 teaspoon dried basil per cup.

Chicken Soup: Add a dash of rosemary, tarragon, or nutmeg. Sprinkle paprika on top for color.

Clam Chowder: Add a dash of caraway seed, sage, or thyme.

Consomme: Dash in basil, marjoram, savory or tarragon.

Fish Chowder: Add bay leaves, curry powder or dill.

Mushroom Soup: Season with curry, oregano or marjoram.

Onion Soup: Add marjoram.

Oyster Stew: Lightly add cayenne, mace, or marjoram.

Potato Soup: Dash with mustard or basil. Top with snipped chives or parsley.

Split - Pea Soup: Add dash basil, chili powder or rosemary.

Tomato Soup: Dash in basil, dill, oregano, sage or tarragon.

Vegetable Soup: Try allspice, oregano, sage or thyme.

Snacks, Dips, Appetizers & Beverages

FUDGE FONDUE

6 oz. chocolate chips   2 T. butter
Melt in small saucepan. Stirring constantly, add these ingredients:

1 can condensed milk   1 t. vanilla
dash salt

Cook about 5 minutes or until mixture is hot and slightly thickened. Keep warm in fondue pot while serving. If it becomes slightly thick, gradually add hot water until it is right consistency.

Substitute:
Fudge mint - 1 t. mint for vanilla
or
Butterscotch - butterscotch chips for chocolate chips

 If you enjoyed today, it wasn't wasted.

1

MOCHA SAUCE

1 can evaporated milk
1/4 c. sugar

2 t. instant coffee
4 sq. chocolate, grated

Put ingredients in fondue pot. Stir until boiling. Reduce heat and simmer gently for 5 minutes, stirring constantly. Stir in 2 t. rum.

Betty Troyer (Kitchen)

RANCH PRETZELS

1 c. vegetable oil
2 T. dill weed

1-16 oz. pkg. ranch dressing
24 oz. pretzels

Stir every 10 minutes until absorbed. Takes about 2 hours until totally absorbed.

Lorena Mast (Waitress)

SPICED PECANS

1 egg white
1/2 c. sugar
1 t. cold water

1 lb. pecan halves
1 t. salt
1/2 t. cinnamon

Beat egg whites slightly. Add water and sugar; beat until frothy, but not stiff. Fold in pecans. Add salt and cinnamon and mix well. Spread on buttered cookie sheet. Bake at 350 degrees for 1 hour.

Ellen Mishler (Hostess/Cashier)

Party and T.V. Snacks

If nature did not give you that which is yours by right,
Just nibble at these dainties to give you an appetite.

TEMPTING APPETIZER PIE

1-8 oz. cream cheese	2 T. finely chopped pepper
2 T. milk	1/2 c. sour cream
1 pkg. dried beef	1/8 t. pepper
2 T. onion	

Soften cream cheese. Add milk and blend well. Stir in beef, onion, chopped peppers, sour cream, and pepper. Mix well. Spoon into 8" glass pie plate. Heat uncovered for 2 1/2 to 3 minutes. Serve warm. Good dip for crackers.

Martha Coblentz (Bakery)

TORTILLA APPETIZERS

Filling

8 oz. sour cream	season salt, to taste
8 oz. cream cheese	garlic powder, to taste

Mix ingredients together and spread filling on 6-8 large tortilla's.

Vegetables

1 can green chili's, diced & drained	1/2 c. chopped green onions
1 c. grated cheddar cheese	4 oz. black olives, drained & chopped

Spread on top of filling on tortillas and roll each one up. Chill for several hours. Slice 1/2"-3/4" thick. Place single layer on a large platter. Electric knife makes cutting them easier.

Jan Bontrager (Waitress)

Those who say they will forgive, but can't forget an injury, simply bury the hatchet while they leave the handle out ready for immediate use. -D.L. Moody

---

BLUBBER BURNER

1 glass water
2 t. vinegar

honey to sweeten
2 t. Realemon

1 glass before each meal.

Erma Yoder (Maintenance)

LIME PUNCH

1 small box lime jello
1 c. sugar

2 c. boiling water

Make sure dry ingredients are dissolved. Add 1 large can (46 oz.) pineapple juice and enough water to make 1 gallon (2 qt.). Stir or shake well before refrigerating. Can be made several days ahead. When ready to use add 1 quart lime sherbet (optional) and 1 qt. lemon-lime soda. Can be made with any flavor jello and sherbet. Yield: 1 1/2 gal.

Mary Schlabach (Waitress)
Carolyn Hershberger (Bakery)

ORANGE JUBILEE

1-6 oz. can orange juice concentrate
1 c. milk
10-12 ice cubes

1/2 c. sugar
1 c. water
1 t. vanilla

Blend all ingredients in a blender.

Rosalie Bontrager (Manager/Inn)

 Macho does not prove mucho

ORANGE LEMONADE

1 3/4 c. sugar
2 1/2 c. water
1 1/2 c. fresh orange juice
from 5 oranges

1 1/2 c. fresh lemon juice
from 8 lemons
2 T. grated lemon peel
2 T. grated orange peel

In medium saucepan, combine sugar and water. Cook over medium heat, stirring occasionally, until sugar dissolves. Cool. Add juices and peels. Cover and let stand at room temperature for 1 hour. Strain syrup and cover and refrigerate. To serve, fill glasses or pitcher with equal amounts of fruit syrup and water. Add ice and serve. Yield: 12 servings

Iva Miller (Kitchen)

PINEAPPLE EGGNOG PUNCH

2 qt. eggnog
2 c. cold lemon-lime soda

3 c. unsweetened pineapple
juice, cold

Mix together. Add ice ring and serve immediately.

Ring

Mix 2 c. eggnog, 2 c. milk, red maraschino cherries, and green mint leaf candy. Decorate bottom of 4 1/2 c. ring mold with cherries and candy. Gently add a little of milk and eggnog mixture. Freeze solid. Add remaining mixture and freeze several hours or overnight.

Jan Bontrager (Waitress)

PUNCH

2 qt. lime or orange Kool Aid
6 qt. ginger ale

4 qt. lime or orange sherbet

Mix Kool Aid according to package directions (use only 3/4 c. sugar). Add ginger ale and sherbet. If sherbet is too firm, chop it up.

Dorothy F. Slabaugh (Bakery)

5

RHUBARB DRINK

Cover 3 quarts of rhubarb, cut in chunks, with water and cook. Let stand 1/2 hour and drain. To this juice add:

1-16 oz. can frozen orange juice
6 c. sugar
2 pkg. tropical Kool Aid

1-12 oz. can frozen lemonade
7 qt. water

Mix all together. You can add lemon-lime soda.

Betty Troyer (Kitchen)

RUSSIAN TEA

2 c. Tang
2 c. sugar
1 c. instant tea

1 pkg. lemonade mix
1 t. ground cinnamon
1 t. cloves

Mix well and store in a jar. Use 2 t. for each cup of hot water.

Gayle Martin (Bakery)

Nothing lies beyond the reach of prayer except that which lies outside the will of God.

BUTTERSCOTCH SAUCE

1 c. brown sugar
1/4 c. rich milk or half & half

1 T. corn syrup
3 T. butter or oleo

Combine all together in a saucepan. Stir over heat until boiling. Simmer 3 to 4 minutes. Good on ice cream.

Ellen Mishler (Hostess/Cashier)

CHIP DIP

2 1/2 c. sour cream

1 pkg. Lipton French Onion
Soup Mix

Stir together and serve.

Wanda Sue Bontrager (Grill Cook)

CHURCH PEANUT BUTTER SPREAD

3 c. brown sugar
5 lb. peanut butter
2 c. light corn syrup

1 lb. butter, melted
1 gallon marshmallow cream
3 c. water

Mix together.

Frieda King (Grill Cook)

CREAM CHEESE AND BEEF DIP

1 pkg. cooked beef
1-8 oz. cream cheese, soft
1/4 t. garlic salt

1/4 t. onion salt
1 T. worcestershire sauce

Tear beef into pieces. Mix all ingredients. Let stand at room temperature
at least 1/2 hour before serving.

Norma Velleman (Cashier/Restaurant Gifts)

DILL DIP

1 c. sour cream
1 T. parsley
1 t. salt

1 T. dill weed
1 t. dried onion, minced
1/3 c. mayonnaise

Mix all ingredients. Chill. Serve with vegetables as a dip.

Norma Velleman (Cashier/Restaurant Gifts)

FRUIT DIP

1 c. brown sugar
1-8 oz. cream cheese, room
temperature

1 t. vanilla

Whip ingredients well. Serve with slices of fresh fruit.

Maritta Helmuth (Waitress)
Rosanne Bontrager (Busser)
Doreen Mast (Cashier/Knot N Grain)

FRUIT DIP

2-8 oz. pkg. cream cheese
1-13 oz. jar marshmallow cream
pinch of ginger

pinch of cinnamon
2 t. strawberry jam

Mix all ingredients together. Good on all fruits.

Martha Coblentz (Bakery)

FRUIT DIP MIX

8 oz. Cool Whip
3 oz. pkg. instant vanilla pudding

juice from 16 oz. can chunk pineapple

Mix all ingredients together until well blended. Use as dip for fruits.

Barb Weaver (Restaurant Gifts)

I didn't have potatoes, so I substituted rice,
I didn't have paprika, so I used another spice.
I didn't have tomato sauce, so I used tomato paste.
A whole can, not a half. I don't believe in waste.

She said you couldn't beat it.
There must be something wrong with her.
I couldn't even eat it!

Betti Kauffman (Cashier/Hostess)

GOURMET SHRIMP SPREAD

1-8 oz. pkg. cream cheese, softened
1/4 c. mayonnaise
1 T. chopped fresh parsley
1/2 t. dill weed
2-4 1/4 oz. cans shrimp, rinsed & drained
1 T. lemon juice

Combine all ingredients and mix on medium speed until well mixed. Chill until ready to serve. Serve on crackers.

Katie Hochstedler (Bakery)

HOT BEAN DIP

3 1/2 c. refried beans
1 lb. sharp cheddar cheese, shredded
hot taco sauce, to taste
2 tomatoes, cut in wedges
1 medium onion, diced

In casserole dish, combine beans, 1/2 lb. cheese, and taco sauce. Bake at 350 degrees for 30 minutes. Mix tomatoes, onions, and remaining cheese together and place this mixture on top of the beans. Return to the oven and bake another 10 minutes.
Yield: 3 c.

Erma Swartzendruber (Office)

LEMON FRUIT DIP

1/2 c. mayonnaise
1/2 c. lemon yogurt

Mix well. Serve chilled with sliced fruit.

Carol Wiggins (Restaurant Gifts)

Some people are making such thorough preparation for rainy days that they aren't enjoying today's sunshine.

MEXICAN BEAN DIP

Brown 1 lb. hamburger. Add 1 pkg. taco mix. Put in baking dish and add in layers:

6 oz. salsa	1 can refried beans
16 oz. sour cream	shredded cheese

Bake at 400 degrees for 10 to 15 minutes. Serve with tortilla chips.

Charlotte Miller (Waitress)

NACHO DIP

1-8 oz. cream cheese	2 c. shredded cheese
1-8 oz. can Hormel Chili, no beans	

Layer in microwave pan: cream cheese followed by chili. Top with cheese. Microwave until cheese is melted. Serve with nacho chips.

Marla Mast (Waitress)

NACHO SPREAD

2 c. sour cream	1 large can refried beans
2 pkg. taco seasoning mix	

Mix together and spread in jelly roll pan. Top with any or all of the following:

shredded lettuce	chopped tomatoes
chopped green peppers	chopped onions
olives	shredded cheese

Serve with nacho chips.

Carol Detweiler (Waitress)

PIZZA DIP

8 oz. pkg. cream cheese
1 c. pizza sauce
chopped onions
chopped olives

chopped peppers
mushrooms
grated cheese

Spread the cream cheese on a platter. Top with pizza sauce. Layer all the toppings on next and top with grated cheese. Spread on crackers.

Rosanne Bontrager (Busser)

SHRIMP CURRY DIP

1 1/3 c. mayonnaise
2 t. lemon juice
1 t. - 1 T. honey
1/2 t. curry powder
salt & pepper, to taste
2 T. catsup
dash tabasco sauce

1 medium onion, diced fine
1-4 1/2 oz. can tiny shrimp pcs.
assorted fresh vegetables—washed
  broccoli, pepper strips, carrots,
  celery, cauliflower, and scallions

Combine all ingredients except vegetables. Mix and refrigerate overnight. Serve cold with vegetables. Can be thinned with milk and used as salad dressing.

DiAnn Beachy (Waitress)

SHRIMP DIP

1-8 oz. pkg. cream cheese
4 T. mayonnaise
2 T. lemon juice
2 T. grated onion

1-5 oz. can shrimp
worcestershire sauce, to taste
salt & pepper

Mix cream cheese, mayonnaise, and lemon juice until smooth. Add onion. Drain and mash shrimp. Add to mixture. Add remaining ingredients and chill.

Nancy Boyer (Waitress)

11

SPINACH DIP

1 1/2 c. sour cream
1 c. mayonnaise
1 envelope vegetable soup mix
10-oz. pkg. chopped spinach
3 green onion (chopped) or
2 t. minced onions

8 oz. can water chestnuts,
drained and chopped
1 loaf sheepherder's bread or
sourdough bread

Thaw spinach and squeeze out liquid. Add remaining ingredients and blend well. Cover; refrigerate at least 2 hours before serving. To serve, carve out center of bread; break into bite size pieces and arrange on a tray around the loaf. Stir dip thoroughly and put into hollowed out loaf. Can also be served with crackers.
Yield: 10-20

Sharman Reimer

TACO DIP

Mix together in a small bowl:

1-16 oz. sour cream
1-8 oz. pkg. cream cheese

1 pkg. taco seasoning

Spread mixture evenly on a jelly roll pan. Spread any or all of the following on top:

chopped lettuce
chopped onion
black olives

chopped tomato
shredded colby cheese
re-fried beans

Use nacho chips to dip mixture out.

Tina Powell (Kitchen)

Good and bad luck are often mistaken for good and bad judgement.
It is better to give than to lend and the cost is about the same.

TEX-MEX CHIP DIP

10 1/2 oz. jalapeno bean dip
2 bell peppers, chopped,
optional

1/2 t. salt
1/4 t. pepper

Mix:

1 c. sour cream
1/2 c. salad dressing

2 T. lemon juice
1 pkg. taco seasoning

Spread bean dip on platter. Put the peppers, salt, and pepper on top of bean dip. Spread sour cream mixture on top of peppers. Top with 8 oz. shredded cheddar cheese, 2 chopped tomatoes, and chopped green onions. Serve with chips.

Glenda Yoder (Waitress)

VEGETABLE DIP

2-8 oz. cream cheese
1-16 oz. pkg. sour cream
2 pkg. tender sliced ham,
turkey, or chicken

1/2 t. chicken base
1/2 t. onion powder
1/2 t. Lawry's season salt
worcestershire sauce, to taste

Mix cream cheese and sour cream together until smooth. Mix in remaining ingredients. Serve with your favorite vegetables.

Ruth Ann Yoder (Bakery)

VEGETABLE DIP

1 pkg. spaghetti sauce mix

16 oz. sour cream

Mix ingredients and chill overnight.

Carol Wiggins (Restaurant Gifts)

VEGETABLE DIP

2 c. sour cream
1 c. real mayonnaise

1 pkg. Hidden Valley Ranch dry mix

Stir together and serve.

Wanda Sue Bontrager (Grill Cook)

VEGETABLE DIP

1-6 oz. cream cheese
1 c. mayonnaise
2 beef bouillon cubes

garlic, to taste
onion, to taste

Mix all ingredients together and serve with fresh vegetables.

Erma Yoder (Maintenance)

Isn't it strange that you are so indispensable when you ask for a day off and so expendable when you ask for a raise.

BANANA BOATS

4 bananas
1 1/2 c. peanut butter

1 pkg. chocolate chips
toothpicks

Peel one side of banana (like a boat) and spoon out part of banana. Spoon peanut butter into boat and cover with chocolate chips. Wrap each in saran wrap and microwave for 30 to 45 seconds on high or until melted.

Jon Helmuth (Host)

CARAMEL CORN

2 c. brown sugar
1/2 c. corn syrup
2 sticks oleo
1 t. salt

1/2 t. soda
1 t. vanilla
7 qt. popped corn

Boil the brown sugar, corn syrup, oleo, and salt for 5 minutes. Take from the heat and add soda and vanilla. Pour over popcorn and mix well. Pour into cake pans and bake in 250 degree oven for 45 minutes to 1 hour, stirring often.

Freda Yutzy (Waitress)
Sophia Helmuth (Mother/Becky Helmuth(Waitress)

CARAMEL CORN (MICROWAVE)

Microwave on high for 4 1/2 minutes the following ingredients:

1 c. brown sugar
1 t. salt

1/4 c. light corn syrup
1 stick butter

Add 1/2 t. soda to the cooked mixture and stir. Pour into a grocery bag containing 5 quarts of popcorn and shake. Microwave on high and shake after 90 seconds, 60 seconds, 40 seconds, and 30 seconds.

Doreen Mast (Knot N Grain)
Susanna Miller (Cook)

CRISPY RICE BARS

1 c. light corn syrup
1 c. sugar
1 c. peanut butter

6 c. crispy rice cereal
1-6 oz. pkg. chocolate chips
1-6 oz. pkg. butterscotch chips

In a large saucepan, bring corn syrup and sugar to boil over medium heat, stirring constantly. Remove from heat. Stir in peanut butter. Fold in cereal. Press into greased 13 x 9 x 2 pan. In small saucepan, melt chocolate and butterscotch chips together over low heat, stirring constantly. Pour over bars. Chill about 15 minutes before cutting.

Dorothy Fern Slabaugh (Bakery)

FRUIT PIZZA

Cream together 1/2 c. brown sugar, 1/2 c. butter, and 1 egg. Add 1 1/3 c. flour, 1 t. baking powder, and a pinch of salt. Press in greased pan. Bake at 375 degrees for 10 minutes or until golden brown.

1/2 c. powdered sugar   1/2 t. vanilla
8 oz. cream cheese   1 T. milk

Spread over crust. Add any fruit.

Millie Whetstone (Kitchen)

GORP

1 large jar dry roasted peanuts   1-1 lb. bag M&M's peanuts
1 large box raisins   1-1 lb. bag M&M's

Mix and serve.

Fannie Yutzy (Bakery)

NUTTYO'S

1/2 c. brown sugar   1/2 t. salt
1/2 c. corn syrup   6 c. Cheerios
1/4 c. butter   1 1/2 c. pecans

Heat oven to 325 degrees. Butter jelly roll pan. Heat sugar, syrup, butter, and salt over medium heat, stirring until sugar dissolves. Cook 5 minutes. Remove from heat. Stir in cereal and nuts. Spread in pan and bake for 15 minutes. Cool for 10 minutes and loosen with spatula. Let stand for 1 hour and store in covered container.

Susanna Miller (Kitchen)

Insect bites: A little dab of toothpaste will take itching and swelling out fast.

ORIENTAL GLAZED NUTS

2 lbs. pecan or walnut halves
or whole blanched peanuts
1/3 c. packed brown sugar

dash cinnamon
safflower oil

Place nuts in large saucepan and add water to cover. Bring to boil. Boil 5 minutes, skimming off solids; drain. Place nuts in bowl and quickly stir in sugar and cinnamon, mixing until all sugar is dissolved. Heat in at least 1/2 inch oil to 375 degrees in large skillet. Add nuts carefully in small batches and cook until golden, 1 to 3 minutes. Stir and watch closely to avoid scorching. Remove with slotted spoon and spread on wax paper to cool. Do not let nuts dry in clumps. Yield: 6 to 8 cups

Jan Bontrager (Waitress)

OVEN CARAMEL CORN

2 c. brown sugar
1/2 c. corn syrup
2 sticks butter or oleo

1 t. salt
1 t. baking soda
nut meats, if desired

Boil brown sugar, syrup, and salt in a 6 quart kettle for 5 minutes. Remove from heat and add baking soda. Stir well. Have popcorn in a greased roaster and pour the hot mixture over popcorn. Place in 200 degree oven for 1 hour, stirring every 15 minutes with greased wooden spoon. Pour on greased tabletop to cool. Store in covered container to keep crisp.

Marietta Helmuth (Waitress)

Patience is the ability to idle your motor when you feel like stripping your gears.
Look for patterns in your life that trigger stress and get rid of them. (This does not include spouse or children!)

OYSTER CRACKERS

1 pkg. Hidden Valley dry
ranch dressing
1 c. vegetable oil
2 bags or 2 boxes oyster crackers

1/2 t. lemon pepper
1/2 t. garlic powder
1/2 t. dill weed

Mix together well. Roast crackers a while in a 250 degree oven until warm through.

Dorothy F. Slabaugh (Bakery)
Marna Schlabach (Kitchen)

OYSTER CRACKERS

3/4 c. vegetable oil
1 pkg. Hidden Valley Ranch
dressing mix, dry

1-12 oz. box oyster crackers
1/4 t. dill weed
1 t. garlic salt

Pour oil into 15 x 10 cookie sheet. Stir in dressing mix, salt, and dill weed. Add crackers. Place in 250 degree oven for 2 hours. Stir every 15 minutes. Store in air tight container.

Cletus Miller (Maintenance)
Betty Troyer (Kitchen)

PEANUT BUTTER POPCORN

1/2 c. light corn syrup

1/2 c. sugar

Mix and bring to soft boil. Add 1/2 c. peanut butter and 1/2 t. vanilla. Pour over 1 popper of popped popcorn and mix thoroughly.

Judy Beachy (Kitchen Manager)

 Lord, when we are wrong, make us willing to change.
And when we are right, make us easy to live with.

18

Soups,
Salads
& Dressings

SEASONING GUIDE

Get acquainted with spices and herbs. Add in small amounts, 1/4 teaspoon for each 4 servings. Taste before adding more. Crush dried herbs or snip fresh herbs before using. If substituting fresh for dried, use 3 time more fresh herbs.

EGGS, CHEESE

Baked Eggs: Sprinkle dash of thyme or paprika over the top.

Creamed Eggs: Add mace.

Deviled Eggs: Add celery seed, cumin, mustard, savory, chili powder or curry powder.

Omelet: Try with dash of marjoram or rosemary (go easy!).

Scrambled Eggs: Sprinkle lightly with basil, thyme, rosemary or marjoram. Add seasoning near the end of cooking.

Souffle: Add 1/4 teaspoon marjoram to 4-egg souffle. To cheese souffle, add basil or savory.

Cheese Casseroles: Spark with dash sage or marjoram.

Cheese Fondue: Try adding a dash of basil or nutmeg.

Cheese Rabbit (rarebit): Try with mace or mustard.

Cheese Sauce: Add mustard or a dash of marjoram or thyme.

Cheese Spread: Blend sage, caraway seed, thyme or celery seed into melted process cheese.

Cottage Cheese: Blend in chives or a dash of sage, caraway seed, dill, anise, or cumin. Prepare several hours ahead of time.

Cream Cheese: Blend in curry powder, marjoram, caraway seed, or dill. Sprinkle paprika or cayenne on top. Use as celery filling or appetizer spread.

Soups, Salads & Dressings

BANANA SOUP

6 bananas
1 c. brown sugar

12 slices of bread
milk

Mash bananas. Stir in brown sugar. Break the bread into bite size pieces. Add the milk until it's the consistency of soup. Serve cold.

Hazel Bontrager (Kitchen)

BROCCOLI SOUP

1 bunch broccoli
3/4 c. butter
2 T. butter
6 c. chicken broth

6 oz. pkg. noodles
6 c. milk
1 lb. Velveeta cheese

Chop and pre-cook broccoli. Saute onion and butter. Bring broth to boil and add noodles and cook until soft. Add milk, cheese, and sauteed onions. Add cooked broccoli and heat. May use half the amount of cheese.

Lorena Mast (Waitress)

CHEDDAR-TUNA CHOWDER

2 c. boiling salted water
1/2 carrot
1 small onion, chopped
1 large potato, chopped
1/2 c. celery, chopped
1/3 c. flour

2 c. milk
1-6 oz. can tuna
1 can cream style corn
pinch of dried rosemary
chopped chives
3/4 lb. cheddar cheese, shredded

Add vegetables to boiling water. Boil and simmer 10 minutes covered. Do not drain. Shake together milk and flour and add to the soup. Add tuna and corn. Cook until thickened. Add cheese and herbs. Makes 2 quarts.

Doreen Mast (Knot N Grain)

CHEESY POTATO SOUP WITH BACON

4 c. diced potatoes
1/2 c. chopped onion
1 t. salt

1/2 c. chopped celery
1 T. butter

Combine ingredients in a saucepan and add just enough water to cover vegetables. Cook until tender, but not mushy. Add 1 quart of milk and 1/2 pound of Velveeta cheese. Stir until cheese is completely dissolved. Have ready, 6 slices of fried bacon, and just before serving, crumble up and add to soup.

Mary Esther Miller(Restaurant/Gifts)

CHILI SOUP

2 lb. browned hamburger ,
drained
1/2 c. brown sugar
5 1/2 - 6 c. water

1 chopped onion
1-50 oz. or 3 lb. 3 qt. tomato soup
1 can (15 3/4 oz) chili beans
chili powder to taste

Mix all ingredients, bring to a boil, simmer if desired.

Teresa Coblentz (Busser)

CREAM OF BROCCOLI SOUP

4 slices of bacon	2 T. flour
1/3 c. onion, chopped	1 T. instant bouillon, chicken
6 c. raw potatoes, shredded	1-13 oz. can evaporated milk
2 t. salt	1 1/2 c. milk
3 c. boiling water	1/2 t. pepper
1-10 oz. pkg. frozen broccoli, chopped	2 t. Accent

Fry bacon in deep skillet. Remove slices, drain and reserve the grease. Add the onions, potatoes, salt and boiling water to the bacon grease. Cover and simmer about 15 minutes. During the last 5 minutes, add the broccoli that has been pureed with water (just enough to puree) in a blender. Melt butter in a seperate saucepan. Blend in flour and boullion. Add milk and cook until thickened. Add to broccoli mixture and heat. Add pepper and Accent. Crumble bacon, fine. Can be added to the soup or added as a garnish.

Note:

Use about 6 medium potatoes for the shredded potatoes. Also fresh broccoli can be used, 1 1/2 c. Serves 8.

Mary A. Bontrager (Waitstaff)

CROCK POT CHILI SOUP

1 1/2 c. onions	1 lb. browned hamburger
4 c. crushed tomatoes	1 t. sugar
1 small clove garlic	2 T. chili powder
2 t. salt	2 c. red kidney beans

Place all ingredients in crock pot and cook all day on low heat.

Ruth Peshina (Waitress)

Many things are opened by mistake--but none so frequently as the mouth.

CUCUMBER & ZUCCHINI SOUP

2 cucumbers, peeled and seeded
1 medium zucchini, seeded
1 chicken bouillon cube,
dissolved in 1 c. water

Salt & pepper, to taste
1/2 t. onion salt

Steam cucumber and zucchini until clear. Put in blender and puree. Add to chicken bouillion in pan and add seasonings. Add 1 quart of milk and heat just to boiling. Serve.

Emma B. Miller (Hostess/Cashier)

GREEN BEAN AND POTATO SOUP

10 stalks celery, chopped
2 bunches green onion, chopped
1/2 c. margarine
3/4 c. flour
4 qt. milk
6 potatoes, diced
2 T. dried parsley

2 T. dill weed
2 t. salt
1/2 t. pepper
2 pkgs. frozen French style
green beans (thawed,
drained, chopped)
2 cans evaporated milk

Saute celery and onion in margarine. Add flour and cook slightly. Add milk slowly, while stirring. Cook until the mixture starts getting hot. Add potatoes, parsley, dill weed, salt, and pepper. Simmer over low heat until potatoes are tender. Add beans and evaporated milk. Cook until beans are tender.

Marsha Gingerich (Bakery)

Since everything is in our heads, we'd better not lose them.

HOT CHICKEN GUMBO

1 chicken, diced	1/4 t. pepper
1 1/2 qt. water	4 c. rice
1/4 can (14-16 oz.) tomatoes	1 lb. okra, sliced
2 c. onions, sliced	3/4 c. green onions
1 T. parsley, minced	1 T. salt

Cook chicken in 1 1/2 qt. water. Cool, remove fat, and chicken from bones. Add other ingredients and cook until soft.

Betti Kauffman (Cashier/Hostess)

NEW ENGLAND CLAM CHOWDER

2 -6 1/2 oz. cans chopped clams	1/8 t. pepper
4 slices bacon, diced	parsley, to taste
2/3 c. chopped onion	1 1/2 c. heavy cream
3 c. potatoes, peeled/diced	1 1/2 c. milk
2 T. cornstarch	1/8 t. hot pepper sauce or to taste
1 t. salt	

Drain clams, reserve liquid. Add enough clam juice and water to measure 2 c. in a 4 quart sauce pan. Cook bacon until crisp. Remove bacon and drain on paper towel. Add onions to bacon grease. Saute 2 to 3 minutes or until tender. Stir in reserved clam liquid and potatoes. Cover and cook 10 to 15 minutes or until potatoes are tender. Stir in corn starch, salt and pepper. Gradually stir in cream and milk until smooth. Stir into saucepan. Stirring constantly, bring to boil over medium low heat and boil 1 minute. Add clams and hot pepper sauce. Stirring occasionally, cook until heated through. Sprinkle bacon over chowder. Makes about 7 cups.

Mary A. Bontrager (Waitress)

I had no shoes and complained, until I met a man who had no feet.

SIMPLE, TASTY POTATO SOUP

1/2 c. carrots, diced
1 T. minced onions
3 T. chicken base

1/2 c. diced potatoes
1/2 c. chopped ham
1 qt. water

Cook all ingredients together until vegetables are soft. Do not drain water. Add 1 quart of milk. Make a mixture of 3/4 c. flour and 3/4 c. milk, like gravy. Add to other mixture. Melt 1 cup Velveeta cheese in soup last. Do not overcook.

Carolyn Hershberger (Bakery)

TURKEY CHOWDER

1 c. diced potatoes
1 c. diced celery
1 qt. chicken or turkey broth

1 c. diced carrots
1 medium onion (diced)
1 qt. water

Combine all ingredients and cook until vegetables are done. Add 6 T. flour and 2 cups of milk. Bring to boil. Add 1 stick of oleo and 1 lb. Velveeta cheese. Do not cook after cheese is added.

Ruth Beachy (Restaurant Gifts)
Alma L. Hershberger (Restaurant Gifts)

Something you can do to keep bacon strips from sticking together in the package is to roll the bacon package in a tube shape and put a rubber band around it before you refrigerate it.

TURKEY CHOWDER

2 turkey wings
1 T. salt
1 medium onion, diced
4 c. turkey broth
1 c. carrots, chopped
1 c. celery, chopped

1 c. potatoes, diced
2 c. milk
6 T. flour
1 c. mild cheese, shredded
1/4 c. margarine

Place wings in large pan. Add water until covered. Add salt and onion. Bring to a boil. Simmer until tender. Remove meat from the bones. Cut in small pieces. To 4 c. broth, add water, if necessary. Add carrots, celery, and potatoes. Simmer until tender. Stir in turkey. Add milk to flour and add it to turkey mixture. Add margarine and cheese. Cook over medium heat, stirring constantly, until thickened.

Walter Lehman (Essenhaus Foods)

WISCONSIN POTATO CHEESE SOUP

2 T. butter or margarine
1/3 c. celery, chopped
1/3 c. onion, chopped
4 c. potatoes, diced & peeled
3 c. chicken broth
2 c. milk

1/4 t. pepper
1 1/2 t. salt
dash of paprika
2 c. cheddar cheese, shredded
fresh parsley, chopped

In a large saucepan, melt butter over medium high heat. Saute celery and onion until tender. Add potatoes and broth. Cover and simmer until potatoes are tender, about 12 minutes. In batches, puree potato mixture in a blender or food processor. Return to saucepan. Stir in milk and seasonings. Add the cheese and heat only until melted. Garnish with parsley and cheese. Yield: 8 servings

Iva Miller (Kitchen)

The only food that doesn't get more expensive is food for thought.

BEST EVER CRANBERRY SALAD

1/2 lb. ground cranberries   2 chopped apples
3/4 c. sugar

Mix and set aside.

2-3 oz. cherry jello   1 c. cold water
2 c. boiling water

Add cranberry mixture to this mixture let thicken. Add a 20 oz. can crushed pineapple, drained, and 1/2 c. chopped pecans. Pour into Pyrex 9 x 13 pan. Let set overnight.

Topping
8 oz. cream cheese   16 large marshmallows, quartered
1 c. Rich's Topping

Whip cream cheese until creamy. Gradually add Rich's Topping. Stir in marshmallows. Put in refrigerator overnight. The next morning, whip mixture until smooth. Pour over jello mixture.

Jan Bontrager (Waitress)

BROCCOLI & CAULIFLOWER SALAD

1 broccoli head   1 cauliflower head
12 pcs. bacon, fried crisp and   1 red onion, chopped
broken in pcs.   1/2 c. raisins
1c. mayonnaise   2 T. vinegar
1/2 c. sugar

Combine and marinate overnight in refrigerator.

Option: May add slivered almonds, shredded carrots, or radishes.

Barb Weaver (Cashier/Restaurant Office)
Ruth Ann Wagler (Kitchen)
Doreen Mast (Cashier/Knot N Grain
Sharon Boley (Waitress)

BROCCOLI SALAD

3 broccoli heads
1 cauliflower head
1 c. raisins

1 1/2 c. sunflower seeds
12 slices bacon, fried &
broken into pieces

Cut broccoli and cauliflower into bite size pieces. Mix with raisins, sunflower seeds, and bacon.

Dressing

1 qt. Miracle Whip
1/3 c. vinegar

2 T. sugar
1/2 c. milk

Mix together and pour over salad mixture.

Judy Beachy (Kitchen Manager)
Bill Burns (Bakery)

Put a tablespoon of butter or oil in the water when cooking rice, dried beans, or macaroni. It will keep it from running over.

CHICKEN SALAD

5 c. chicken, cooked/cubed
2 T. salad oil
2 T. orange juice
2 T. vinegar
1 T. salt
1-11 oz. can mandarin oranges, drained

1-13 oz. can pineapple tidbits, drained
1 c. toasted slivered almonds
1 1/2 c. small green grapes
1 1/2 c. mayonnaise
1 1/2 c. celery, sliced
3 c. cooked rice

Combine chicken, salad oil, orange juice, vinegar, and salt. Let stand while preparing remaining salad ingredients or over night. Gently toss all ingredients.

Walter Lehman (Essenhaus Foods))

CRAB AND AVOCADO SALAD

Dressing

16 oz. bottle of thousand island salad dressing

7 oz. bottle of ketchup
3 T. horseradish

Mix these ingredients and pour over:

2 lb. crab or imitation crab, cut in small pieces

3 avocadoes, cubed
2 c. celery, chopped fine

Sue Miller (Manager)

CRANBERRY SALAD

1/2 lb. or less cranberries
1 medium apple
Grind all together, peelings and all.

1 medium orange

1 small can crushed pineapple
4 pcs. celery, cut fine

1 c. pecans, cut fine

Grind and mix together. Add sugar and let stand.

2 pkg. raspberry jello,
  (prepared per pkg.directions)

3 c. sugar, scant

When jello starts to set, mix all the above ingredients with jello. May put in a mold or dish.

Topping
1 pkg. lemon jello
13 1/2 oz. can crushed pineapple, drained
2 c. miniature marshmallows

1-8 oz. cream cheese
1/2 c. dairy sour cream
dash of salt
1/2 c. whipping cream

Dissolve jello in 1 c. boiling water. Add marshmallows. Stir until melted. Add pineapple juice to jello. Blend cream cheese, sour cream, and salt. Stir in pineapple. Chill until partly set. Fold in whipped cream. Pour over set jello mixture.

Walter Lehman (Essenhaus Foods)

CREAMED LETTUCE

3 c. early leaf or 1/2 head lettuce
1/2 t. salt
1 T. vinegar
1/4 c. cream
2 T. sugar

Cut the lettuce coarsely. Add sugar, cream, and salt to the vinegar. Pour cream dressing over lettuce. Toss lightly and serve. May be served over potatoes boiled in salt water or slice 2 hard boiled eggs over lettuce and use as tossed salad.

Mary Arlene Bontrager (Waitress)

CRYSTAL SALAD

1-3 oz. pkg. lemon jello
1 1/4 c. boiling water
1/2 c. pineapple juice
1/2 c. whipping cream, whipped
1/2 c. salad dressing
1/2 c. diced red apples, unpeeled
1/2 c. crushed pineapple
1/2 c. diced celery
1 c. mini marshmallows

Dissolve jello in boiling water. Add pineapple juice. When this begins to gel, add whipped cream. Mix salad dressing, apples, pineapple, celery, and marshmallows. Combine both mixtures. Chill until firm.

Betti Kauffman (Hostess)

DOUBLE CHEESE SALAD

1 20 oz. can crushed pineapple,
drain & reserve juice
2 T. plain gelatin
1/2 c. cold water
1 c. pineapple juice
3/4 c. sugar
1/2 pt. heavy whipped cream
1/2 lb. cottage cheese
juice of 1 lemon

Drain pineapple, reserving juice. Soften gelatin in cold water. Combine fruit juices and heat. Dissolve gelatin and sugar in fruit juices. Chill. When gelatin mixture begins to thicken, add remaining ingredients. Pour into a mold. Chill until firm.

Mattie Marie Diener (Waitress)

FALL FRUIT SALAD RING

1-6 oz. pkg. red jello
1/2 c. banana slices
10 sliced apples or pears
1/4 c. chopped celery

ice cubes
1 1/2 c. boiling water
1 c. cold grapefruit juice

Completely dissolve jello in boiling water. Combine juice and ice cubes to make 2 1/2 c. Add to gelatin and stir until slightly thickened. Remove any unmelted ice. Fold in fruit and celery. Pour into 6 c. ring mold. Chill until firm. Yield: 12 servings

Mattie Marie Diener (Waitress)

FRESH APPLE SALAD

1 egg, beaten
1 c. sugar
2 T. vinegar
1 t. vanilla

2 c. water
2 T. clear jel, heaping
1 T. butter

Cook until thick and cool completely. Add:

diced apples, 6 to 8, depending on size
3-4 bananas
red or green grapes,

1/2 c. celery
1 c. miniature marshmallows
small can pineapple chunks, optional drained

Mary Esther Miller (Manager/Restaurant Gifts)

FROZEN BREAKFAST TREAT

2 c. mashed bananas
2 c. orange juice, frozen concentrate

1-2 T. lemon juice
1 c. sugar, scant
1 c. crushed pineapple

Thoroughly mix all ingredients with orange juice (fixed according to package directions). Freeze. Strawberries, blueberries, raspberries, or maraschino cherries may be added for garnish.

Marietta Helmuth (Waitress)

FRUIT COMPOTE

1 c. sliced strawberries
1 c. orange-pineapple juice or
orange juice
1/4 t. finely chopped orange peel

1/2 c. sliced peaches
1/2 c. blueberries
toasted coconut

In large mixing bowl, combine all ingredients. Cover and chill for 1 hour.
Sprinkle with toasted coconut.

Elma Miller (Waitress)

FRUIT SALAD

1 lb. green grapes
1 lb. red seedless grapes
4 apples, chopped

1-16 oz. can fruit cocktail
4 bananas, sliced
1-8 oz. tub Cool Whip

Rinse fruit well. Mix all ingredients in large bowl and keep cool. Do not
prepare earlier than 1-1 1/2 hours before serving, or bananas will turn.

Pamela Frey (Bakery)

FRUIT SALAD

2 c. water

2 c. sugar

Heat to boiling. Mix in:

2 T. corn starch
1/2 t. salt
2 t. vinegar

1/2 c. cream
2 t. vanilla

Add to above mixture and boil until thickens. Cool and pour over
prepared fruit. (Apples, grapes, bananas, celery, pineapple, and nuts, if
desired)

Lena Lehman

33

FRUIT SLUSH

2 3/4 c. white sugar
1 1/2 c. frozen orange juice
1 qt. crushed pineapple

6 c. hot water
3 1/2 lb. bananas, mashed

Freeze. Serve partially thawed.

Erma Yoder (Maintenance)
Martha Coblentz (Bakery)

GRANDMA'S CREAMED CUCUMBERS

4 medium cucumbers
2 medium onions, diced
3 t. salt

1 c. heavy cream
3 T. vinegar
3 T. sugar

Peel and thinly slice cucumbers. Place cumbers and onions in large bowl. Add salt, stirring to coat. Cover with dish to weigh down. Let set for 12 to 18 hours, draining periodically. Cucumbers will be limp but crunchy. Drain cucumber mixture. Add cream, vinegar, and sugar. Chill. Serve over boiled new potatoes. Sprinkle with paprika. 6 servings

Mary A. Bontrager (Waitress)

GRAPEFRUIT SALAD

Soak 3 T. plain gelatin in 1 c. cold water in a bowl. Boil together 3 c. sugar and 2 c. water for 3 minutes. Pour this over gelatin. Let cool. Then add 1 c. orange juice, 1/2 c. lemon juice, 1 t. salt, and 3 c. drained grapefruit, spooned out like you would eat it.

Becky Helmuth (Waitress)

 People who light up your life usually know where the switch is.

GRAPE SALAD

1-8 oz. cream cheese, softened   1 c. sour cream
1 1/2 c. powdered sugar   1 t. lemon juice

Beat ingredients together. Fold in 1 large container of Cool Whip and 4 lbs. whole, seedless grapes.

Viola Miller (Ned Miller's Wife/Essenhaus Foods)

HAM - RONI - SALAD

1 c. diced ham   1 c. chopped green pepper
2 c. macaroni, quick cooked   1 T. mayonnaise
3/4 c. chopped celery   1 1/2 T. barbecue sauce
1 c. grated carrots   1 t. prepared mustard
1/4 c. chopped onions   salt & pepper

Combine ham, macaroni, celery, carrots, salt, pepper, and onion. Combine mayonnaise, barbecue sauce (optional), catsup, and mustard. Mix thoroughly. Add to other mixture.

Millie Whetstone (Kitchen)

HOT CHEESE AND POTATO SALAD

8 lg. Idaho potatoes - boiled   1 lb. Velveeta or colby cheese
w/or without skin. Dice   1 c. mayonnaise
after cooking   salt & pepper, to taste
3/4 c. chopped onions

Mix ingredients and place in 9 x 13 pan. Crumble 1/2 lb. cooked bacon over the top. Slice black or green olives and place on top. Bake at 350 degrees, covered, for 30 minutes, uncovered, for 30 minutes more.

Dana Graber (Decorating)

35

HOT TACO SALAD

1 bag Doritos	1/2 lb. shredded cheese
2 lb. hamburger	1 c. sour cream
1 pkg. taco seasoning	1/2 head lettuce
1 can hot chili beans, heated	chopped tomatoes

Crush taco chips in bottom of 9 x 13 pan. Prepare hamburger and taco seasoning. Pour meat and beans over chips. Add cheese and put in a 375 degree oven until cheese melts. Add sour cream and return to oven until sour cream melts. Just before serving, add lettuce and tomatoes. Serve with taco sauce.

Freda Yutzy (Waitress)

HOLIDAY SHERBET SALAD

1-16 oz. pkg. raspberry or strawberry gelatin	1-15 oz. can drained mandarin oranges
2 c. boiling water	1 c. miniature marshmallows
1 pt. raspberry sherbet	1-8 oz. Cool Whip
1-20 oz. can drained pineapple	

Dissolve gelatin in boiling water. Stir sherbet into hot gelatin. Chill 45 minutes or until partially set. Add fruits and marshmallows. Fold in whipped topping. Chill until firm.

Pamela Frey (Bakery)

KIDNEY BEAN SALAD

1 14 oz. can kidney beans, about 1 3/4 to 2 c.	1/4 t. salt
2 pcs. sliced celery	1/8 t. pepper
2 hard cooked eggs, chopped	1/4 t. onion powder or
2 dill pickles, diced	1/4 c. chopped onion

Drain beans. Rinse and drain again. Combine beans with celery, eggs, pickles, and seasonings. Add mayonnaise or Italian dressing to your taste.

Mary Arlene Bontrager (Waitress)

ITALIAN SALAD BOWL

1/2 clove garlic	1 1/2 T. vinegar
1/4 t. prepared mustard	1/2 t. worcestershire sauce
1 t. salt	4 T. corn oil
few grains pepper	1 qt. assorted salad greens

Drop garlic clove in wooden bowl. Add prepared mustard, salt, a few grains of pepper. Blend thoroughly with fork. Add vinegar, worcestershire sauce, and corn oil. Beat with fork until thoroughly mixed. Add crisp and well drained salad greens, broken into bite-sized pieces. Toss lightly until all greens glisten. Serve at once. Yield: 4 servings

Mary Arlene Bontrager (Waitress)

LIME PEAR SALAD

1-6 oz. box lime jello	1 c. pear juice
1 pt. sliced pears, reserve juice	1 T. butter
1/2 c. sugar	1 c. whipped topping
2 T. flour	

Mix jello according to directions on box. Cool. Add sliced pears and let set. Boil together 1/2 c. sugar, 2 T. flour, and 1 c. pear juice. When thick, remove from heat and add 1 T. butter. Cool and add 1 c. whipped topping. Put on top of jello.

Luella Yoder (Kitchen)

It is a good idea to keep your words soft and sweet; you never know when you may have to eat them.

LIME WHIP JELLO SALAD

1 large pkg. lime jello,
may use other flavors
1-16 oz. container Cool Whip
1-16 oz. container cottage
cheese, small curd
1/2 c. mayonnaise, optional

1 can crushed pineapple
drain some juice
1 c. chopped pecans
Optional: coconut,
marshmallows, cherries

Blend jello, Cool Whip, cottage cheese, mayonnaise, and pineapple.
Blend in nuts. May add optional items at this point. Cover and refrigerate
for at least 1 hour or until firm.

Vyvyan Dunlap (Decorating Department)

LINGUINE SALAD

1 lb. liguine cooked & salted
1 1/2 bunches green onions
2 cucumbers, sliced

1 1/2 c. fresh broccoli
16 oz. Italian dressing

Put cooked and salted linguine in colander and run cold water over it.
Add other ingredients. Better made days ahead.

Lorena Mast (Waitress)

MIXED VEGETABLE SALAD

2-16 oz. cans mixed vegetables
1 sm. onion, chopped
1 c. chopped celery
1-16 oz can kidney beans
1 small green pepper, chopped

1/2 c. vinegar
1/2-3/4 c. sugar
1 T. prepared mustard
2 T. flour

Drain vegetables, add onions, peppers, and celery. Set aside. Combine
vinegar, sugar (to taste), mustard, and flour in a saucepan. Cook until
thickened. Cool. Pour over vegetables and refrigerate overnight.

Lena Miller (Meatroom)

PARTY SALAD

1-3 oz. box lime jello
1 c. hot water
1 c. mini marshmallows
1 can crushed pineapple

1 c. shredded cabbage
1/2 c. chopped nuts
1 c. whipped cream
1/4 c. salad dressing

Dissolve jello with 1 c. hot water. Add marshmallows while jello is still hot. When thick, add the rest of ingredients.

Rosanna Miller (Kitchen)

Break fluid: A new name for coffee

PATIO CHICKEN SALAD

1 1/2 c. pineapple juice   1 t. curry powder

Bring to boil. Add 1 1/3 c. instant rice, cover, and remove from heat. Let set for 5 minutes and fluff.

1 1/2 c. diced cooked chicken
1/2 c. dill pickles, diced
1-10 oz. pkg. peas, cooked, cooled

1/2 c. celery, diced
1 t. grated onion
3/4 c. mayonnaise

Mix all gently with a fork. Chill. Serve on greens. Garnish with tomatoes and peach halves filled with chutney.

Mary Arlene Bontrager (Waitress)

39

PEACH JELLO SALAD

2 pkg. peach jello
3 c. boiling water

1 can pineapple, reserve juice
1 can fruit cocktail or bananas

Dissolve jello in hot water. Pour into 9 x 14 pan. Add fruit and chill.

1 c. pineapple juice
1/2 c. sugar

1/2 T. flour
1 egg

Mix and bring to boil. Cool.

1 c. liquid whipping cream

8 oz. cream cheese

Whip whipping cream until stiff. Whip in cream cheese. Mix with second mixture. Spread on set jello and top with grated cheese.

Carlene Miller (Restaurant Reservations)

PEAR SALAD

2-16 oz. cans pears, reserve juice
3 oz. lemon jello

3 oz. lime jello
1-8 oz. cream cheese
12 oz. whipped topping

Blend pears in blender. Pour pear juice in pan and heat to boiling. Add jello and stir until dissolved. Add cream cheese. Blend this mixture in the blender. Add to pears. Beat in whipped topping with a whisk or hand beater.

Betti Kauffman (Cashier/Hostess)

The riches that are in the heart cannot be stolen.

PINK SALAD

1-13 1/2 oz. can pineapple,
with juice
1-3 oz. pkg. strawberry jello
16 large marshmallows

1-8 oz. pkg. cream cheese
1/4 c. milk
1-8 oz. carton Cool Whip

Combine crushed pineapple with juice, jello, and marshmallows. Heat until melted and then cool. Combine cream cheese and milk. Mix until smooth. Add Cool Whip to cream cheese mixture. Combine both mixtures until well blended. Pour into mold.

Laura Hochstetler (Laundry)

POTATO SALAD

1 1/2 c. sugar
1 t. celery seed
1/2 t. celery salt

1/4 t. salt
1/2 c. salad dressing
2 t. mustard

Cook 6 large potatoes. Cool and peel. Cook 1 c. macaroni in salt water. Drain and cool. Cook 5 eggs. Cool and peel. Dice potatoes, eggs, and 1/4 c. onions. Combine all ingredients. Let set a couple of hours - if too dry add a little milk.

Fannie Yutzy (Bakery)

POTATO SALAD (FOR 50 PEOPLE)

10 lbs. potatoes, cooked/diced
1 bunch celery, diced
1 dozen eggs, hard boiled/diced
1 small onion, diced
4 c. Miracle Whip

1/2 c. vinegar
1/4 c. salt
1/8 c. mustard
3 c. sugar

Mix all together. Best if refrigerated for a day or two.

Luella Yoder (Kitchen)

41

RED APPLESAUCE SALAD

2 c. boiling water
1/4 c. red hots candies

2-3 oz. pkgs. cherry jello
4 c. applesauce

Dissolve red hots in boiling water. Add cherry jello, stirring until dissolved. Add applesauce. Pour into dish and refrigerate.

Agnes Cross (Bakery)

RICE SALAD

2 c. chicken broth
1 chicken bouillon

1 c. rice

Boil and cool.

1 c. olives
3/4 c. celery
1/2 c. green onions
1 pt. lima beans + juice

2 t. curry powder
1/2 c. parsley
1 pt. Hellman's mayonnaise

Mix all ingredients together and serve.

Becky Helmuth (Waitress)

SEAFOOD AND RICE OR PASTA SALAD

2 c. cooked spiral pasta or
1 c. cooked rice *
2 t. onion, chopped
1/2 lb. shredded imitation crab, 10 sticks
1 c. celery chopped

1/8 t. pepper, optional
2 t. Dijon mustard
3 T. bottled Italian dressing
1/2 c. salad dressing
1 t. catsup

Mix and refrigerate.

* 1 c. of cooked rice will make 2 c.

Betti Kauffman (Cashier/Hostess)

SKILLET SALAD

4 slices bacon
1/4 c. vinegar
1 T. brown sugar
1 t. salt

1 T. onion, chopped
4 c. shredded cabbage
1/2 c. chopped parsley

Cook bacon until crisp. Remove from skillet and crumble. Add vinegar, sugar, salt, and onion to bacon fat. Add bacon. Heat thoroughly. Take from stove and toss cabbage and parsley in hot dressing.

Mary Arlene Bontrager (Waitress)

SOUR KRAUT SALAD

2 c. sour kraut, drained
1/2 c. celery, chopped fine
1 medium onion, chopped fine

1 large green pepper,
chopped fine
1/2 c. sugar

Mix all ingredients and let set in refrigerator for 6 hours.

Leola Kauffman (Laundry)

Take Time

Take time to think. . .It is the source of power
Take time to play . . . It is the secret of perpetual youth
Take time to read . . . It is the fountain of wisdom
Take time to pray . . . It is the greatest power on earth
Take time to love and be loved . . .It is a God-given privilege
Take time to be friendly . . . It is the road to happiness
Take time to laugh . . . It is the music of the soul
Take time to give . . . It is to short a day to be selfish
Take time to work . . . It is the price of success
Take time to do charity . . . It is the key to heaven

STUFFED EGGS

Basic recipe

6 hard cooked eggs	1/4 c. Miracle Whip
1/4 t. salt	dash of pepper

Mix well with egg yolk and fill egg white centers.

Variations:

Pizza Style

2 T. Miracle Whip	2 T. catsup
1 t. oregano	1/8 t. garlic powder

Mix well with egg yolk and fill egg white centers.

Bacon

1/4 c. Miracle Whip	1/4 t. salt
3 t. bacon	

Mix well with egg yolk and fill egg white centers.

Bacon and Peanut Butter

1/4 c. Miracle Whip	3 t. bacon
2 T. peanut butter	1/4 t. salt

Mix well with egg yolks and fill egg white centers.

Martha Coblentz (Bakery)

 Life is like a sandwich. The more you add to it, the better it becomes.

TASTY MACARONI TOSS

1-7 1/4 oz. pkg. macaroni
and cheese dinner
1/2 c. celery slices

1 c. frozen peas, thawed/drained
1 c. creamy cucumber dressing
1 c. radish slices

Prepare dinner as directed on package. Add remaining ingredients. Mix
lightly. Chill. Yield: 6-8 servings

Mary Arlene Bontrager (Waitress)

VEGETABLE SALAD

1 pkg. California blend vegetables
1 can red beans, rinse & drain
1 small onion, chopped
1/4 c. celery

2 T. flour
1 c. sugar
2 T. prepared mustard
1/2 c. vinegar
1/2 c. water

Cook vegetables; drain. Add beans, onion, and celery. Combine
remaining ingredients and cook until thick. Pour over vegetables and let
set for 24 hours.

Pamela Frey (Bakery)

VEGETABLE SALAD

1 pkg. mixed vegetables,
cook, cool & drain
1 small green onion, chopped

1 c. celery, chopped
1 small green pepper, chopped
1 can dark red kidney beans

Dressing

3/4 c. sugar
1 1/2 T. flour
1 1/2 T. prepared mustard

3/8 c. vinegar
3/8 c. water

Cook until thick. Cool and pour over vegetables. Let set overnight in a
covered dish.

Leola Kauffman (Laundry)

45

YUM - YUM SALAD

1 small box lemon jello
2 t. sugar
pinch of salt
1 c. hot water

1/2 c. cold water
2 t. vinegar
1 small can pineapple

Let this start to thicken. Add 1 c. whipped cream and 1/2 c. grated cheese.

Rosanne Bontrager (Busser)

DRESSING FOR POTATO SALAD

3/4 c. sugar
1 c. salad dressing
2 T. vinegar

2 t. mustard
1/2 t. celery seed

Mix all ingredients together and mix with cooked, diced potatoes.

Ruthann Wagler (Kitchen/Bakery)

HONEY & OIL DRESSING

1/2 c. sugar
1 t. dry mustard
1 t. paprika
1 t. celery salt
1/4 t. salt

1/3 c. honey
1/3 c. vinegar
1 T. lemon juice
1 t. grated onion
1 c. salad oil

Mix all ingredients, except oil, until sugar is dissolved. Slowly add oil and beat with beater until well mixed. Yield: 2 c.

Mary Esther Miller (Manager/Restaurant Gifts)

 Be wiser than other people if you can. But, do not tell them so.

HOT BACON DRESSING FOR LETTUCE OR COOKED DICED POTATOES

4 slices bacon
1/2 t. salt
1 egg
1/2 t. celery seed

1/2 c. sugar
1 T. cornstarch
1/4 c. vinegar
1 c. milk

Fry bacon. Combine all ingredients , except bacon. Mix well. Add milk and cook until thick. Add crumbled bacon.

Betti Kauffman (Cashier/Hostess)

POPPY SEED DRESSING

1 c. Miracle Whip
1/3 c. vegetable oil
1 onion, grated
1 1/2 c. sour cream

1 c. sugar
1/4 c. vinegar
1 t. salt
2 t. poppy seed

Mix together.

Rosanna Miller (Kitchen)

SALAD DRESSING

1 T. or more brown sugar, to taste
1/2 c. light corn syrup
1/2 c. Miracle Whip

Mix all ingredients together and use on any salad.

Ellen Mishler (Cashier/Hostess)

Do your duty that is best;
Leave unto the Lord the rest.

SAUCE FOR APPLE SALAD

1 c. sugar   1 c. water
2 T. cornstarch

Boil this together until thickens. Then beat 1 egg and pour the above mixture into eggs and beat well. Put mixture back on stove and bring to a boil. Remove from the stove and add 1 1/2 T. vinegar and 1 T. butter. Cool and pour over chopped apples.

Ellen Mishler (Cashier/Hostess)

Breads,
Rolls, Cereals
& Pancakes

SEASONING GUIDE

Get acquainted with spices and herbs. Add in small amounts, 1/4 teaspoon for each 4 servings. Taste before adding more. Crush dried herbs or snip fresh herbs before using. If substituting fresh for dried, use 3 time more fresh herbs.

BREADS, PASTA

Biscuits: Add caraway seed, thyme or savory to flour. Serve with meat.

Bread: Make each loaf a surprise by adding caraway seed, cardamom or poppy seed.

Coffee Cake: Mix crushed aniseed in batter. For variety, sprinkle cinnamon-sugar mixture on top or add poppy seed filling.

Corn Bread: Add poultry seasoning or caraway seed to dry ingredients. Be adventuresome! Add 1/2 teaspoon rosemary to batter.

Croutons: Toss toast crumbs in melted butter seasoned with basil, marjoram or onion salt.

Doughnuts: Add mace or nutmeg to dry ingredients. After frying, roll in cinnamon sugar.

Dumplings: Add thyme or parsley (fresh or flakes) to batter.

Muffins: Blueberry-add dash of nutmeg to dry ingredients. Season plain muffins with caraway seed or cinnamon.

Noodles: Butter, then sprinkle with poppy seed.

Rolls: Add caraway seed or sprinkle with sesame seed.

Spaghetti: Toss with butter, Parmesan and snipped chives.

Waffles: Add poultry seasoning to batter; serve with creamed chicken. Or add cardamom to honey; pour over waffles.

Breads, Rolls, Cereals & Pancakes

BLUEBERRY CREAM MUFFINS

4 eggs
2 c. sugar
1 c. vegetable oil
1 t. vanilla
4 c. all-purpose flour

1 t. salt
1 t. baking soda
2 t. baking powder
2 c. (16 oz.) sour cream
2 c. fresh blueberries

In a mixing bowl, beat eggs. Gradually add sugar. While beating, slowly pour in oil. Add vanilla. Combine dry ingredients. Add alternately with the sour cream to the egg mixture. Gently fold in blueberries. Spoon into greased muffin tins. Bake at 400 degrees for 20 minutes. Yield: 24 muffins

Iva Miller (Kitchen)

Kindness is the golden chain by which a community is bound together.

BLUEBERRY MUFFINS

1 egg
1/2 c. milk
1/4 c. vegetable oil
2 t. baking powder

1/2 c. sugar
1 1/2 c. flour
1/2 t. salt
1 c. fresh blueberries, drained

Heat oven to 400 degrees. Grease bottom of baking cups or use paper baking cups.

Beat egg with fork. Stir in milk and oil. Blend in combined dry ingredients, stirring just until flour is moistened. Batter will be lumpy. Do not over-mix. Fold in blueberries. Fill muffin cups about 2/3 full. Bake 20 to 25 minutes or until golden brown. Loosen immediately with spatula. Yield: 12 muffins

Ellen Mishler (Hostess-Cashier)
Pamela Frey (Bakery)

DALLAS'S OATMEAL CARROT MUFFINS

1 c. quick cooking oats
(not instant)
1 c. buttermilk
1 egg, beaten
1/3 c. melted butter or oleo
1/2 c. brown sugar
1 c. finely shredded carrots

1 t. vanilla
1 t. grated orange rind
1 c. whole wheat or all purpose flour
2 t. baking powder
1 t. soda
1 t. salt

Pour buttermilk over oats in bowl. Add beaten egg, melted butter, sugar, carrots, vanilla, and orange rind. Mix thoroughly. Combine flour, baking powder, baking soda, and salt. Mix. Add to oat mixture, stirring just until moistened. If desired, add raisins and dates. Fill greased muffin cups 3/4 full. Bake at 375 degrees for 15 to 20 minutes.

Becky Helmuth (Waitress)

A good life is like a good watch: open face, busy hands, pure as crystal, and full of good works.

GINGERSNAP RAISIN MUFFINS

1/4 c. margarine	1 t. salt
1/4 c. white sugar	1/2 t. cinnamon
1 egg	1/2 t. ginger
1/2 c. molasses	1/4 t. cloves
1 c. all-purpose flour	1/2 c. hot water
1 t. baking soda	1 c. raisins

Cream margarine and sugar. Add eggs and molasses and beat. Stir together flour, baking soda, salt, cinnamon, ginger, and cloves. Stir into molasses mixture, gradually . Add hot water and stir until smooth. Stir in raisins. Fill greased muffin cups and bake at 375 degrees for 20 minutes.

Becky Helmuth (Waitress)

MORNING GLORY MUFFINS

2 1/2 c. sugar	4 c. shredded carrots
4 c. flour	2 apples, shredded
4 t. cinnamon	1 c. pecans
4 t. baking soda	6 eggs, lightly beaten
1 t. salt	2 c. vegetable oil
1 c. shredded coconut	1 t. vanilla
1 c. raisins	

Sift together into a bowl the sugar, flour, cinnamon, baking soda, and salt. Add coconut, raisins, carrots, apples and pecans. Stir well. Add eggs, oil, and vanilla. Stir until blended. Spoon into greased muffin tins and bake in a pre-heated 375 degree oven for 20 minutes.

Viola Miller (Wife of Ned Miller-Essenhaus Foods)

Hail to the girl who's learned the art
Of cooking her way to her husbands heart.
She gives him roast and pies for dinner.
He couldn't be happier, but he could be thinner.

RAISIN BRAN MUFFINS

5 c. flour	4 eggs
6 t. baking soda	1 c. oil
3 c. sugar	10 oz. box raisin bran flakes
3 t. salt	extra raisins (if desired)
1 qt. buttermilk	

Mix and fill muffin cups 3/4 full. Bake 400 degrees for 12 to 15 minutes. Makes 6 dozen. Dough will keep in refrigerator up to 6 weeks.

Anna M. Slabaugh (Bakery)

Preserving Children

1 large grassy field	1/2 doz. children-all sizes
1 dog	1 long narrow brook

Mix children with other ingredients and empty them in the field. Stir continuously. Sprinkle with flowers. Pour brook gently over pebbles. Cover all with a deep blue sky and bake in a hot sun. When children are well browned, they may be removed. Cool in a bath tub with lots of soap and warm water.

BISCUITS

ALABAMA BISCUITS

1 pkg. yeast	1/4 c. shortening, melted
1 c. warm water	2 1/2 - 3 c. flour
2 t. sugar	2 t. baking powder, scant
pinch of salt	

Dissolve yeast in water. Add sugar, salt, and shortening. Sift flour and baking powder. Add to yeast. Knead 10 times. Roll out and cut with cutter. Butter both sides and fold over. Let rise for 1 hour. Bake at 350 degrees until brown. Do not over-bake.

Carolyn Hershberger (Bakery)

CHEESE GARLIC BISCUITS

2 c. Bisquick
2/3 c. milk
1/2 c. shredded cheddar cheese

1/4 c. butter, melted
1/4 t. garlic powder

Mix Bisquick, milk, and cheese until soft dough formed. Beat for 30 seconds. Drop dough by spoonful on un-greased baking sheet. Bake 8 - 10 minutes at 450 degrees or until golden brown. Mix butter and garlic powder. Brush on top of warm biscuits before removing from baking sheet. Serve warm. Yield: 10-12

Sharon Boley (Waitress)
Lori Miller (Waitress)
Charlotte Miller(Waitress)

MELT-IN-YOUR-MOUTH BISCUITS

2 c. flour
2 t. baking powder
1/2 t. cream of tartar
1/2 t. salt

2 T. sugar
1/2 c. Crisco shortening
2/3 c. milk
1 egg, beaten

Sift dry ingredients together and cut in shortening until mixture resembles coarse meal. Pour milk in slowly. Add eggs and stir well. Bake 10 to 15 minutes in a 450 degree oven.

Fannie Lehman (Meatroom)

Recipe for Happiness

(You do not need a bowl, spoon, or mixer; but it works.)

*Take two heaping cups of patience
*One heartful of love
*Two handfuls of generosity
*Dash of laughter
*One headful of understanding

Sprinkle generously with kindness and add plenty of faith. Mix well. Spread over a period of a lifetime. Serve to everyone you meet.

DOUBLE QUICK DINNER BUNS

3/4 c. water
1 pkg. dry yeast
1/4 c. sugar
1 t. salt

2 1/4 c. sifted bread flour
1 egg
1/4 c. shortening, soft

Dissolve yeast in water. Add sugar, salt, and about 1/2 of flour. Beat thoroughly for 2 minutes. Add egg and shortening. Gradually beat in the rest of the flour until smooth. Let rise 40 - 45 minutes in a warm place. Stir down batter and drop in greased muffin cups. Let rise until double in size, about 30 minutes. Bake 10 minutes in hot oven.

Joann Bontrager (Busser)

The Kitchen Prayer

Lord of pots and pans and things,
Since I've not time to be
A saint who's doing lovely things
Or watching late with thee
Or dreaming in the dawning light
Or storming heavens gates,
Make me a saint who's getting meals
And washing up the plates.
Although I must have Martha's hands
I have a Mary mind,
And when I black the boots and shoes
Thy sandals, Lord, I find.
I think of how they trod the earth
What time I scrub the floor.
Accept this meditation, Lord,
I haven't time for more.
Warm up my kitchen with they love
And light it with thy peace.
Forgive me all my worrying
And make my grumbling cease.
Thou who didst love to give men food
In room or by the sea,
Accept this service that I do.
I do it unto thee.

SUPERB GOLDEN CRESCENTS

4 c. sifted Gold Medal flour
1/2 c. sugar
2 pkg. yeast
1 t. saltwater

1 1/2 c. lukewarm milk
(I make it warmer)
1/2 c. shortening
2 eggs (or 4 yolks + 2 T.)

Measure flour called for in recipe. Place 1/3 of it in a bowl and set remainder aside. For instance, if your recipe calls for 6 c. flour, place 2 c. in a bowl. Measure remainder dry ingredients and add to flour in bowl. Stir in specified amount of dry yeast just right from envelope. Heat liquids and fat called for in the recipe over low heat until warm, being sure that you include the liquid that you would have normally used, for dissolving the yeast. Fat does not need to melt. Add warm liquid to dry ingredients in bowl. Turn on electric mixer and beat for 2 minutes at medium speed, scraping sides of bowl occasionally. Stop mixer, add 1/2 c. of reserved flour or enough to make a thicker batter. If eggs are called for, add here. Beat on high speed for 2 minutes, scraping sides of bowl occasionally. Stop mixer and stir in by hand the remaining flour to make a soft dough. (You may not need all the flour, for usually it takes a bit less when this short cut method is followed.) Let rise once. Divide dough into three equal parts, roll out into a 12" circle. Cut each circle into 16 pie shaped pieces, begin at rounded edge, roll up each piece so that the long point winds up on the underneath side. Place on greased cookie sheet, one inch apart. Cover with cloth and let rise about one hour. Bake 10 to 15 minutes in pre-heated 375 degree oven or until golden brown. Brush with melted butter. Yield: 4 dozen rolls.

Wanda S. Bontrager (Kitchen)

Things You Just Can't Do

Sow bad habits and reap good character.
Sow jealousy and hatred and reap love and friendship.
Sow dissipation and reap a healthy body.
Sow deception and reap confidence.
Sow cowardice and reap courage.
Sow neglect of the Bible and reap a well-guided life.

BROWN BREAD

1/2 c. white sugar   1/2 c. oleo
3 t. salt

Combine these three ingredients in bowl. Then pour 1 1/2 c. hot water over it to melt oleo. When sugar and salt is dissolved, add 1 1/2 c. cold water to make warm to the touch. Pour 3-3 1/2 c. white flour over the water. On top of this sprinkle 1 1/2 T. or 2 pkg. yeast. Stir , beat with egg beater until lumps disappear. Add 3 c. whole wheat flour. Stir with wooden spoon. Add 1 c. white flour. Knead until it does not stick to hands. Grease top and cover with plastic lid and let rise. Punch down in half an hour and let it rise again until it reaches the top of the bowl. Punch down again and put in pans. Let rise again. Bake in 400 degree oven for 45 minutes.

Mary K. Schmucker (Kitchen)

DATE NUT BREAD

2 c. boiling water   2 t. soda
2 heaping T. butter   2 c. dates, cut up

Combine and let cool.

2 heaping T. butter   1 t. vanilla
2 c. sugar   4 c. sifted flour
2 eggs   chopped nuts
1 t. salt

Cream butter and sugar. Add eggs, salt, and vanilla. Then add date mixture. Mix together well. Add flour and nuts. Pour into 6 well greased 1 lb. tin cans. Bake 1 1/2 hours at 300 degrees. Makes 6 nice round loaves that are ideal for gifts at Christmas.

Marilyn M. Kehr (Restaurant Gifts)

FRENCH HERB BREAD

5 to 6 c. flour
2 pkgs. dry yeast
1 pkg. dry ranch style
  buttermilk salad
  dressing mix (reserve 1 t.)

1 1/2 c. buttermilk
1/2 c. water
1/4 c. shortening
1 egg
1 T. melted butter

In large mixer bowl combine 2 c. flour, yeast, and 3 t. salad dressing mix. Mix well. Heat buttermilk, water, and shortening until warm, 120 to 130 degrees (shortening does not have to melt). Add to flour mixture. Add egg. Blend until moistened; beat 3 minutes at medium speed. Gradually stir in enough remaining flour to make a firm dough. Knead on well-floured surface until smooth, approximately 8 to 10 minutes. Place in greased bowl, turning to grease top. Cover; let rise in warm oven (turn oven to lowest setting for 1 minute, turn off) for 20 minutes. Punch down dough; divide into 2 parts. On lightly floured surface roll or pat each half to a 12 x 7 inch rectangle. Roll lightly, sealing edges and ends. Place seam down on greased cookie sheet. Make diagonal slashes about 2 inches apart in tops of loaves. Cover - let rise in warm oven until light and doubled about 30 minutes. Bake at 375 for 25 to 30 minutes. While warm, brush with melted butter and sprinkle remaining 1 t. salad dressing mix.

Erma Swartzendruber (Office)

How To Preserve A Husband

Be careful in your selection. Do not choose too young and take only such as have been reared in a good moral atmosphere. Some insist on keeping them in a pickle, while others keep them in hot water. This only makes them sour, hard, and sometimes bitter. Even poor varieties may be made sweet, tender, and good by garnishing them with patience, sweetening them with smiles and flavoring them with kisses to taste. Then wrap them in a mantel of love; keep warm with a steady fire of domestic devotion; and serve with peaches and cream. When thus prepared, they will keep for years.

OATMEAL BREAD

Mix together until dissolved:

2 1/2 c. hot water   2 pkg. yeast

Add:

2 c. oatmeal   1/4 c. brown sugar
1 T. salt   2 T. soft shortening

Then add 5 1/2 to 6 c. flour. Mix until batter is stiff. Let rise until doubled. Shape into 2 loaves or make into dinner rolls. Easy to make and never fails. Bake bread at 450 degrees for 50 minutes, until golden brown. Bake rolls at 450 degrees for 15 to 20 minutes.

Connie Bowers (Kitchen Supervisor)

RAISIN BREAD

2 pkg. yeast   1/2 c. vegetable oil
1 c. warm water   2 eggs, beaten
2 c. milk   3 lb. flour
1 c. sugar   1 1/2 c. seedless raisins
1 T. salt

Combine all ingredients, except raisins. Heat mixture to scalding. Let rise, then stir in raisins. Place on floured board and knead. Place in greased loaf pans. Bake at 300 degrees for 40 minutes.

Cletus Miller (Maintenance)

Jewish Penicillin

For bronchitis and other respiratory diseases: Season chicken soup with plenty of black pepper and garlic. Add a little curry powder. This combination increases secretions to help clear the airways. It is also good for the common cold.

Katie Hochstedler (Bakery)

TOMATO BREAD

2 c. tomato juice	1/2 t. basil
2 T. butter	1/4 c. grated cheese
3 T. sugar	1 pkg. yeast dissolved in
1/4 c. catsup	1/4 c. warm water
1/2 t. oregano	1 t. salt

Heat tomato juice and butter until butter melts. Add other ingredients, except yeast and flour. Cool to lukewarm. Add yeast and 3 c. flour. Beat well. Add remaining flour. Knead. Bake at 375 degrees for 30 minutes. Yield:2 loaves

Irene Schrock (Kitchen)

WHITE BREAD

1 pkg. dry yeast	2 1/2 c. warm water
1/3 c. sugar	2 1/2 T. vegetable oil
2 t. salt	7 c. flour

In large bowl combine yeast, sugar, salt, water, and oil. Gradually add 3 c. flour to form a soft dough. Beat 2 minutes with a mixer. Gradually add flour. Turn out onto a floured surface and knead until smooth. Place in greased bowl. Cover and let rise about 2 hours. Punch down. Divide into 2 portions and form loaves. Place in greased bread pans. Prick tops with fork. Let rise until higher than pans (about 2 hours). Bake at 350 degrees for 25 - 30 minutes. Cool 10 minutes. Butter tops of loaves. Place pans on sides until loosened. Remove bread and cool completely.

Mary A. Bontrager (Waitress)

When you have work to do,
Do it with will.
They who reach the top
Must first climb the hill.

ZUCCHINI BREAD

2 c. sugar
3 eggs, beaten
1 c. oil
2 c. flour
1/4 t. baking soda

1 t. salt
1 c. quick oats
2 c. zucchini, grated
1 t. vanilla

Cream sugar, eggs, and oil. Add dry ingredients, quick oats, zucchini, and vanilla. Grease pans. Bake at 350 degrees an hour or longer.

Pamela Frey (Bakery)

There are three kinds of people:
Go - Go
Go - Slow
No - Go

APPLE FRITTERS

1 1/2 c. flour
1 T. sugar
1 T. baking powder
1/2 t. salt
2 eggs beaten

3/4 c. milk, scant
1 T. hot salad oil
3 c. apples, peeled &
finely chopped
powdered sugar

Combine dry ingredients. Add eggs, milk, salad oil, and apples. Stir until moistened. Drop batter by teaspoonful into 1/2 inch hot oil. Cook until brown, 3 to 4 minutes each side. Drain and then roll in powdered sugar. Yield: 3 dozen

Wanita Yoder (Kitchen)

CINNAMON ROLLS OR TWISTS

Combine in small bowl: 1 c. warm water, 2 T. yeast, 2 T. white sugar, and 1 c. flour. Mix well and let rise while heating 2 c. milk. In large bowl combine: 2/3 c. white sugar, 1 stick oleo, and 2 1/2 t. salt. Add boiling hot milk and stir to dissolve sugar and oleo. Add 2 beaten eggs and your yeast mixture. Mix well and add 7 1/2 c. flour. Let rise once. This dough can be used for rolls or twists.

Mix 1 1/2 c. brown sugar and 2 T. cinnamon. Pull off dough size of a walnut. Roll into ball. Dip in oleo then sugar mixture. Twist into oblong twists and place on greased baking sheet. Bake at 350 degrees. Glaze while still warm.

Glaze

1/2 c. hot water
1 t. vanilla

2 T. white corn syrup
pinch salt

Mix together. Add powdered sugar to desired thickness, approximately 2 1/2 to 3 c.

Lena Lehman

"It's Up To You"

Have you made someone happy or made someone sad?
What have you done with the day that you had?
God gave it to you to do just as you would.
Did you do what was wicked or do what was good?
Did you lift someone up or put someone down?
Did you hand out a smile or give them a frown?
Did you lighten some load or some progress impede?
Did you look for a rose or just gather a weed?
What did you do with your beautiful day?
God gave it to you. Did you throw it away?

No Name

FOUNDATION SWEET ROLLS

1 c. scalded milk
1/2 c. sugar
1 1/2 t. salt
1/2 c. shortening
2 cakes yeast (or 2 T. dry)

1 c. lukewarm water
2 eggs, beaten
1/2 t. nutmeg
7 c. flour

Pour scalded milk over sugar, salt and shortening. Dissolve yeast in lukewarm water. Add yeast and beaten eggs. Beat well. Add flour gradually, beating well. Knead lightly, working in just enough flour so the dough can be handled. Place dough in a greased bowl, cover and let rise, about 1 1/2 hours (double size). Make into cinnamon rolls by dividing into 2 portions. Roll into oblong pieces 1/4" thick. Brush with 6 T. butter and sprinkle with 1 1/2 brown sugar and 1 T. cinnamon. Roll and cut in 1" thick slices. Let rise about 1 hour. Bake at 325 degrees for 15 to 20 minutes. Frost with powdered sugar frosting.

Powdered Sugar Frosting

1 t. vanilla
1 T. margarine

2 c. powdered sugar

Mix and add milk until is consistancy to spread.

Ida Weaver (Waitress)

FRUIT TWISTS

3-4 oz. pkg. crescent rolls
1-3 oz. pkg. cream cheese, soft
1/4 c. chopped nuts

1/3 c. raspberry, peach, cherry
or apricot preserves

Unroll crescent dough. Seal perforation to form rectangles from each pkg. Pat each into and 8 x 4 inch rectangle. Spread cream cheese on each one. Top with fruit and nuts. Cut each rectangle into 4 8x1 inch strips (total of 24 strips). Fold each strip in half, crosswise, and twist. Put on lightly greased foil lined baking sheet. Bake at 375 degrees for 8 to 10 minutes or until golden brown.

Betty Troyer (Kitchen)

MONKEY BREAD

1 c. milk, scalded
1/3 c. brown sugar
1/3 c. butter, melted
1/2 t. salt

1 pkg. yeast, dissolved
in 1/4 c. warm water
3 eggs, well beaten
3 3/4 - 4 c. flour (may use
whole wheat)

Set aside a mixture of sugar and cinnamon to dip the dough balls in. Mix
1 1/2 c. white sugar, 1/2 c. chopped nuts, and 6 T. cinnamon. Add sugar,
butter, and salt to scalded milk. When lukewarm, add dissolved yeast,
eggs, and just enough flour for stiff batter (dough is sticky). Cover and let
rise until double (about one hour). Knead and let rise again for 45
minutes. Roll into small balls of dough about the size of a walnut. Dip
balls into butter, then roll in sugar/cinnamon mixture. Pile balls loosely
into ungreased angel food cake pan and let rise again for 30 minutes.
Bake at 400 degrees for 10 minutes. Reduce heat to 350 degrees for
another 20 minutes or until golden brown. Remove immediately. Serve
warm.

Irene Schrock (Kitchen)

A Happy Home Recipe

4 c. of love
2 c. of loyalty
3 c. forgiveness
1 c. friendship

5 T. of hope
2 T. tenderness
4 qt. faith
1 barrel of laughter

Take love and loyalty and mix thoroughly with faith.
Blend with tenderness, kindness, and understanding. Add
friendship and hope. Sprinkle abundantly with laughter.
Bake with sunshine. Serve generous helpings daily.

Leola Kauffman (Laundry)

STRAWBERRY BRAID

1/2 c. warm water
2 pkgs. active yeast
1/2 c. sugar
1/2 c. lukewarm milk,
scald, then cool
1/2 c. margarine, softened
2 T. milk

2 eggs
1 t. salt
1 1/2 c. whole wheat flour
3 1/2 c. all-purpose flour
1 1/2 c. powdered sugar
1-12 oz. jar strawberry jam

Dissolve yeast in warm water in large bowl. Stir in sugar, 1/2 c. milk, butter, eggs, salt, whole wheat flour, and 1 c. all-purpose flour. Beat until smooth. Stir in enough of the remaining flour to make dough easy to handle. Turn dough onto lightly floured surface. Knead until smooth and elastic, about 5 minutes. Place in greased bowl, turning greased side up. Cover and let rise in warm place for about 1 1/2 hours. Grease 2 baking sheets. Punch down dough and divide in half. Roll each half into a rectangle, 15 x 9 inches, and place on cookie sheet. Make 2" cuts at 1" intervals on long sides of rectangle with scissors. Reserve 2 T. jam. Spread remaining jam lengthwise down center of rectangles. Criss-cross strips over jam. Let rise 40 minutes. Heat oven to 375 degrees and bake until light brown or 20 to 25 minutes. Mix powdered sugar, 2 T. milk, and the reserved jam. Drizzle over braids while warm.

Karen Hochstedler (Bakery)

HINTS FOR BAKING BREADS

1. Kneading the dough for a half minute after mixing improves the texture of baking powder biscuits.
2. Use cooking or salad oil in waffles and hot cakes in the place of shortening. No extra pan or bowl to melt the shortening and no waiting.
3. When bread is baking, a small dish of water in the oven will help to keep the crust from getting hard.
4. Dip the spoon in hot water to measure shortening, butter, etc., the fat will slip out more easily.
5. Small amounts of leftover corn may be added to pancake batter for variety.
6. When you are doing any sort of baking, you get better results if you remember to preheat your cookie sheet, muffin tins, or cake pans.

SWEDISH ROLLS

1/2 c. sugar	1 pkg. yeast
4 c. flour	1 c. warm milk
1 t. salt	2 eggs
1 c. oleo or butter	

Mix sugar, flour, salt, and butter as for pie dough. Add yeast softened in the cup of warm milk. Add eggs and mix thoroughly. Keep in refrigerator overnight or at least 6 hours. Divide dough into 4 parts. Roll into circle. Spread with melted butter and brown sugar and cinnamon mixture. Cut circle into 16 pieces, roll starting from big end. Place on greased cookie sheet and bake at 350 degrees for 10-12 minutes. Frost and put coconut on some and nuts on others.

Frosting

1 1/2 c. sifted confect. sugar	1 1/2 T. butter
3 T. cream	1 t. vanilla

John & Lois Sauder (General Manager)

If you spend most of your time improving yourself, you won't have as much time to criticize others.

OVEN TEMPERATURE CHART

Breads	Minutes	Temperature
Loaf	50-60	350 - 400 degrees
Rolls	20-30	400 - 450 degrees
Biscuits	12-15	400 - 450 degrees
Muffins	20-25	400 - 450 degrees
Popovers	30-40	425 - 450 degrees
Corn Bread	25-30	400 - 425 degrees
Nut Bread	50-75	350 degrees
Gingerbread.	40-50	350 - 370 degrees

SWEDISH TEA RINGS

1/2 c. milk	1 pkg. yeast
1/2 c. shortening	1/4 c. warm water
1/2 c. sugar	2 eggs, beaten
1/2 t. salt	3-3 1/2 c. flour

Scald milk. Add shortening, sugar, and salt. Stir until sugar dissolves. Cool until lukewarm. Dissolve yeast in 1/4 c. water. Combine with milk mixture. Add eggs and beat well. Add enough of the remaining flour to make a soft dough. Let rise. Roll out in rectangular shape and spread with 1/3 c. melted butter, 2/3 c. brown sugar, nuts, and cinnamon. Roll up as a jelly roll and put into a greased pie pan in a ring. Press edges together to seal. Cut with scissors 1/2" apart. Bake and spread with thin brown sugar glaze.

Brown Sugar Glaze

Melt 1 pkg. or 1/4 oz. gelatin in 3/4 c. hot water. Add 1 T. melted lard, 1 1/4 lbs. powdered sugar and vanilla to taste.

Irene Schrock (Kitchen)

HOMEMADE PANCAKES

2 1/4 c. flour	2 eggs
1 t. salt	5 T. salad oil
3 T. baking powder	2 c. milk
1/2 c. sugar	

Mix dry ingredients first, then add wet ones. Fry on hot griddle.

Betty Troyer (Kitchen)

The man who minds his own business generally has a good one.

HOMEMADE WAFFLES

3 eggs, separated
1/4 t. salt
3 t. baking powder
1 T. sugar

3 c. milk
3 c. flour
3 or 4 T. butter, melted

Mix all ingredients together. Beat egg whites until stiff. Fold into other ingredients. Pour into waffle maker.

Connie Bowers (Kitchen Supervisor)

Church members are either pillars or caterpillars. The pillars hold up the church; the caterpillars just crawl in and out.

PANCAKES

2 c. flour
1 t. soda
2 t. baking powder
1/2 t. salt

2 eggs
2 c. buttermilk
4 T. butter, melted

Sift together flour, soda, baking powder, and salt. Beat eggs. Add buttermilk and melted butter. Mix in dry ingredients. Fry on griddle at 375 degrees.

Glenda Yoder (Waitress)

MAPLE SYRUP

Combine 1 c. light corn syrup, 1/2 c. brown sugar, and 1/2 c. water. Cook and stir until 210 degrees on candy thermometer. Add a few drops maple flavor. It is ready to serve. A few drops of vinegar will keep the syrup for a while (stops crystallization).

Susanna Miller (Kitchen)

PANCAKE SYRUP

1 1/4 c. brown sugar
1/3 c. light corn syrup

3/4 c. white sugar
1 c. water

Boil together 5 minutes. Add 1 t. vanilla.

Delores Wagler (Maintenance)

BAKED OATMEAL

1c. brown sugar
1/2 c. melted butter

2 eggs, beaten

Mix together and add:

3 c. oatmeal
1 t. salt

2 t. baking powder
1 c. milk

Blend and pour into greased 13" x 9" glass pan and bake at 350 degrees
for 30 minutes.

Sharon Boley (Waitress)
Doreen Mast (Knot N Grain)

GRANOLA

3 c. whole wheat flour
3 t. soda
2 t. salt
3 c. brown sugar

12 c. quick oats
2 c. melted butter
2 c. coconut

Mix all together, by hand. Toast in oven at 250 degrees for 1 1/2 hours
or until golden brown and crispy. Stir every 15 to 20 minutes. Add
slivered almonds, chocolate chips, or raisins after toasted.

Mattie M. Diener (Waitress)
Freda Yutzy (Waitress)

Meats,
Poultry
& Main Dishes

FOOD QUANTITIES FOR SERVING 25, 50, 100 PEOPLE

FOOD	25 SERVINGS	50 SERVINGS	100 SERVINGS
Meat, Poultry, or Fish			
Wieners (beef)	6 1/2 pounds	13 pounds	25 pounds
Hamburger	9 pounds	18 pounds	35 pounds
Turkey or Chicken	13 pounds	25 to 35 lbs.	50 to 75 pounds
Fish, large whole (round)	13 pounds	25 pounds	50 pounds
Fish Fillets or Steaks	7 1/2 pounds	15 pounds	30 pounds
Salads, Casseroles			
Potato Salad	4 1/4 quarts	2 1/4 gallons	4 1/2 gallons
Scalloped Potatoes 1 12x20" pan	4 1/2 quarts	8 1/2 quarts	17 quarts
Spaghetti	1 1/4 gallons	2 1/2 gallons	5 gallons
Baked Beans	3/4 gallons	1 1/4 gallons	2 1/2 gallons
Jello Salad	3/4 gallons	1 1/4 gallons	2 1/2 gallons
Ice Cream			
Brick	3 1/4 quarts	6 1/2 quarts	12 1/2 quarts
Bulk	2 1/4 quarts	4 1/2 quarts or 1 1/4 gallons	9 quarts or 2 1/2 gallons
Beverages			
Coffee	1/2 pound and 1 1/2 gal. wat.	1 pound and 3 gal. water	2 pounds and 6 gal. water
Tea	1/2 pound and 1 1/2 gal. wat.	1 pound and 3 gal. water	2 pounds and 6 gal. water
Lemonade	10 to 15 lemons 1 1/2 gal. water	20 to 30 lemons 3 gal. water	40 to 60 lemons 6 gal. water
Desserts			
Watermelon	37 1/2 pounds	75 pounds	150 pounds
Cake	1 10x12" sheet cake 1 1/2 10" layer cake	1 12x20" sheet cake 3 10" layer cakes	2 12x20" sheet cakes 6 10" layer cakes

Meats, Poultry & Main Dishes

BAKED CHICKEN

12 oz. fresh mushrooms
1 chicken, boned & cut up
1 qt. chicken broth

8-12 oz. Mozzarella cheese, shredded

Put a layer of mushrooms in a 9 x 13 pan; add the chicken. Put cheese on chicken. Add broth and the rest of the mushrooms. Bake until chicken is done.

Jan Bontrager (Waitress)

BAKED CHICKEN AND RICE

1 c. raw rice
2 can cream of mushroom soup
2 c. milk

chicken, cooked & de-boned cubed/desired quantity
1 envelope Lipton onion soup mix

Wash rice and put in bottom of large buttered cake pan. Mix 1 can cream of mushroom soup with 2 c. milk. Pour over rice. Lay cut up chicken on top. On top of chicken sprinkle 1 envelope of Lipton onion soup mix. Cover with foil and bake 1 1/2 hours at 350 degrees.

Mel Lambright (Dishwasher)

73

BAKED CHUCK ROAST

3 to 5 lb. beef roast
1 pkg. onion soup mix

12 oz. cola drink

Place unseasoned roast in baking dish. Sprinkle with onion soup mix. Pour cola drink over roast. Cover and seal tightly with aluminum foil. Bake at 300 degrees for 3 1/2 hours or until tender. This has an excellent flavor.

Edna Nissley (Waitress)

BARBECUED LIVER AND ONIONS

2 T. butter
1 medium onion, sliced
1/2 lb. liver, cut in 1/2" strips

2 T. catsup
2 T. vinegar
1 T. worcestershire sauce

Saute onion in butter until golden. Add 1/2 lb. liver, cut in strips 1/2" wide, and brown just until red disappears. Mix and add remaining ingredients. Heat and serve.

Betti Kauffman (Hostess)

Sermon in soap

Duz you Dreft along with the Tide? Vel, now is the time for all to cheer up, if you want real Joy. The Trend is to Breeze to church regularly on Sunday morning. But, too many people Woodbury their heads in the pillow or work in their yards like Handy Andy or make their cars Sparkle, forgetting that the Lord's day was made for Lestoil. When the Lord is put first, a Dove will never need to be bent S.O.S. Don't trust your Lux by neglecting worship on Sunday. Maybe we ought to Dial you to remind you of Ivory palaces up yonder. This isn't just Bab-O, worship will add you your life Buoy. So Whisk yourself out of bed next Sunday morning, dress-up Spic-N-Span, and Dash like Comet to Sunday school and church. As you sing praise to God, it will bring Cleanser to your soul and you will feel like Mr. Clean all week. Pledge yourself and Pride of comfort and conscience will be yours. What's more, your Life will become full of Zest.

Judy Beachy
Betti Kauffman

74

BARBECUED MEATBALLS

Meatballs

3 lbs. ground beef
1 c. oatmeal
2 eggs
1/2 t. garlic
1/2 t. pepper

1-12 oz. can evaporated milk
1 c. cracker crumbs
1/2 c. chopped onions
2 t. salt
2 t. chili powder

Sauce

2 c. catsup
1/2 t. liquid smoke, to taste
1/4 c. chopped onion

1 c. brown sugar
1/2 t. garlic powder

To make meatballs, combine all ingredients (mixture will be soft) and shape into walnut size meatballs. Place meatballs in a single layer on wax paper lined cookie sheets. Freeze until solid. Store frozen meatballs in freezer bags until ready to cook. To make sauce, combine all ingredients and stir until sugar is dissolved. Place frozen meatballs in a 13 x 9 x 2 inch baking pan. Pour on the sauce. Bake at 350 degrees for 1 hour. Yield: 80 meatballs

Walter Lehman (Essenhaus Foods)

BARBECUE SAUCE

1 c. catsup
1 t. liquid smoke
2 T. light brown sugar
1/4 t. seasoned salt

pinch of dried parsley
1 T. finely chopped onion
1/4 t. dried garlic

Combine all ingredients and brush on chicken, beef, or pork during the last 10 minutes on the grill.

Dana Graber (Decorating Department)

If there were more self-starters, the boss wouldn't have to be a crank.

BARBECUE SAUCE (CHICKEN)

4 c. water
2 sticks margarine
5-6 T. worcestershire sauce

2 c. white vinegar
4 T. salt
1 T. garlic salt

Mix all ingredients. Add chicken pieces. Boil 10 minutes. Cover and soak overnight. No need to refrigerate. Grill chicken 20 minutes, occasionally dipping in sauce the chicken soaked in.

Randi Yoder (Supervisor Restaurant)

BARBECUE SAUCE (CHICKEN)

1 c. water
1/2 c. vinegar
2 T. salt
1 T. sugar
3/4 t. garlic powder

1/4 t. pepper
1/4 lb. butter
3/4 t. worcestershire sauce
1/2 t. tabasco

Mix ingredients together in a saucepan and simmer several minutes.

Mary A. Bontrager (Waitress)

BARBECUE MEAT BALLS

1 c. milk
3 lb. hamburger
2 c. oatmeal
2 eggs
1 c. chopped onion

1/2 t. garlic powder
2 t. salt
1/2 t. pepper
2 t. chili powder

Mix and shape into balls.

Sauce

2 c. catsup
1 1/2 c. brown sugar (scant)

2 T. liquid smoke
1/2 t. garlic powder

Bake at 350 degrees for 1 hour.

Noah (Amanda) Lehman

76

BEEF & CHEESE MACARONI

1 lb. macaroni
2 qt. beef broth
1T. beef base or bouillion

salt & pepper to taste
1 lb. processed cheese
2 cans cream of mushroom soup

Cook macaroni in beef broth seasoned with beef base, salt & pepper.
Add soup and cheese when macaroni is soft. Mix well.

Sue Miller (Manager)

BEEF JERKY

Sauce

1/4 c. soy sauce
1 T. garlic powder
1 t. hickory smoked salt

1 T. pepper
1/2 t. onion powder

Cut 1 1/2 to 2 lbs. boneless flank round steak into 1"x 1/4" or 1/2" strips.
Cut while partially frozen. Remove all fat. Mix meat in sauce and cover
tightly. Refrigerate 5 hours. Stir or shake every so often. Set oven at
lowest temperature. Meat will dry in 4 to 6 hours. Arrange meat close
together on rack. Check often.

Wanda S. Bontrager (Kitchen)

BEEF SAUSAGE

1 lb. ground beef
1/4 t. nutmeg
1/4 t. sugar

1 t. salt (scant)
1/4 t. sage

Mix well. Shape into patties and fry.

Marsha Gingerich (Bakery)

77

BREADED FISH

Dip fish in a mixture of 1 1/2 c. milk and 1 egg. Then dip in following mixture:

3 c. flour	2 T. paprika
1 t. sage	1 t. red pepper
1 t. thyme	4 T. Lawry's salt
1 T. chili powder	

Deep fat fry fish.

Walter Lehman (Essenhaus Foods)

People are like stained glass windows; they sparkle and shine when the sun is out, but when the darkness sets in their true beauty is revealed only if there is a light within.

CHICKEN ALA-KING

1 chicken	1 T. margarine
2-10 oz. pkg. peas and carrots	1 1/2 qt. chicken gravy
2 T. onion, chopped	salt/pepper, to taste
2 T. green peppers, diced	

Cook chicken until tender. Remove meat from bones. Cook the peas and carrots until almost tender. Saute onions and peppers in margarine for a few minutes. Mix all ingredients together and place in a greased casserole. Bake at 350 degrees for about 45 minutes. Good with bread crumbs or biscuits on top.

Betti Kauffman (Hostess)

CHICKEN BREADING

1 lb. crackers, crushed fine
4 t. garlic salt
4 t. salt

1 lb. Rice Krispies, crushed fine
12 t. Lawry's salt

Dip chicken pieces in equal amounts of butter and milk (heated). Roll in the above breading mixture and bake at 425 degrees for 20 minutes on cookie sheet. Then put in roaster and bake at 350 degrees for 1 1/2 hours.

Mrs. John H. Hochstetler (Mother-Lynn Hochstetler/Dishwasher)

CHICKEN BREAST ROLLED IN PARMESAN & BREAD CRUMBS

1 egg
1/8 t. salt
1/2 t. olive oil
1/2 c. parmesan grated cheese
1/2 c. fine white bread crumbs

4 boneless chicken breasts
1/4 t. salt
pinch of pepper
1 c. flour, spread on plate

Mix 1 egg, 1/8 t. salt, and 1/2 t. olive oil. Mix 1/2 c. parmesan cheese and fine white bread crumbs. Season chicken with salt and pepper. One at a time, roll chicken in flour and shake off excess. Dip in beaten egg. Then roll in cheese and bread crumbs. Lay on wax paper and allow to set for 10 to 15 minutes or several hours. Saute on both sides in butter, 4 minutes each side.

Rosie Eash (Waitress)

One of the hardest exercises to perform is to keep the jaw muscles in a closed position.

CHICKEN IN BARBECUE SAUCE

Sauce
1 pkg. Lipton onion soup mix	2 T. mustard
1 1/2 c. water	2 t. salt
1/2 c. vinegar	1 t. pepper
1/2 c. margarine or butter	1c. ketchup
1/4 c. sugar	

Simmer sauce 10 minutes. Place chicken pieces (1 chicken cut into serving pieces) in a pan with melted butter. Spread with 1/2 barbecue sauce and place in oven at 400 degrees for 30 minutes. Turn and spread other side with sauce and bake at 300 degrees for 1/2 hour longer, until sauce has cooked down enough to become brown and syrup-like and not watery. This sauce is also delicious on pork chops or round steak or cheaper cuts of beef.

Sue Miller (Manager)

The Heavenly Grocery Store

I had walked down life's highway quite some distance before
I spied a lovely building labeled, "Heaven's Grocery Store."
As I drew a little nearer, the door swung open wide,
And before I had a chance to think, I found myself inside.

I saw a host of angels. The were standing everywhere
One handed me a basket saying, "Child shop with care."
All the things I ever needed were in that grocery store.
I gathered up a basketful and then came back for more.

I selected a pound of patience, needed in every trial.
Further on was understanding. Love was also in that aisle.
I grabbed a box or two of wisdom, and a bag or two of grace,
And stopped to pick up strength and courage to help me win the race.

I weighed up mustard seeds of faith to help me fight off sin.
Then I found a sack of prayer. I just had to put that in.
Peace and joy were stacked up tall on the last and highest shelf.
And songs of praise were hanging there, so I just helped myself.

When I asked the check-out angel, "How much money do I owe?",
He answered with a smile, "Share them everywhere you go."
Again I turned to him and asked, "But how much do I owe?"
He answered with a smile, "Share them everywhere you go."
Again I turned to him and asked, "But how much do I owe?"
"My child, Jesus paid your bill a long long time ago."

Luella Yoder, revised by Fannie Beauchamp

CRISPY HERB BAKED CHICKEN

2/3 c. Idaho "Spuds" potato flakes
1/4 c. grated parmesan cheese
2 t. dried parsley flakes
1/4 t. garlic salt

1/8 t. paprika
dash of pepper
1/3 c. margarine/butter, melted
3 to 3 1/2 lbs. chicken, cut up, skinned, rinsed and patted dry

Heat oven to 375 degrees. Grease or line with foil a 15 x 10 x 1 baking pan or 13 x 9 pan. In medium bowl, combine dry ingredients. Stir until well mixed. Dip chicken pieces into margarine. Roll in potato flake mixture to coat. Place in greased pan. Bake at 375 degrees for 45 to 60 minutes or until chicken is tender and golden brown. 4-5 servings.

Walter Lehman (Essenhaus Foods)

If we fill our hours with regrets of yesterday and with the worries of tomorrow, we have no today in which to be thankful.

CURRY CHICKEN (QUICK)

6 skinned and boned chicken breasts (boil until tender)
1 c. mayonnaise (optional)
1 t. curry (to taste)

1-8 oz. pkg. noodles or pasta
1 can cream of mushroom soup
1 T. lemon juice
1 1/2 c. shredded cheddar cheese

Combine all ingredients (except 1/2 cheese) and pour into buttered baking dish (chicken breasts on top of noodle mixture). Sprinkle with rest of cheese and bake at 350 degrees for 30 minutes.
Serve with steamed broccoli or another vegetable and warm bread or rolls.

Vyvyan Dunlap (Decorating Dept.)

DAD'S FAVORITE STEAK

Chill a beef top round steak, swiss steak, or arm roast. Cut 1 1/2 to 1 3/4 inches thick. Score both sides in diamond pattern, 1/8 inches deep.

Marinade

1/2 c. water	1/2 c. soy sauce
1/4 c. salad oil	1/4 c. lemon juice
2 T. brown sugar	1/2 t. ginger
1 clove garlic, minced	10 drops hot sauce

Cook marinade slowly for 10 minutes. Chill. Place steak in plastic bag, add marinade, press out air, tie securely, and place in pan in refrigerator for 6 to 8 hours or overnight. Remove steak from marinade, reserving marinade, and place on grill over ash covered coals or on a rack in broiling pan so surface meat is 4 to 5 inches from heat. Broil at moderate temperature rare or medium (25 to 30 minutes, depending on thickness of steak and doneness desired), brushing with marinade and turning occasionally. Carve in thin slices, diagonally against the grain.

Dick Carpenter (Material Handling)

DAVID LANE'S BARBECUE SAUCE

1/2 c. KC barbecue sauce	1/2 c. catsup
1/4 c. white or brown sugar	1/2 t. yellow plain mustard
1/2 t. worcestershire sauce	1/2 t. Lawry's seasoned salt
1/2 stick oleo/butter, melted	1/4 c. raisins
1/4 c. pineapple juice	dash of salt, pepper,
4 T. Holland House red	onion powder, and
cooking wine,	ground cinnamon

Combine all above ingredients and use as a sauce over 2 to 8 pounds of meat. Good for venison, wild game, beef, pork, or poultry. Cook at 275 degrees in a covered oven pan for about 3 hours, depending on how much meat is used.

David Lane (Maintenance)

82

EASY CHICKEN

Place 4 chicken legs and thighs (skinned) in a baking dish. Pour a small bottle of Italian dressing over the chicken. Bake at 350 degrees for 30 minutes. Turn chicken over and bake another 30 minutes.

Walter Lehman (Essenhaus Foods)

FRUITED CHICKEN

3/4 c. sifted flour
1/4 t. garlic salt
1/4 t. ground nutmeg
1/4 t. salt
1/4 t. celery salt
1/3 c. soy sauce

2 1/2 to 3 lbs. chicken, cut into chunks
1/2 c. butter or margarine
2-20 oz. cans pineapple chunks in heavy syrup
3 T. flour
1 T. sugar

In a plastic bag mix 3/4 c. flour and seasonings. Add chicken pieces, a few at a time. Shake to coat. Brown chicken in margarine, reserving drippings. Place chicken pieces in 13 x 9 inch baking dish. Drain fruit, reserving 1 1/2 c. syrup. Arrange fruit over chicken. Stir 3 T. flour and fried chicken drippings. Add 1 1/2 c. syrup and 1/3 c. soy sauce. Stir until thickened and bubbly. Spoon over chicken. Cover with foil. Bake at 350 degrees for 1 hour. Serves 8.

Anne Yoder (Restaurant Manager)

GLAZED MEATLOAF

2 eggs, beaten
2/3 c. milk
2 t. salt
1/4 t. pepper
3 slices bread, cut into small pieces
2/3 c. carrots, shredded

2/3 c. onion, chopped
1 1/2 c. shredded cheddar cheese
2 lb. hamburger
1/4 c. brown sugar
1/4 c. catsup
1 T. mustard

Stir together eggs, milk, salt, pepper, and bread. Add carrots, onions, cheese, and hamburger. Mix well. Form into a loaf. Bake at 350 degrees for 1 hour and 15 minutes. Combine brown sugar, catsup, and mustard. Spread over meat loaf and bake 15 minutes longer. About 10 servings.

Marsha Gingerich (Bakery)

83

GLAZED MEATLOAF

4 1/2 lb. hamburger
2-2 1/2 c. cracker crumbs
4 1/2 t. salt

4 eggs, beaten
2 c. milk
1 t. pepper

Mix well. Bake until almost done. Add glaze over top the last 15 minutes.

Glaze:

1 c. brown sugar
1/2 c. catsup

2 t. mustard

Cook and stir until sugar is dissolved.

Jan Bontrager (Waitress)

Yesterday is gone, forget it. Tomorrow will never come, don't worry about it. Do a master job today.

GREAT BARBECUE RIBS

Sauce

1 gallon any kind BBQ sauce
1 can cola drink
1/4 c. worcestershire sauce

1 can beer
1 c. brown sugar
8 oz. grape jelly

Mix all ingredients and simmer for at least 4 hours.

Ribs

Bake ribs at 350 degrees until very tender, about 1 1/2 hours. Drain and cover with sauce. Broil or use open grill to brown and serve. You may like sauce on the side for dip.

Frances Blough (Waitress)

GRILLED HAMBURGERS

3 lb. ground chuck   1/2 c. water
1 pkg. onion soup mix   salt & pepper, to taste

Mix all ingredients. Make into patties. Grill.

Katie Miller (Shop Director)

HAM LOAF OR BALLS

4 lb. ham loaf (mix 60 %   1 small can pineapple,
ground ham, 40 % sausage)   drained (use juice only)
2 c. bread crumbs *   1 1/2 c. corn flake crumbs *
3 eggs, beaten   1 1/2 c. milk

Mix and shape into balls. Place on shallow baking dish. Bake at 350
degrees for 1 hour. Drizzle with sauce and continue baking for another
hour.

Sauce
1 1/2 c. pineapple juice   1/2 c. brown sugar
2 T. clear jel   1/3 c. dark corn syrup
1 t. dry mustard   2 T. vinegar

Heat slowly until thickened. Spoon over balls when half baked.

* 1 c. each of graham crackers and soda cracker crumbs instead of corn
flakes and bread crumbs.

Millie Whetstone (Kitchen)

KOREAN BEEF PATTIES

1 lb. ground beef   4 T. soy sauce
2 T. sugar   1 T. toasted sesame seed, crushed
black pepper, to taste   2 1/2 T. chopped green onion
1 T. toasted sesame oil   1 T. garlic, minced

Combine all ingredients. Form into four balls and flatten into patties.
Broil, grill or pan fry until done.

Iva Miller (Kitchen)

LEMON HERB GRILLED CHICKEN

Marinade

3/4 c. vegetable oil
2 t. seasoned salt
2 t. sweet basil
1/2 t. garlic powder

3/4 c. lemon juice
2 t. paprika
2 t. thyme

Combine ingredients. Marinate in refrigerator several hours or overnight. Broil or grill 2 to 2 1/2 lbs. of chicken pieces 4" from heat source for 15 to 20 minutes per side or until done. Baste often with marinade.

Nancy Boyer (Waitress)

MAINE SHANTY FISH LOAF

1 lb. cooked fish
1 1/2 c. soft bread crumbs
3/4 c. milk
1 egg , beaten
1 T. lemon juice
2 T. chopped green pepper
salt and pepper, to taste

1 1/2 T. parsley
1/2 t. baking powder
1/2 c. finely chopped celery
1/3 c. minced onion
2 T. pimento
1/2 t. "Old Bay" seafood seasonings

Mix all ingredients. Pour into greased loaf pan. Bake at 350 degrees for 1 hour.

Vyvyan Dunlap (Decorating Dept.)

 Contentment is not found in having everything, but in being satisfied with everything you have.

MARINADE FOR STEAK ON THE GRILL

1 1/2 c. salad oil
2 t. salt
2 cloves garlic, crushed
2 T. dry mustard
2 t. dried parsley flakes

3/4 c. soy sauce
1/2 c. wine vinegar
4 T. Worcestershire sauce
2 t. coarse black pepper
1/3 c. lemon juice

Combine all ingredients. Stir to blend. Make this sauce the day before using, if possible. Makes 3 cups. Two hours is the minimum time to marinade steak.

Mary A. Bontrager (Waitress)

Wisdom - Knowing what to do
Skill - Knowing how to do it.
Virtue - Doing it.

MARINADE SAUCE FOR GRILLED CHICKEN

1 pt. vinegar
1/3 c. salt
3 pt. water

1/2 c. margarine
4 T. worcestershire sauce

Mix all ingredients; bring to a boil. Add chicken pieces and bring to a boil again. Cover and let set for 1 hour (grilling time approximately 15 minutes). Make enough marinade sauce to cover chicken. Can be re-used if stored in refrigerator. This is a good and quick way to make barbecued chicken.

Betti Kauffman (Hostess)

MEATLOAF

1 1/2 lbs. hamburger
3/4 c. quick rolled oats
1/4 c. onion, chopped
1 egg, beaten

1 1/2 t. salt
1/4 t. pepper
3/4 c. milk
1/2 c. pizza sauce

Mix ingredients well and pack firmly in a baking dish. Mix the following sauce and pour over meatloaf:

1/3 c. catsup
1 T. mustard

2 T. brown sugar

Bake at 350 degrees for 1 1/4 hours.

Mary A. Bontrager (Waitress)

PARMESAN CHICKEN

1 c. grated parmesan cheese
2 c. soft bread crumbs
1/3 c. butter or oleo, melted

1/2 c. regular or Dijon mustard
6 chicken breasts, halved,
boned, skinned

Combine cheese, bread crumbs, and butter. Coat chicken breast with mustard, then dip in crumb mixture. Place breaded chicken in a 9 x 13 baking dish. Bake at 425 degrees for 15 minutes or until chicken is done. Makes 6 servings.

DiAnn Beachy (Waitress)

You can't change the past, but you can ruin a perfectly good present by worrying about the future!

POPPY SEED CHICKEN

2 lbs. cooked & boned chicken
or turkey
1-10 1/2 oz. cream of chicken soup
1 c. sour cream

1 stick butter, melted
1 1/2 c. crushed Ritz crackers
poppy seeds, to taste

Put 2 lbs. of cooked and boned chicken or turkey into a buttered
8" x 8" dish. Mix chicken soup and sour cream. Pour over chicken. Melt
butter or margarine and add to crushed Ritz crackers. Put on top and
bake at 350 degrees for 40 minutes. Double ingredients for 13" x 9"
pan. Sprinkle generously with poppy seeds before baking.

Mary. A. Schlabach (Waitress)

QUICK AND HEALTHY BAKED CHICKEN

1 whole chicken
1 c. milk

Lawry's salt

Wash chicken and remove skin. Dip in milk and sprinkle seasoned salt
on both sides. Place in a casserole and pour remaining milk in bottom of
pan. Bake at 350 degrees for 1 1/2 to 2 hours. When done, you have a
nice clear broth for gravy.

Amanda Miller (Bakery)

QUICK CHICKEN STIR FRY

2 T. oil
3 boneless, skinless,
halved chicken breasts
1 garlic clove, minced
1 c. red pepper strips
1/4 c. onions, diced

1 c. broccoli florets
1 c. carrot slices
1/2 c. Miracle Whip
1 T. soy sauce
1/2 t. ground ginger

Heat oil in skillet. Cut chicken in strips and put into skillet with garlic. Stir
fry for 3 minutes. Add vegetables. Stir fry for 3 minutes. Reduce heat to
medium and stir in Miracle Whip, soy sauce, and ginger. Simmer 1
minute. Serve over rice. Serves 4.

Lorena Mast (Waitress)

SALMON LOAF

1 can salmon
2 egg yolks, well beaten
1 T. lemon juice
2 T. butter melted in 1/2 c. hot milk

1 c. cracker crumbs
1 t. chopped parsley
2 egg whites, beaten stiff

Remove skin and bone salmon. Add all ingredients except egg whites. Fold in beaten egg whites last. Bake in buttered casserole at 350 degrees for 1 hour.

Katie Miller (Bakery)

SAUSAGE BALLS

1 lb. sausage
3 c. baking mix

1 lb. cheddar cheese
1 T. water

Mix together well. Roll into small balls. Let rise until almost double in size. Bake at 350 degrees for 15 to 20 minutes. Good snack.

Martha Coblentz (Bakery)
Sue Miller (Manager)

SEASONED BAKED CHICKEN

Mix

4 c. corn flakes
3 t. paprika
3 t. onion powder
2 T. sugar

4 t. salt
2 t. garlic powder
4 c. cracker crumbs
1/4 c. vegetable oil

Soak chicken strips from 2 medium size fryer chickens in 3/4 c. tender quick, 5 c. water, and 4 t. liquid smoke overnight.

Dip meat strips in warm vegetable oil and roll in mix. Put on greased pan and brown 1 hour at 370 degrees.

Esther Nisley (Bakery)

SLOPPY JOE'S

2 lb. ground beef   1 lb. ground pork
1 can tomato soup   1 onion, grated
1 carrot, grated   1 egg
1 c. bread crumbs

Mix all but bread crumbs and bake for 1 hour at 350 degrees. Add bread crumbs when ready to serve.

Wilma Weaver (Waitress)

SPICY BUFFALO CHICKEN WINGS

Butter Sauce

1 c. hot pepper sauce   8 oz. butter
1/2 c. vinegar

Cut tips of 10 lbs. of chicken wings and halve wings at joint. Cook wings for 10 to 15 minutes and dry thoroughly. Combine hot sauce, vinegar, and butter and heat. Fry wings and coat with butter sauce mixture.

Judy Beachy (Kitchen Manager)

TASTY LIVER

1 lb. beef liver   flour for dredging
1 1/2 c. milk (enough to cover)   salt & pepper, to taste
4 strips of bacon

Place liver in bowl and cover with milk. Let soak at least 15 minutes. While liver is soaking, fry bacon. Pour off fat, leaving enough to fry liver. Remove liver from milk, dredge in seasoned flour and fry until brown on both sides. Pour the milk the liver was soaking in into a skillet. Let simmer until milk disappears. Makes liver so tasty and tender.

Lena Miller (Meat Room)

VENISON JERKY

Slice meat 1/2" thick. Remove fat. Lay in single layer. Baste with liquid smoke and melted butter or margarine. Salt generously. You can add onion or garlic powder. Put strips in large bowl,* weigh down. Let stand overnight at room temperature. Put strips on oven rack. Bake at 150 degrees for 11 hours. After 6 hours, turn over. "Good Luck" and enjoy the taste.

*Do not use aluminum bowl.

David M. Lane (Material Handling)

WESTERN MEATBALLS

3 lb. ground beef
1 c. rolled oats
2 eggs
1 t. garlic powder
1 t. pepper

1 1/2 c. milk
1 c. cracker crumbs
1/2 c. chopped onions
1 t. salt
1 T. chili powder

Mix well and form into small balls.

Sauce

1 c. brown sugar
2 T. catsup
1/2 t. liquid smoke

1/2 c. chopped onion
1 t. garlic powder

Mix ingredients and cover meatballs. Bake at 350 degrees for 1 hour.

Ruthann Wagler (Kitchen & Bakery)

If you can't forgive others, you have burned the bridge over which you must pass.

AUNT ROSIE'S BAKED BEANS

4 c. pork & beans
1 t. dry mustard
1/2 c. catsup

3/4 c. brown sugar
3 slices chopped bacon (fried)
salt & pepper to taste

Combine all ingredients. Place in casserole dish and bake uncovered at 325 degrees for 2 1/2 hours.

Cletus Miller (Maintenance)

There's a difference between good sound reasons and reasons that sound good.

BACHELOR'S SURPRISE

2 lb. ground beef
4 c. minute rice
1/2 c. diced onion
salt & pepper to taste

1 can pork & beans
1 can stewed tomatoes
1/2 c. diced green beans

Optional: dash of catsup, mustard, and tabasco sauce

Brown beef. Cook rice. Combine all ingredients and season to taste. Simmer 1/2 hour. When ready to serve, add grated cheese. Serves 4 to 5 people or 1 bachelor for a week.

Jon Helmuth (Host/Waiter)

BAKED BEANS

1 can butter beans,
drained (30 oz. can)
1-43 oz. can baked beans
1 med. onion fried w/bacon
1 c. brown sugar
1 T. mustard

1 can chili hot beans,
not drained (22 oz.)
1/2 lb. fried bacon and
drippings
1 c. catsup

Mix all ingredients and bake uncovered at 350 degrees for 1 hour or 250 degrees for 3 to 3 1/2 hours. Serves 26.

Mary K. Schrock (Kitchen)

Blessed is he who expects nothing for he shall never be disappointed.

BAKED BEAN COMBO

8 slices bacon
2 large onions, sliced
1 c. brown sugar
1 t. mustard

1/2 t. garlic powder
1/2 c. vinegar
1 t. salt

1-16 oz. can green lima beans,
drained
1-16 oz. can kidney beans,
drained

2-15 oz. cans Great Northern Beans,
drained
1-28 oz. can pork & beans,
un-drained

Fry bacon and crumble. To bacon drippings add onions, brown sugar, mustard, garlic powder, salt, and vinegar. Heat for 20 minutes. Add all beans at once and bacon. Place in casserole dish and cover. Bake at 350 degrees for 2 hours. Makes 2 1/2 to 3 quarts.

Irma Stutzman (Bakery)

BAKED BROCCOLI CASSEROLE

1 10 oz. frozen broccoli,
thawed
3 T. flour
2 T. melted butter
2 c. potato chips, crushed

1 lb. cottage cheese
3 eggs, beaten
salt & pepper to taste
1/4 lb. Velveeta cheese

Mix all ingredients. In microwave, cook on high setting for 12 to 15 minutes, stirring half way through time. Add chips during the last 2 minutes.

Martha Coblentz (Bakery)

BAKED EGGS

8 slices bread
1 lb. cooked ham, bacon, or
sausage
2 c. grated cheese
7 eggs

3 c. milk
1 t. salt
1 c. corn flakes
1/2 stick butter

Crumble slices of bread in greased 9 x 13 inch pan. Add ham, bacon, or sausage. Add grated cheese. Another layer of bread can be added here, if desired. Beat eggs, milk, and salt. Pour over the top of bread mixture. Cover and refrigerate overnight. Next morning, sprinkle cereal on top, anything crunchy, usually corn flakes. Melt butter and pour over this. Bake, uncovered, for 1 hour at 300 degrees. Serves 12 to 15

Anna M. Slabaugh (Bakery)

Temptation becomes a sin when you yield to it.

BAKED FRIES

2 large baking potatoes,
scrubbed
1 T. margarine, melted

1/2 t. paprika
1/4 t. salt
parmesan cheese, to taste

Cut potatoes in half, lengthwise. Cut each half into 4 spears. Cook in pot of lightly salted water for 3 minutes. Drain. Toss with margarine, salt, and paprika. Spread on cookie sheet which has been coated with cooking spray. Bake in 400 degree oven for 15 minutes or until tender. Place in towel lined basket. Sprinkle with parmesan cheese.

Hope Miller (Kitchen Supervisor)

BAKED GREEN BEANS AND MUSHROOMS

2 c. bread crumbs
1/2 c. melted butter
4-3 oz. cans sliced mushrooms,
drained
3-15 oz. cans cut green beans,
drained
1/2 lb. bacon, cut & fried

1/4 t. salt
1/8 t. pepper
2/3 T. chopped onion
2-10 oz. cans cream of mushroom
soup
1 c. milk
1/2 c. toasted slivered almonds,
optional

Combine bread cubes with butter; place half the mixture in greased 13x9x2 casserole. Add mushrooms and beans; sprinkle with salt, pepper and onion. Combine soup and milk; pour over mixture. Sprinkle with remaining bread crumbs; sprinkle with almonds. Bake at 400 degrees for 30 minutes. Yield: 12 servings.

Sue Miller (Manager)

If the T.V. set and the refrigerator weren't so far apart, some of us wouldn't get any exercise at all.

BAKED PIZZA SANDWICH

1 lb. ground beef
1 t. oregano leaves
1 pt. pizza sauce
2 c. Bisquick
1 egg

2/3 c. milk
1-8 oz. pkg. cheddar cheese, shredded
1 1/4 c. parmesan cheese, optional

Cook and drain meat. Stir in oregano leaves and half of pizza sauce. Heat to boiling. Mix Bisquick, egg, and milk. Measure 3/4 of batter in a greased casserole. Pour remaining pizza sauce over batter. Spread some shredded cheese, meat mixture, soup, and remaining cheese and put the rest of the batter on top by spoonfuls. Sprinkle with parmesan. Bake uncovered until brown in 425 degree oven.

Marietta Helmuth (Waitress)

BAKED POTATO WEDGES

Arrange 5 or 6 potatoes (cut into wedges) that have been scrubbed clean (skin side down) in shallow baking pan. Mix the following ingredients together and brush or pour over potatoes:

2 T. parmesan cheese
1 t. salt
1/2 t. pepper

1/2 t. garlic powder
1/2 t. paprika
1/2 c. oil

Bake at 375 degrees for 45 minutes.

Alice Risser (Dutch Country Gifts Cashier)

BAKED SQUASH

1 large squash
1/2 c. packed brown sugar
1/4 t. cinnamon

1/4 t. nutmeg
1/4 c. butter, melted
2 t. lemon juice

Place squash in 2 qt. casserole dish. Sprinkle with spice and sugar. Drizzle with butter and lemon juice. Bake at 350 degrees until squash is soft.

Betty Troyer (Kitchen)

BEEF AND NOODLES CASSEROLE

1 lb. hamburger
1/2 c. chopped onion
8 oz. pkg. cream cheese
3/4 c. milk

1 can cream of mushroom soup
8 oz. pkg. noodles, cooked
1 can green beans or corn,
drained

Optional: 1/4 c. chopped green pepper or pimento

Brown meat, add onion and cook until tender. Stir in cream cheese and milk until well blended. Add remaining ingredients. Bake in 2 quart dish at 350 degrees for 30 minutes.

Jan Bontrager (Waitress)

BREAKFAST CASSEROLE

1 lb. sausage, ham, bacon,
or hamburger
6 eggs
2 c. milk

1 t. salt - dash pepper
1 t. dry mustard
6 slices bread, cubed
1 c. cheddar cheese, grated

Brown meat (if using raw meat) drain and set aside. Beat eggs and add milk, salt, pepper, and dry mustard. With hands , add bread and "mush" until bread is mixed well. Add cheese and meat. Refrigerate overnight. Bake in 9 x 9 pan at 350 degrees for 45 minutes. Serves 6

Barb Weaver (Restaurant Gifts)

BREAKFAST HAYSTACK

1 qt. home fries
6 to 8 oz. mushrooms,
sliced & fried in butter
2 c. toasted croutons

12 eggs, scrambled
1 c. ham, chopped; or 1 c.
sausage, fried & crumbled;
or 1/2 bacon, fried & crumbled

Put this in layers like haystack and serve with cheddar cheese sauce on top. Yield: 6 people

Ruth A. Yoder (Bakery)

98

BREAKFAST PIZZA

1 lb. bulk sausage
1 pkg. Jiffy pizza crust mix
1 c. potatoes, cooked & shredded
1-4 oz. pkg. shredded cheddar
cheese

4 eggs
3 T. milk
1/2 t. salt
1/8 t. pepper
2 T. grated parmesan cheese

Brown sausage and drain. Cool. Prepare crust as directed on package. Spoon cooled sausage over crust. Sprinkle with potatoes and cheddar cheese. Beat eggs, milk, salt and pepper together. Pour over potatoes and cheese. Sprinkle with parmesan cheese. Bake at 375 degrees for 30 minutes. Slice and serve.

Marietta Helmuth (Waitress)

BREAKFAST SOUFFLE

16 slices of bread
1-12 oz. can Spam
1/2 onion, diced
1/2 green pepper, chopped
1-4 oz. can mushrooms, drained
8 oz. cheddar cheese, grated

6 large eggs
3 1/4 c. milk
1/4 t. pepper
1 t. salt
2 c. corn flakes, crushed
1/3 c. melted butter

Remove crusts from bread. Butter one side. Place half of bread, buttered side down, in a 9 x 13 pan. Slice Spam into 12 slices and place on bread. Sprinkle the onion, green pepper, mushrooms, and cheese over the Spam mixture. Place remaining bread on top, buttered side up. Beat eggs. Add milk and seasonings. Pour over bread. Refrigerate over night. Remove one hour before baking. Top with crushed corn flakes and melted butter. Bake at 350 degrees for one hour or until set.

Nancy Boyer (Waitress)

 What you are is God's gift to you; what you become is your gift to God.

99

BROCCOLI CHEESE CASSEROLE

16 oz. frozen broccoli, thawed
1/2 c. onion
2 cans mushroom soup

1 c. celery
1 c. melted butter
2 c. minute rice
1-16 oz. Cheese Whiz

Mix everything. Bake at 350 degrees for 1 hour. Can be made in a crock pot.

Edna Nissley (Waitress)

BROCCOLI AND HAM POT PIE

1 small pkg. frozen broccoli,
cooked and drained
2 c. ham, cooked and cubed
3 T. onions, chopped
2 c. swiss cheese, shredded

1 1/4 c. half & half
3 eggs, slightly beaten
salt & pepper, to taste
1-10" pastry shell

Mix first 4 ingredients. Scald milk and add eggs to milk. Pour over vegetable and meat. Bake at 350 degrees approximately 45 minutes or until brown on top.

Amanda Miller (Bakery)

BROCCOLI BACON QUICHE

4 slices bacon
4 eggs
1 c. half & half
1 c. grated swiss cheese

2 c. broccoli florets
1/4 t. salt
1/8 t. garlic powder
1/8 t. lemon pepper

Preheat oven to 350 degrees. Cook bacon until crisp and set aside. Beat eggs with half & half and cheese. Stir in broccoli, salt, garlic powder and lemon pepper. Crumble bacon. Stir 1/2 crumbled bacon into egg mixture. Pour mixture in a 9 inch pie plate. Bake at 350 degrees for 30 to 35 minutes or until knife inserted halfway between center and edge comes out clean. Top with remaining bacon.
Yield: 4 servings

Barbara Miller (Maintenance)

BROCCOLI CASSEROLE

1 c. rice
1 can cream of chicken soup
1 can mushroom soup
1 small jar Cheese Whiz
2 c. chicken, cooked & diced

1/2 c. chopped onion
1 10 oz. frozen broccoli
1/4 c. milk
1 can french fried onion rings

Cook rice. Mix all ingredients together, except onion rings. Spread in a greased 9 x 13 pan. Bake 25 minutes at 350 degrees. Place onion rings on top and bake 20 more minutes.

Barb Weaver (Restaurant Gifts)

BURRITO CASSEROLE

Mix 2 cans cream mushroom soup mixed with 16 oz. sour cream. Brown 3 lbs. hamburger with 2 packages taco seasonings. Mix refried beans with hamburger if you want. Cover with soft burrito shells. Bake at 350 degrees for 45 minutes to 1 hour. Layer cheese over top when done baking and it's still hot so cheese can melt. When ready to serve top with lettuce and tomatoes. This makes a big roaster 1/2 full.

Ruth Ann Schrock (Bakery)

BURRITOS

2 c. all-purpose flour
1/3 c. oleo
1/2 c. milk, or more for right consistency

1/2 t. salt
1 t. baking powder

Mix all ingredients to make a soft dough (or use 8 -10 soft tortilla shells).

1 lb. hamburger, browned
1 16 oz. can refried beans
3 tomatoes
shredded mozzarella & cheddar cheeses

1 pkg. taco seasonings
1 can pizza sauce or salsa
1 pepper, chopped

Mix above ingredients and fill dough or tortilla shells in layers and fold over top and pinch to seal edges. When using the dough brush top with milk. Bake at 325 to 350 degrees. Serve immediately with sour cream, lettuce, tomatoes, and taco chips if desired.

Ruth A. Yoder (Bakery)

BURRITOS

1 1/2 lb. hamburger   1 med. onion

Brown and drain. Add 1 package burrito mix, 1 c. water, and 1-15 oz. can refried beans. Simmer for 10 minutes. Heat 12 tortilla in un-greased pan, 1 at a time. Fill with hamburger mixture.

Sauce:

24 oz. can tomato sauce   1 pkg. taco seasoning

Pour sauce over tortillas. Top sauce with 12 oz. American cheese. Bake at 350 degrees for 30 minutes. Serve with chopped lettuce, tomatoes, and sour cream.

Katie Miller (Shop Director)

BURRITO'S

1 lb. hamburger   1 c. chopped onions

Fry. Add 1 can refried beans. Season with salt, pepper, cumin, and hot pepper. Lastly, add shredded cheddar cheese, any amount. Fill 10 or 12 flour tortilla and put on cookie sheet with sides. (Spray pan with cooking spray)

Sauce:
Fry 2 medium onions and 1/2 green pepper in 3 T. butter. Add 2-8 oz. tomato sauce, 1 c. water, 1 small green hot pepper, and 1 T. chili powder. Cook for 30 minutes on low heat. Makes 3 c. Put sauce on top of burritos and top with shredded cheese and bake at 350 degrees until cheese is melted. They are ready to serve.

Bertha Miller (Noodle House)

 If it goes in one ear and out the mouth - it's gossip.

BURRITOS

2 lb. hamburger
1 T. season salt
1 t. red pepper
3 cans refried beans
1/2 c. green peppers, chopped
1/2 c. onion, chopped
8 slices Velveeta cheese

1/2 c. tomatoes, chopped
2 pkgs. Ortega flour shells
1 qt. pizza sauce
1 can nacho cheese sauce
1 pkg. mozzarella cheese,
shredded

Brown hamburger with salt and red pepper. Drain grease. Add 3 cans refried beans, chopped tomatoes, pepper, onion to your taste; mix together. Spread 1 T. mixture on each shell. Roll up the shells and put in greased pan. Spread mixture of 1 qt. pizza sauce and 1 can nacho cheese sauce over burritos. Bake at 400 degrees until sauce bubbles. Spread Velveeta cheese slices and mozzarella cheese over the top. Melt then serve. Good with cottage cheese or sour cream and taco sauce.

Martha Miller (Dishwasher)

CASHEW CHICKEN WITH SNOW PEAS

4 T. peanut oil
4 oz. raw cashews
1/2 lb. snow peas drained

4 oz. can button mushrooms,
drained
15 oz. can bamboo shoots,

Seasoning Sauce

1 c. chicken broth
1 T. cornstarch
1/2 t. sugar

3 T. soy sauce
1/2 t. salt

Marinate 3 chicken breasts (boned and sliced) in 1 T. soy sauce and 1 T. cornstarch. Make seasoning sauce. Fry nuts in 4 T. hot oil. Remove when light brown. Add marinated chicken to hot oil. Cook until white. Add peas, mushrooms, and bamboo shoots. Stir-fry 2 minutes. Add seasoning sauce. Cook until bubbly and thickened. Put on serving plate and top with nuts. Serve with white rice.

DiAnn Beachy (Waitress)

CELERY-MUSHROOM POULTRY STUFFING

1/4 lb. oleo or butter
2 c. onion, finely chopped
2 c. celery, chopped
2 c. mushroom soup
6 c. cooked rice

2 t. salt
1/2 t. black pepper
3 t. sage or to taste
1 t. poultry seasoning
1 c. chicken broth

Melt oleo in 2 quart saucepan. Add onions, celery, and mushrooms (if use fresh mushrooms). Cover and cook slowly until tender. Add rice, salt, pepper, seasoning and broth. Immediately, stuff into fowl. Bake covered in the oven.

8 c. dressing is enough for a 9 to 10 lb. hen
1 c. uncooked rice = 3 c. cooked rice
   Option: chicken base, in place of poultry seasoning
   mushroom soup in place of chicken broth

Esther Nisley (Bakery)

CHEESE POTATOES

8-10 potatoes
1-8 oz. pkg. cream cheese
1 c. sour cream
paprika

1 or 2 T. butter
salt
garlic salt

Boil potatoes, drain and mash. Beat sour cream and cream cheese until blended. Add to hot potatoes, beating constantly until light and fluffy. Season to taste with salt and garlic salt. Put in 2-quart casserole. Sprinkle with paprika and bake at 350 degrees until slightly brown. These can also be refrigerated several days then baked. Also can be frozen then baked for an hour or heated in a crockpot.

Sue Miller (Manager)

Happiness is not having what you want, but in wanting what you have.

CHEESY POTATO CASSEROLE

6 potatoes, cooked, peeled, sliced
1 c. cheddar cheese, shredded
1/3 c. onion, chopped
1 can cream of chicken soup

1/4 c. butter
1 c. sour cream
1 t. salt

Mix together potatoes, half of cheese, and remaining ingredients. Put in casserole dish and sprinkle with rest of cheese. Bake at 400 degrees for 45 minutes.

Sharon Boley (Waitress)

CHEESY POTATO CASSEROLE

6 med.potatoes, cooked, peeled, sliced
1 c. cheddar cheese, shredded
1 c. sour cream

1 can cream of chicken soup
1/3 c. chopped onion
1/4 c. butter
1 t. salt

Mix together potatoes, half of cheese, and the remaining ingredients. Put into casserole dish and sprinkle with remaining cheese. Bake at 400 degrees for 45 minutes.

Viola Miller (Wife of Ned Miller-Essenhaus Foods)

CHEESY VEGETABLE CASSEROLE

1/2 lb. American cheese
1/2 c. butter or margarine
1 c. crushed butter crackers

1-16 oz. bag frozen vegetables,
(broccoli, cauliflower, and
carrots) thawed & drained

Cut cheese into cubes. Place in saucepan with 1/4 c. butter. Heat over medium heat until melted and smooth, stirring often. Place vegetables in a 1 quart casserole dish. Pour cheese mixture over and mix well. Melt remaining butter. Stir in cracker crumbs. Sprinkle over top of casserole. Bake uncovered at 350 degrees for 20 to 25 minutes. Serve at once.

Barbara Miller (Maintenance)

CHICKEN CASSEROLE

1/2 loaf white bread, cubed
1 1/2 c. cracker crumbs, divided
3 c. chicken broth
3 eggs, lightly beaten
1 t. salt
3/4 c. celery, diced
2 T. onion, chopped
3 c. chicken, cooked & cubed
1-8 oz. can sliced mushrooms, drained
1 T. butter or oleo

In mixing bowl combine bread cubes and 1 c. cracker crumbs. Stir in broth, eggs, salt, celery, onion, chicken, and mushrooms. Spoon into a greased 2 quart casserole. In a saucepan, melt butter and brown remaining crackers crumbs. Sprinkle over casserole. Bake at 350 degrees for 1 hour. 6-8 servings

Treva Yoder (Miller's Housekeeper)

CHICKEN GUMBO CASSEROLE

Put 9 broken slices of bread on bottom of loaf pan. Add 4 c. chicken pieces. Mix together 1/4 c. melted oleo, 1/2 c. salad dressing, 4 beaten eggs, 1 c. milk, 1 c. broth, and 1 t. salt. Put mixture on top of chicken and bread. Top with slices of Velveeta cheese and two cans of cream of celery soup. Buttered crumbs on top. Cover. Refrigerate overnight. Bake at 350 degrees for 1 1/4 hour.

Treva Lehman (Waitress)

Casseroles

Let's pour some happy spirit
In a great big mixing bowl,
Then add a few ingredients,
And lo! A casserole!

CHICKEN POT PIE

6 c. flour   3/4 t. salt
1 c. oleo   3 t. baking powder
3/4 c. milk

Roll out and press in glass pie pans.

Gravy
1 qt. chicken broth   1 1/2 c. cooked chicken

Filling

1 1/2 c. potatoes, cooked & cubed 1 c. carrots, cooked
1 c. celery, cooked   1 c. frozen peas

Mix gravy with vegetable filling and pour into shells. Top with crust.
Bake at 350 degrees for 1 hour.

Carolyn Hershberger (Bakery)

CHICKEN RICE CASSEROLE

2 c. cooked rice   3/4 c. mayonnaise
2 T. diced onion   1 can cream of chicken soup
1 c. diced celery   2 c. cooked chicken

Cook rice and set aside. Mix all ingredients together and place in 9 x 13
baking dish.

Topping:

2 T. melted butter   1 c. corn flake crumbs

Mix together and sprinkle on top of casserole. Bake at 350 degrees for
1 hour. Serves 8-10.

Lena Miller (Kitchen)

Good exercise for the heart; bending down and helping
another up.

CHICKEN SPAGHETTI CASSEROLE

1 green pepper, diced
1 c. celery, diced
1 medium onion, diced
1 lb. Velveeta cheese
1 can mushroom soup
1 can cream of chicken soup

1 lb. spaghetti
1 c. chicken, cooked &
de-boned (save broth)
1 small jar pimento's
1 c. mushrooms, drained
1 can Rotel

Saute peppers and celery in butter. Melt 1 lb. Velveeta cheese with soups. Add sauteed onions, green peppers, and celery. Cook spaghetti in chicken broth and drain. Mix together and put in un-greased 9 x 13 pan. Top with 1 c. grated cheddar cheese. Bake at 350 degrees for 30-35 minutes.

Judy Beachy (Kitchen Manager)

CHILI EGG PUFF

10 eggs
1 t. baking powder
1 pt. creamed cottage cheese
1/2 c. butter or margarine

1/2 c. flour
1/2 t. salt
1 lb. shredded cheese
2-4 oz. cans diced green chili's

Combine all ingredients. Heat and pour into 9 x 13 inch pan. Bake at 350 degrees for 35 minutes. Serves 10 to 12. Good with salsa.

Viola Miller-Wife of Ned Miller (Material Handling)

CHINESE CASSEROLE

1 can cream of chicken soup
1 can of water
1 can Chinese vegetables

1 can cream of mushroom soup
1/2 c. dry rice

Mix with 1 lb. browned hamburger. Bake at 350 degrees for 1 hour. Add Chinese noodles on top and brown for 10-15 minutes.

Cecelia Berkey (Office)

CHINESE DISH

1 lb. ground hamburger	1 c. rice
1 small onion	1 c. water
1 large can chopped suey vegetables	1 large can sprouts
1 T. soy sauce	1 can cream of mushroom soup
	chow mein noodles

Cook hamburger and onion. Drain. Combine other ingredients (except for noodles) in a greased casserole. Bake 1 hour at 375 degrees. Add noodles at the table.

Marietta Helmuth (Waitress)

CORNED BEEF CASSEROLE

1-6 oz. pkg. macaroni	1 can cream of mushroom soup
1-12 oz. can corned beef	1 c. whole milk
1/4 lb. American cheese	butter cracker crumbs for topping
1 can cream of chicken soup	

Cook macaroni and drain. Chop corned beef and cube cheese. Combine all ingredients and put in casserole dish. Top with butter crumbs. Bake 1/2 hour at 350 degrees.

Bill Burns (Bakery)

CORN FRITTERS

1 1/2 c. flour	2 t. baking powder
1/2 t. salt	1 egg
1 c. fresh or frozen corn	milk, enough for stiff dough

Mix all ingredients together. Fry by tablespoon in deep fat. Serve with syrup.

Leola Kauffman (Laundry)

CORNMEAL MUSH

4 1/2 c. corn meal
3 c. cold water
2 1/2 t. salt

6 c. boiling water
3 c. milk

Mix corn meal, cold water, salt. Stir into boiling water and milk. Bring to boil while stirring. Turn heat on low and cook about 45 minutes, slowly. Stir occasionally. Then pour out in pans. To keep the top soft, put a bar of oleo on the top of the mush. Lay a sheet of wax paper over pan to cool.

Ida Weaver (Waitress)

CRUSTY MEXICAN BEAN BAKE

Crust

1/2 c. flour
1/2 c. sour cream
2 T. shortening or margarine

1/2 t. baking powder
1/2 t. salt
1 egg, beaten

Stir together all ingredients (may be slightly lumpy). Spread thinly with back of spoon on bottom and sides of a shallow greased 2 quart casserole. (Crust may be stirred together in advance. Refrigerate until ready to use.) Fill with bean mixture.

Filling

3/4 lb. ground beef
1/2 c. onion
2 c. un-drained & cooked kidney beans

1 t. salt
2 t. chili powder
3/4 c. (6 oz.can) tomato paste

Brown ground beef and onion in skillet. Add the rest of the ingredients. Spoon into crust and bake at 350 degrees for 30 minutes. Sprinkle top with 1/2 c. grated cheese, lettuce, and/or 1 c. chopped tomatoes.

Marilyn Bontrager (Waitress)

EASY MEATBALL STROGANOFF

1 lb. ground beef
1/4 c. fine dry bread crumbs
1/4 onion, chopped fine
1 egg
1/4 t. salt

1 can cream of mushroom soup
1/2 c. sour cream
1/4 c. water
8 oz. noodles, cooked

Mix thoroughly: beef, crumbs, onion, egg, and salt. Shape into 16 meatballs. Brown in skillet (use shortening if necessary). Pour off fat. Add soup, sour cream, and 1/4 c. water. Cover and simmer for 20 minutes. Stir often. Serve with noodles.

Vada Whetsone (Bakery)

EASY PIZZA

1 1/2 c. flour
1/2 t. salt
1 t. oregano

2 eggs
1 c. milk
2 t. baking powder

Mix together above ingredients and pour onto cookie sheet. Fry together 1 lb. hamburger and 1 medium onion. Put on crust. Bake at 400 degrees for 20-25 minutes. Top with pizza sauce and cheese. Put in oven until cheese melts.

Delores Wagler (Maintenance)

EASY PIZZA DOUGH

2 c. flour
2/3 c. milk
1/2 c. oil

1 T. baking powder
1 t. salt

Mix ingredients and knead. Spread on pizza pan.

Erma Yoder (Maintenance)

FETTUCCINE ALFREDO WITH CRAB

1/2 c. butter, melted
1/2 c. heavy cream
1/3 c. shredded mozzarella cheese
1 t. chopped parsley

1 pkg. imitation crab
meat, chunk style
3 c. cooked fettuccine noodles
1/4 c. parmesan cheese

Combine butter, cream, mozzarella cheese and cook over low heat until cheese melts and cream bubbles and thickens.

Add parsley and crab. Stir and heat until meat is heated through. Arrange fettuccini noodles on a large plate or shallow dish. Pour mixture over noodles and garnish with parsley and parmesan cheese. Serve at once. Serves 4.

Malinda Eash (Knot N Grain)

GOLD RUSH BRUNCH

Cook and prepare 4 large potatoes for hash browns or use frozen hash browns. Fry lightly and add 2 T. onion and 2 T. parsley. Put into a greased 9 x 13 inch pan. Top with the following in layers:

1 lb. ham or Canadian bacon,
cubed

8 hard boiled eggs, sliced
1 1/2 lb. cheddar cheese ,shredded

Heat and dissolve in sauce pan and pour over the above:

1/4 c. melted butter
1/4 t. salt
1 c. sour cream

1/4 c. flour
1 3/4 c. milk
pepper

Bake at 400 degrees for 30 to 40 minutes. It can be made ahead and refrigerated (allow more heating time).

Marsha Gingerich (Bakery)

The Christian's walk should contrast with the world, not blend with it.

GOULASH

3 c. dry macaroni
1 lb. hamburger
1 medium onion, diced
salt & pepper, to taste

1 pepper, diced
1 pkg. taco seasoning mix
1 quart tomato juice

Boil macaroni in water until soft. Brown together hamburger, onion, pepper, and taco seasoning. Drain hamburger and macaroni. Mix together. Add tomato juice and heat.

Petrina Morton (Kitchen)

GRANDMA'S DUMPLINGS

1-14 oz. can chicken broth
1 can cream of celery soup
1 1/4 c. water
2 T. butter or margarine
1 egg

3/4 c. milk
1 1/2 c. all purpose flour
1 1/4 t. baking powder
1 t. dried parsley flakes
1/2 t. salt

In a 5 quart Dutch Oven or heavy saucepan over medium heat, stir soup and water and butter until smooth. Bring to a boil. Reduce heat to low and simmer. Meanwhile, in a liquid measuring cup beat egg. Add enough milk to measure 1 c. Combine flour, baking powder, parsley, and salt. Stir in egg mixture just until flour is moistened. (Dough will be soft and sticky) Drop dough into simmering liquid. Cover and let simmer for 10 minutes.

Anna M. Slabaugh (Bakery)

GRANDMA'S KNEE SLAPPING CHICKEN AND DRESSING

8 oz. chicken flavored stuffing
1 stick butter, melted
1- 3 lb. cooked chicken

4 oz. sour cream
1 can cream of celery soup
2 c. broth

Mix melted butter with stuffing. Put 1/2 of stuffing in bottom of 9 x 13 pan. Add chicken layer. Pour 1 c. broth over chicken and stuffing. Mix sour cream, soup, and 1 c. broth and pour over chicken and stuffing. Top with rest of stuffing. Bake at 350 degrees for 30 to 45 minutes.

Martha Coblentz (Bakery)

GREEN TOMATO PIE

3 c. sliced green tomatoes   1 1/2 c. sugar
1/4 t. salt   3 T. flour
3 T. vinegar

Stir together in a bowl and put in an uncooked pie shell. Add 3 T. butter and 1 t. cinnamon. Put on top crust. Bake at 400 degrees for 20 minutes. Turn down heat to 350 degrees and bake until brown.

Gayle Martin (Bakery)

GROUND BEEF STEW

2 lb. ground beef   6 medium potatoes, unpeeled
1 small onion, chopped   6 medium carrots, unpeeled
1 t. seasoned salt

Brown ground beef with onion and seasoned salt. Drain grease. Wash potatoes and carrots. Cut in thick slices and layer with ground beef. Cover with beef gravy and bake at 350 degrees for 45 minutes. Reduce heat to 250 degrees and bake for 2 hours or until done.

Beef Gravy

4 c. beef broth   4 T. cornstarch
2 T. instant beef bouillon   1/3 c. cold water

Bring broth and bouillon to a boil. Remove from heat. Mix cornstarch with water and add to broth. Return to heat and simmer. Add salt, if needed.

Wilma Yoder (Cashier-Hostess)

How come if the shoe fits, it's ugly.

GROUND BEEF IN SOUR CREAM

1 c. onion, chopped	1 1/2 t. celery seed
2 T. fat or oil	dash of pepper
1 lb. ground beef	1/4 to 1/2 c. green peppers,
3 c. medium wide noodles	chopped
2 t. worcestershire sauce	1 c. sour cream
1 t. salt	1-3 oz. can mushrooms

Cook onion in hot fat until tender. Add beef and brown lightly. Layer noodles over meat. Combine worcestershire sauce and seasoning. Pour over noodles. Bring to a boil. Cover and simmer on low heat 20 minutes. Add green peppers. Cover and cook for 10 minutes. Stir in sour cream and mushrooms. Heat through.

Rosalie Bontrager (Inn Keeper)

A leader should not get too far ahead of his troupes or he might get shot in the rear.

HAM AND SCALLOPED POTATOES

Melt 1 c. butter. Stir in 1 1/2 c. flour, 4 t. salt, 1 T. mustard powder, onion, salt, and pepper. Gradually add 1 gallon of milk. Cook until thickened. Optional: 1 1/2 lb. diced Velveeta cheese). Stir until melted. Layer 20 lb. potatoes (cooked and sliced) with chopped ham. Pour sauce over all. Bake 1 hour at 350 degrees or longer at lower temperature. Serves 50.

Betti Kauffman (Host/Cashier)

HAMBURGER CASSEROLE WITH BALLARD BISCUITS

1 1/2 lb. hamburger
1 c. onion, chopped
1 t. salt
1 c. mushroom soup
1 can cream of chicken soup

2-3 oz. pkg. cream cheese
1/4 c. milk
1/4 c. catsup
1 tube biscuits

Brown hamburger, onion, and salt until meat is done. Add soups, cream cheese, milk, and catsup. Heat until cream cheese is melted and mixture is hot. Pour into cake pan and place biscuits on top. Bake at 375 degrees for 15-20 minutes or until biscuits are golden brown.

Carol Detweiler (Waitress)

HEARTY POTATOES (MICROWAVE)

5-7 small potatoes, peeled &
cut in wedges
1/2 pkg. dry onion soup mix

3 T. margarine, melted
dash of pepper
2 T. water

Combine all ingredients in 1/2 quart casserole. Mix well. Cover and bake on full power for 7 to 10 minutes or until potatoes are tender. Stir twice during cooking time to coat potatoes with butter sauce.

Alice Risser (Dutch Country Gifts)

The Silence Breaker

Impudent tummy,
How do you dare
Rumble when everyone's
Wrapped in prayer?

HAMBURGER AND VEGETABLE CASSEROLE

1 1/2 lb. hamburger
salt & pepper, to taste
5 drops tabasco sauce
1 large tomato, chopped
1 pepper, diced

2 c. cabbage, cut up
4 medium potatoes, sliced or shoestring
2 carrots, chopped
1 small onion, chopped
1 can cream of mushroom soup

Press raw hamburger in a 3 quart or larger casserole. Add salt and pepper. Mix 5 drops of tabasco sauce with chopped tomatoes and put on top of hamburger. Add layers of raw vegetables in order given. Salt and pepper to taste. Top with cream of mushroom soup. Bake at 350 degrees for an hour.

Rosanna Miller (Kitchen)

Good window wash:

To about 2-3 qt. water add: t. cornstarch and a little Joy. The windows will not rain spot so soon.

HAMBURGER PIE

1 lb. ground beef
1/2 c. onions, chopped
1-10 oz. can tomato soup
1 egg, beaten
1 c. milk

1-16 oz. can cut green beans, drained
3 medium potatoes, cooked, peeled & mashed
1/2 c. American cheese, shredded

Fry onion and beef together and drain. Add tomato soup, mixed with egg and milk. Put in bottom of casserole pan. Layer green beans on top and then mashed potatoes. Top with cheese. Bake at 350 degrees for 25-30 minutes.

Wilma Weaver (Waitress)

HESS MESS

1 1/2 lb. hamburger
1 large onion, chopped
salt and pepper, to taste
1 can tomato soup
1 can cream of chicken soup

1 can cream of celery soup
1 can cheddar cheese soup
10 oz. spaghetti
4 oz. grated mozzarella cheese

Brown hamburger, onion, salt, and pepper. Add soups, combining well. Cook spaghetti and add to meat mixture. Put in 9 x 13 inch pan and top with cheese. Combine 1/2 c. milk and 1 can of mushroom soup and spread over the top. Bake at 350 degrees for 20-30 minutes.

Fannie Lehman (Meatroom)
Ruth Beachy (Restaurant Gifts)

Every evening I turn my worries over to God - because He's going to be up all night anyway.

HOBO DINNER

Place a cabbage leaf on a piece of tin foil 12" x 12". Have the foil large enough so you can wrap up your meal. On cabbage leaf put 6 oz. hamburger pattie, sliced or shredded potatoes, sliced carrots, chopped onion, salt and pepper to taste. Add 1 slice of Velveeta cheese and cover with another small cabbage leaf. Wrap tight in foil. These can be baked or they can be cooked on a grill if you are camping. Be sure to turn them every 15-20 minutes. It takes at least an hour to cook these on an open fire, depending on how hot the fire. It's best not to cook them on a real hot fire to keep them from scorching. If you bake them in the oven, bake approximately 1 hour at 350 degrees.

Mary Esther Miller (Restaurant Gifts Supervisor)

118

HUSBAND'S DELIGHT

1 lb. hamburger
2 cans tomato or pizza sauce
1 t. salt
1/4 t. garlic salt
1 T. sugar

1 T. worcestershire sauce
1 t. pepper
1/2 of 16 oz. carton sour cream
1/2-8 oz. pkg. cream cheese
1 onion, finely chopped
1-8 oz. pkg. noodles

Brown hamburger and drain. Add tomato sauce and seasoning. Simmer 15 minutes. Blend in sour cream and cream cheese; add onion. Cook noodles and drain. Place a layer of noodles in buttered baking dish. Cover with layer of meat mixture. Top with cream cheese mixture. Repeat process. Bake at 350 degrees for 30 minutes.
6 servings

Mary K. Schrock (Kitchen)

INDIANA BAKED BEANS

2 1/2 qt. dried navy beans
4 qt. water
2 T. salt
3 1/2 t. prepared mustard

2 c. catsup
1 c. molasses
1 large onion

Soak beans overnight in water. Simmer 1 hour in water in which they soaked. Mix all the rest of ingredients together except onion. Add to beans. Lay onion on top. Bake in 300 degrees for 5 hours. Add water during baking if necessary to keep beans from becoming too dry. Remove the onion if you wish to can them.

Clara Yoder (Kitchen)

 Your life is in the hands of any fool who can make you lose your temper.

INDIAN CASSEROLE

1-16 oz. can white hominy
1-16 oz. can cream style corn
or 1 pt. frozen corn
1/4 c. onion, chopped

1 t. sugar, optional
salt, to taste
3 T. butter
4 slices of bread, cubed

In shallow buttered baking dish stir together hominy, corn, onion, sugar, and salt. In separate dish, melt butter and stir in bread cubes. Sprinkle over hominy mixture. Bake in 350 degree oven about 30 minutes. Serve hot.

Dick Carpenter (Material Handling)

IMPOSSIBLE PIZZA PIE

1 lb. hamburger
1 1/2 c. onion, chopped
1/2 t. salt
1/4 t. pepper

1 1/2 c. milk
3 eggs
3/4 c. Bisquick

Heat oven to 400 degrees. Grease glass pie plate. Brown beef and onion. Drain. Add salt and pepper. Spread in pan. Beat milk, eggs, and Bisquick until smooth; one minute with mixer. Pour onto plate. Bake for 25 minutes. Top with pizza sauce below:

3/4 c. catsup
1 1/2 t. vinegar

1/2 t. oregano
garlic

Add cheese and bake 5 - 8 minutes more. Cool 5 minutes and serve.

Tina Bobeck (Cashier/Busser)

When a man says it's a silly, childish game, it's probably a game his wife can beat him at.

JON'S SWEET AND SOUR CHICKEN - STIR FRY ADVENTURE

1 pkg. chicken breast filets
1 c. sweet & sour salad dressing
2 c. teriyaki sauce

1 1/2 c. minute rice
1 c. pineapple chunks

Begin by inviting a favorite friend to dinner.

1. Your friend marinates the breast strips in teriyaki sauce.
2. You fry the strips in skillet with pineapple.
3. Your friend cooks the Minute Rice.
4. Serve the dish as follows:
Spoon rice onto large plate. Top with chicken, pineapple, and sweet and sour sauce.
5. Share the plate with your friend using two forks!

Enjoy!

Jon Helmuth (Restaurant)

MAKE-AHEAD POTATOES

12 large potatoes, boiled
in salt water & peeled
1-8 oz. carton sour cream
1-8 oz. cream cheese, softened

1 t. onion powder
1/4 c. margarine, melted
paprika, to taste

Combine cooked potatoes, sour cream, cream cheese, and onion powder and whip or mash until fluffy. Add small amount of milk if necessary. Spread in a buttered 9 x 13 inch pan and refrigerate or freeze until needed. When ready to use, drizzle melted margarine over top and sprinkle with paprika. Bake at 350 degrees for 1 hour. Delicious with any meat. No gravy is needed.

Edna Nissley (Waitress)

If your knees are knocking, kneel on them.

MANICOTTI

8 manicotti shells or
8 large shell macaroni
1 lb. ground beef
2-6 oz. cans tomato paste
1/2 c. onions, chopped
1/3 c. parsley, snipped
1 T. dried basil, minced
1 1/2 t. salt

1 large clove garlic, minced
2 c. water
2 eggs, beaten
3 c. ricotta cheese or 24 oz.
cottage cheese, drained
1/4 t. salt
3/4 c. grated romano or parmesan
cheese

Cook manicotti shells in boiling salted water until just tender, 15-20 minutes. Drain. Rinse shells in cold water. Meanwhile, in a 3 qt. saucepan, brown meat lightly. Drain of grease. Stir in tomato paste, onion, half of parsley, basil, 1 1/2 t. salt, garlic, water, and dash of pepper. Mix eggs, cottage cheese, salt, half of the parsley, and 1/2 c. romano cheese. Stuff cooked manicotti shells with cheese mixture, using a small spoon. Pour half of tomato-meat sauce into 12x7 1/2 baking dish. Put stuffed shells on and top with the remaining sauce. Sprinkle with the remaining 1/4 c. cheese. Bake at 350 degrees for 40-45 minutes, uncovered. Let stand 10 minutes before serving. Is better yet to make it a day ahead of time. Then just reheat.

Rossanna Miller (Kitchen)

MEXICAN LASAGNA

1 lb. beef
3/4 c. onion, chopped
1-16 oz. can refried beans
2 t. oregano
12 uncooked lasagna noodles

2 1/2 c. water
2 1/2 c. pizza sauce
2 c. sour cream
1 c. shredded cheese

Combine beef, onion, beans, and oregano. Place 4 noodles in bottom of 9 x 13 inch pan. Spread half of beef over noodles. Top with 4 more noodles and then remaining beef. Cover with 4 more noodles. Combine water and pizza sauce and pour over top. Cover lightly with foil. Bake at 350 degrees for 1 1/2 hours. After baked, spoon sour cream over casserole and top with cheese. Bake until cheese is melted (5 minutes).

Ruth Ann Yoder (Bakery)

MOM'S POTATO WEDGES

6 medium potatoes	1/2 t. dried thyme leaves
3 T. oil	dash of cayenne pepper
1/2 t. salt	1/3 c. grated parmesan cheese
1/2 t. dried oregano leaves	2 T. grated cheddar cheese

Scrub un-peeled potatoes well. Cut each potato in half, lengthwise. Then cut into even wedges. Boil potato wedge for 5 minutes in un-salted water. Drain and pat dry. Spread potato wedges in single layer on a lightly greased baking sheet. Sprinkle with oil, spices, and herbs. Bake at 425 degrees for 15 minutes. Sprinkle with cheeses. Bake at 425 degrees for another 10 to 12 minutes or until potatoes are golden brown and cheeses are melted. Serve as a snack or with pork chops, chicken, meat loaf or hamburger. Yield: 4 servings

Barbara Miller (Maintenance)

A road hog is a motorist who is entitled to half of the road and takes it right out of the middle.

MUSH

3 c. corn meal	1 c. flour
2 t. salt	2 1/2 c. cold water

Mix ingredients and stir into 5 c. hot or boiling water. Cook until thick. Stir until you can see the bottom of the pan, 5 to 8 minutes after boiling.

Joann Bontrager (Busser)

If you meet someone without a smile, give him yours.

MY OWN QUESADILLA SPECIALS

8 large flour or corn tortillas
1 lb. grated cheese

1 can refried beans
1 lb. ground beef, cooked &
mashed fine; or beef or chicken,
shredded

Stir Fry

1 c. onion, chopped
1 c. tomatoes
1 c. mushrooms

1 c. green peppers, chopped
1 c. black olives
jalapeno pepper, chopped, to taste,
(optional)

Condiments: salsa, sour cream, and guacamole.

Do the stir fry first. Then, in a hot oiled skillet, place 1 or 2 tortillas, open. Fill each with beans, cheese, meat and fold in half. Gently fry on both sides until golden brown. Remove from skillet and allow to set 1 to 2 minutes on plate. Start next group. To serve, place shredded lettuce on a plate, then lay the quesadilla on top. Spoon the vegetables over it and top with sour cream, salsa, and guacamole.

NOTE: The stir fried vegetables can be put inside the tortilla, then fried.

Vyvyan Dunlap (Decorating)

Never spend your money before you have it earned.

NAVAJO TACOS

1 lb. hamburger, fried & seasoned   1-15 oz. can ranch style beans
                                     or chili hot beans

Simmer together 15 minutes.

Cheese Sauce

3 T. margarine   2 T. flour
1 t. salt   2 c. milk
1/8 t. pepper   1 1/2 c. grated cheddar cheese

Crush 1 bag tortilla chips. Shred 1/2 head lettuce. Grate 1/2 lb. mild
cheddar cheese. Dice 2 medium tomatoes. Dice 1 c. onions.

Melt margarine over low heat. Add flour and seasoning. Stir until well
blended. Gradually add milk , stirring constantly. Cook until thick. Add
cheese and stir until blended.

When ready to eat put on plates in order given: chips, lettuce, meat,
cheese, tomatoes, onions and top with cheese sauce.
Serves 6 -8

Lena Miller (Meat Room)

NIGHT BEFORE CASSEROLE

1 3/4 c. uncooked elbow macaroni 2 c. chicken, cut up
2 cans mushroom soup   1/2 lb. Velveeta cheese, cut up
1 1/2 c. milk

Combine all ingredients in a casserole dish. Let stand in refrigerator over
night. Bake at 350 degrees for 1 hour and 15 minutes.

Barb Weaver (Restaurant Gifts)

125

OVERNIGHT CASSEROLE

2 c. raw macaroni
1 onion, chopped
4 hard cooked eggs, chopped
1/2 lb. cheese, cubed

1 can Spam or
2 c. cubed ham
1 can cream of mushroom soup
3 c. milk

Combine all ingredients and put into a greased 2 1/2 quart casserole. Let stand in refrigerator for 8 hours or overnight. Bake 1 hour at 350 degrees. Serves 8

Fannie Lehman (Meatroom)

PICKLED CABBAGE

1 large head of cabbage
1 T. caraway seeds
1 T. salt

4 T. sugar
4 T. vinegar
1 large onion, chopped, browned

Put 2 T. margarine in a pot. Slice cabbage and add to the pot with caraway seeds and salt. Cook for 15 minutes or until tender, stirring often. Add sugar and vinegar and cook 5 more minutes. Add browned onion and cook 5 more minutes. Freezes well.

Becky Helmuth (Waitress)

PIZZA BURGERS

1 lb. hamburger
1 small onion, chopped
1 small can mushrooms
1/4 t. oregano
salt & pepper to taste

1/4 t. garlic salt
1-8 oz. can pizza sauce
hamburger buns
1/2 lb. grated cheese

Saute hamburger and onion until brown. Add mushrooms, spices and pizza sauce. Cool the meat mixture. Spread on halves of the buns and top with cheese. Place under broiler until cheese is bubbly and edges of bun are toasted.

Lena Miller (Meatroom)

PIZZA CUPS

3/4 lb. ground beef
1-6 oz. can tomato paste
1 T. instant minced onion

1 t. salt
1 t. Italian seasoning
1-10 oz. can refrigerator biscuits

Brown and drain beef. Stir in tomato paste, onion, and seasoning (mixture will be thick). Cook over low heat for 5 minutes, stirring frequently. Place biscuits in a greased muffin tin, pressing to cover bottom and sides. Spoon about 1/4 c. of meat mixture into biscuit lined cup and sprinkle with cheese. Bake at 400 degrees for 12 minutes or until golden brown.
Yield: 12 pizza cups

Iva Miller (Kitchen)

PIZZA MACARONI CASSEROLE

1 lb. hamburger
1/2 c. onion, chopped
8 oz. macaroni, uncooked
1-15 oz. can tomato sauce
1/4 c. water
6 oz. mozzarella cheese, shredded

1/2 t. garlic salt
1/2 t. basil
1/4 t. oregano
1 small can mushrooms
pepperoni, to taste

Cook macaroni and combine all ingredients. Pour into a 9 x 13 pan. Place pepperoni and cheese on top. Bake 15 minutes at 375 degrees.

Barb Weaver (Restaurant Gifts)

Do more than exist — live
touch — feel
look — observe
read — absorb
hear — listen

PIZZA POTATOES

1 pkg. scalloped potatoes,
with sauce mix
1-16 oz. can tomatoes
1 1/2 c. water

1/4 t. oregano leaves
1-4 oz. pkg. sliced pepperoni
1-4 oz. pkg. shredded mozzarella cheese

Heat oven to 400 degrees. Empty potato slices and packet of seasoned sauce mix into greased 1 quart casserole. Heat tomatoes, water and oregano to boiling. Stir into potato mixture. Arrange pepperoni on top and sprinkle with cheese. Bake uncovered for 30 to 35 minutes. Makes 4 servings.

Viola Miller (Ned Miller's wife, Material Handling, Essenhaus Foods)

Variations:

Hamburger Pizza Potatoes: Substitute 1/2 lb. ground beef, browned and drained, for pepperoni. Mix into potato mixture.

Sausage Pizza Potatoes: Substitute 1/2 lb. bulk pork sausage, browned and drained, for pepperoni. Mix into potato mixture.

Alice Risser (Dutch Country Gifts)

POPPY SEED CHICKEN

1 chicken, cooked
1 can cream of celery soup
1 sm. pkg. slivered almonds

1 sm. carton sour cream
1 can cream of mushroom soup
1 tsp. poppy seeds

Mix above ingredients. Top with mixture of 32 crushed Ritz Crackers mixed with 1 stick of melted butter. Bake at 350 degrees for 30 minutes or more.

Pamela Frey (Bakery)

A man wrapped up in himself makes a very small package.

POP OVER PIZZA

1 lb. ground beef
1/2 c. onion, chopped
1 T. vegetable oil

1 c. Bisquick
2 eggs
1 c. milk

Brown ground beef with onion and put in bottom of cake pan. Put one or more pints pizza sauce over hamburger and top with cheese. Mix Bisquick mixture and pour over meat mixture. Bake at 400 degrees for 30 minutes.

Noah (Amanda) Lehman
Judy Beachy (Kitchen Manager)

PORK STEAK AND NOODLE CASSEROLE

2 lb. pork steak, cubed
2 c. dried celery
2 c. dried onions

2 cans cream of mushroom soup
salt & pepper, to taste
1 large pkg. wide noodles

Brown meat and add celery and onions. Saute until almost tender. Add soup and salt and pepper. Boil noodles 5 minutes in salt water. Drain and mix with mixture. Pour into large pan. May add milk if you like more moist. Top with Velveeta cheese slices and crushed potato chips. Bake at 350 degrees for 2 hours.

Mel Lambright (Dishwasher)

PORCUPINES

1 1/2 lb. hamburger
1/2 c. uncooked rice
1 small onion, chopped fine
2 slices bread soaked in 1/2 c. milk

1 c. celery, chopped fine
1/2 t. salt
1 egg

Mix well and shape into balls. Place in baking dish and pour 2 1/2 c. tomato juice over balls. Bake at 300 degrees for 1 1/2 to 2 hours. Best if simmered a while.

Mary Esther Miller(Manager Restaurant Gifts)

PORK CHOP CASSEROLE

6 pork chops
sliced raw potatoes,
enough to cover bottom of pan

2 cans green beans
4 cans cream mushroom soup

Brown pork chops. Layer potatoes and green beans on top of chops in a 9 x 13 pan. Pour mushroom soup on top. Top with toasted bread cubes. Bake at 350 degrees until potatoes are done.

Hazel Bontrager (Kitchen)

Paint spots on clothing will come out with several applications of equal parts of ammonia and turpentine. Then wash in soap suds.

QUICK SUPPER

1 can Spam or Treet
mashed potatoes

cheese

Slice meat 1/4" thick and place on cookie sheet. Top with a spoonful of mashed potato and a slice of your favorite cheese. Bake for 30 minutes at 350 degrees.

Microwave: Heat meat in microwave. Top with warm mashed potatoes and cheese. Microwave until cheese starts to melt.

Katie Hochstedler (Bakery)

RANCH POTATO CASSEROLE

6 to 8 medium red potatoes
1/2 c. sour cream
1/2 c. prepared ranch salad
dressing

1/4 c. bacon bits or cooked &
crumbled bacon
2 T. minced parsley
1 c. (4 oz.) cheddar cheese, shredded

Topping:

1/2 c. shredded cheddar cheese
1/4 c. melted butter

2 c. lightly crushed corn flakes

Cook potatoes until tender. Quarter (leaving skins on) and set aside. Combine sour cream, dressing, bacon, parsley, and 1 c. cheese. Place potatoes on greased 9 x 13 inch baking dish. Pour sour cream mixture over potatoes and gently toss. Top with 1/2 c. of cheese. Combine corn flakes and butter. Sprinkle over casserole. Bake at 350 degrees for 40 to 45 minutes. 8 servings

Walter Lehman (Noodle House)

RICE CASSEROLE

1 medium onion, chopped
1 1/2 stick margarine
1-5.2 oz. box quick cooking
long grain wild rice
chicken stock

1 can cream of chicken soup
1 can consomme' soup
1 soup can full of water,
w/dash salt & pepper
1-4 oz. can mushrooms,
pieces & stems

Saute onion in margarine until melted. Mix all ingredients in a 2 qt. casserole. Bake for 45 minutes at 375 degrees. Stir every 15 minutes.

Norma Velleman (Restaurant Gifts)

When looking for faults, use a mirror not a telescope.

REUBEN CASSEROLE

1-32 oz. jar sauerkraut, drained
2 medium tomatoes, sliced thin
2 T. 1,000 island dressing

4 pkgs. sliced corned beef
2 c. shredded swiss cheese
1-10 oz. can refrigerated biscuits

Optional:

2 rye crackers, crushed

1/4 tsp. caraway seeds

In 9 x 13 pan, spread sauerkraut, arrange tomato slices, spread with dressing, and dot with butter. Cover with corn beef and cheese. Separate each biscuit into 3 thin layers and arrange over casserole. Sprinkle with crumbs and caraway seeds. Bake at 425 degrees for 10 minutes or until biscuits are golden.

Edna Hochstetler (Crafts)

One thing we all know about the speed of light is that it gets here too early in the morning.

SALMON ZUCCHINI

1-14 oz can salmon, drained
flaked
4 T. grated parmesan cheese
1 c. mayonnaise

2 1/2 c. grated zucchini
1 c. fine dried bread crumbs
2 T. lemon juice

Blend all ingredients, reserving a small amount of the parmesan for the top. Spoon into a 2 quart oiled casserole. Sprinkle with freshly grated parmesan. Bake at 350 degrees for 30 minutes. Serves 6-8

Emma B. Miller (Hostess/Cashier)

SAUSAGE & NOODLE BAKE

Brown 1-1 1/2 pounds of sausage with 1 small chopped onion.

Prepare 8 oz. or more fine noodles (cooked and drained) with 1 t. seasoned salt.

Heat and blend:

1 can cream chicken soup   1 can milk
1 c. shredded cheese

Combine all of the above. Top with buttered bread crumbs. Put in 9 x 13 inch pan. Bake at 350 degrees for 40 minutes.

Ronda Yoder (Waitress)

SCALLOPED CABBAGE

Shred a head of cabbage (coarsely). Cook in small amount of water with salt added. Drain. Put in casserole dish.

Mix and add:

1 heaping T. flour   1 T. butter
2 eggs, beaten   1/2 c. sugar
1/4 c. vinegar   seasonings to taste

Sprinkle grated cheese on top. Bake at 350 degrees for 30 to 45 minutes.

Alice Risser (Dutch Country Gifts)

Just when you are successful enough to sleep late you're so old you always wake up early.

SCALLOPED CORN CASSEROLE

1 can cream style corn
1 c. sour cream
1 box corn mix

1 can whole kernel corn
2 eggs
1 stick margarine, melted

Mix all ingredients together. Pour into 9 x 13 baking dish. Bake at 350 degrees for 40 minutes. When done, sprinkle shredded cheddar cheese on top and put back in the oven long enough to melt cheese.

Pamela Frey (Bakery)

SCALLOPED POTATOES

8-10 lb. potatoes, cubed or shoestring
4 lbs. cubed ham
2 cans cream of chicken soup
1 lb. cheese (Velveeta)
1 heaping T. taco seasonings

2 cans cream of celery soup
1 can cream of onion soup
2 cans milk

Mix everything except cheese in roaster. Put cheese on top and bake for 1 hour at 350 degrees.

Treva Yoder (Miller's Housekeeper)

SCALLOPED POTATOES

Sauce:

3 cans cream of mushroom soup
1 c. butter
2 t. salt
1 c. cream or Milnot

3/4 box Velveeta cheese
2 t. onion flakes
1/2 t. pepper

Place a package of shoestring potatoes in an 8 quart container. Pour the above sauce over the potatoes. Add some milk if needed. Bake for 1 hour and 1/2 at 350 degrees. Makes full roaster.

Frieda King (Grill Cook)

SCALLOPED POTATOES

3/4 bushel potatoes cooked
4 cans cheddar cheese soup

4 cans mushroom soup
6 medium onions, chopped
pepper, to taste

Cooked white sauce:

5 T. margarine

5 T. flour

Add milk for a thick sauce (gravy). Stir and bring just to boil. Pour over potatoes in roaster. Stir carefully to mix. Bake at 350 degrees for 1 hour or more. Stir occasionally. Break down for smaller groups.

Barb Weaver (Restaurant Gifts)

Nothing is all wrong: even a clock that has stopped running is right twice a day.

SEAFOOD PASTA

1/2 c. butter
2 cloves of garlic
8 t. flour
1/2 c. half & half
2 to 3 c. milk
2 cans minced clams

1-8 oz. pkg. noodles, cooked
2 cans medium shrimp, drained
2 cans crab meat, drained
basil, to taste
parsley, to taste
lemon juice, optional

Melt butter; add garlic. Mix in flour; add half & half. Slowly add milk, stirring until thick. Add clams with juice. Mix to medium consistency. Add noodles, shrimp, crab, basil, parsley, and lemon juice to taste. Yield: 10-12 servings

Katie Hochstedler (Bakery)

135

SOUR CREAM POTATO PATTIES

1 c. water
2 T. butter
1/2 t. salt
1 1/2 c. instant potatoes

1/2 c. milk
1/2 c. sour cream
1 egg

Heat water and add butter and salt. Remove from heat and add potatoes, milk, and sour cream. Stir in egg. Drop by rounded tablespoon into hot skillet using about 2 T. butter. Fry until golden brown.

Katie Hochstedler (Bakery)

SPAGHETTI PIE

6 oz. spaghetti
2 T. oleo
1/3 c. grated parmesan cheese
2 eggs, well beaten
1 c. cottage cheeese
1 lb. ground beef or
bulk pork sausage
1/2 c. chopped onion

1/4 c. green peppers, chopped
8 oz. can tomatoes, cut up
6 oz. tomato paste
1 t. sugar
1 t. dried oregano, crushed
1/2 t. garlic
1/2 c. shredded mozzarella cheese

Cook spaghetti according to directions and drain. (Should have about 3 c. cooked spaghetti.) Stir in oleo until melted. Stir in parmesan cheese and eggs. Form spaghetti mixture into a "crust" in a buttered 10 inch pie plate. Spread cottage cheese over the bottom of spaghetti crust. In a skillet, cook meat, onion, and green pepper until cooked. Drain off fat. Stir in un-drained tomatoes, tomato paste, sugar, oregano, and garlic salt. Heat through. Add meat mixture over cottage cheese in "crust." Bake uncovered at 350 degrees for 20 minutes. Add mozzarella cheese on top and bake for 5 minutes longer. Serves 6

Jan Bontrager (Waitress)

A journey of many miles begins with a single step.

SPANISH RICE

1/4 c. bacon drippings	1 1/3 c. minute rice
2 lb. hamburger	1 3/4 c. hot water
1/2 green pepper, chopped	1 c. tomato juice
1/2 red pepper, chopped	1 t. salt
1 medium onion, chopped	1 t. mustard

Place bacon drippings, hamburger, peppers, and onions in frying pan and fry. Add rice, hot water, tomato juice, and seasonings. Mix well and bring to a boil. Cover tightly and simmer 10 minutes. Serves 6

Betty Troyer (Kitchen)

STUFFED GREEN PEPPERS

6 large green peppers	1 t. salt
5 c. boiling salt water	1/8 t. garlic salt
1 lb. ground beef	1 c. rice, cooked
2 T. onion, chopped	15 oz. tomato sauce

Heat oven 350 degrees. Cut a thin slice off the stem end of the green pepper and remove all seeds. Cook peppers in the boiling salt water 5 minutes and then drain. Brown beef and onion in skillet until onion is tender. Drain off fat. Stir in salt, garlic salt, rice and 1 c. tomato sauce. Heat through. Lightly stuff peppers with meat mixture. Stand peppers upright in un-greased baking dish. Pour remaining tomato sauce over peppers. Cover and bake 45 minutes. Uncover and bake 15 minutes longer.

Rosanna Miller (Kitchen)

You cannot do a kindness too soon because you never know how soon it will be too late.

SWEET AND SOUR CABBAGE

4 c. shredded cabbage	2 T. sugar
1 c. water	2 T. vinegar
4 T. butter	3 T. sour cream
salt, to taste	

Put cabbage, water, butter, and salt in pan and cook until cabbage is tender. Then mix the remaining ingredients together and stir into cabbage. Serve hot.

Ellen Mishler (Hostess/Cashier)

SWEET POTATO SURPRISE

1 can sweet potatoes, mashed and seasoned with salt and pepper. Form into balls, placing a marshmallow in the center of each one. Roll in cracker or toast crumbs. Place in baking dish and pour melted butter over balls. Brown in oven, just before serving.

Leola Kauffman (Laundry)

TATOR TOTS AND HAMBURGER

2 eggs	salt & pepper, to taste
3 lb. hamburger	2 cans cream of chicken soup
1 small onion, chopped	tator tots, enough to cover

Beat eggs slightly. Add hamburger, chopped onion, and salt and pepper. Mix well. Form into small meat balls and place in bottom of baking dish. Pour soup over meat balls. Place tator tots over the top, covering completely. Bake at 350 degrees for 1 hour.

Anna Marie Slabaugh (Bakery)

TACO BAKE

2 lb. hamburger
1 1/2 c. onion
1-15 oz. can tomato sauce
2 c. red kidney beans, drained
2 t. chili powder
1/2 t. salt

1/2 t. pepper
1-5 oz. pkg. taco shells
2 c. shredded cheese
2 medium tomatoes, small pieces
1/2 small head lettuce, chopped

Brown hamburger and onions and drain. Stir in tomato sauce, kidney beans, chili powder, salt, and pepper. Break each taco shell in half and fold. Arrange on bottom and sides of 9 x 13 inch pan. Spoon meat mixture evenly over shells. Sprinkle with cheese. Bake at 350 degrees for 20-25 minutes. Top with lettuce and tomatoes after removing from oven. Good served with sour cream.

Teresa Coblentz (Busser)

TACO CASSEROLE

2 lb. hamburger
2 pkgs. taco mix
2 c. cooked minute rice
1-22 oz. can chili beans
1 pkg. shredded mozzarella cheese

1 pkg. Doritos
shredded lettuce
chopped tomatoes
taco sauce

Brown hamburger and add to mix as directed. Let simmer for 10 minutes. Put ingredients in a 9 x 13 inch pan in order given here:
rice, chili beans, cheese, hamburger mixture, and crushed chips. Bake at 350 degrees for 20 minutes. Lettuce, tomato, and taco sauce are added after it is baked. We usually let each individual add his own to taste. Is good served with a hot cheese sauce over the top.

Lena Miller (Meatroom)

Housework is something you do that nobody notices until you don't do it.

TACO PIE

1 lb. ground beef
2-8 oz. can tomato sauce
1 pkg. taco seasoning mix

1-8 oz. can crescent rolls
1/2 lb. Velveeta cheese

Brown meat and drain. Stir in tomato sauce and season mix. Simmer 5 minutes. Press dough on pizza pan. Bake at 375 degrees for 10-12 minutes. Cover with meat mixture and top with cheese. Continue baking until cheese is melted. Top with 1 c. shredded lettuce, 1/2 c. tomatoes, and 1/2 c. pitted olives. Serve with sour cream.

Anna Marie Slabaugh (Bakery)

One reason why a dog is such a lovable creature is that his tail wags instead of his tongue.

TATOR TOT CASSEROLE

1 lb. ground beef
1/2 c. onion, chopped
1 lb. tator tots

1-10 1/2 oz. can cheddar cheese soup
1/2 c. milk
1 t. salt, scant

Mix vegetables or green beans (any amount). Brown beef and onion together. Put in layers on the bottom of small roaster or casserole dish, starting with beef, vegetables, and ending with tator tots on top. Cover with soup and milk mixture. Bake at 350 degrees for 45 minutes. May substitute mushroom soup for cheese soup. Then add processed cheese slices on top of vegetables and just before serving, more cheese on top.

Mary Ann Slabach (Waitress)

TEXAS POTATOES

2 lb. pkg. frozen hash brown
potatoes, thawed
1-16 oz. carton sour cream
1 can cream of chicken soup
1/2 c. onion, chopped

1 t. salt
1/4 t. pepper
1 stick margarine
2 c. crushed Ritz crackers

Mix thawed potatoes with sour cream, soup, onion, and seasonings. Put in a 9 x 13 inch baking pan. Top with cracker & margarine mixture. Bake at 350 degrees for one hour. 6-8 servings

Emma B. Miller (Hostess/Cashier)

TUNA CASSEROLE

2 cans tuna
1 can cheddar cheese soup
1 small onion
1 1/2 lb. cheddar cheese, shredded

1 can cream mushroom soup
12 oz. frozen peas
1 1 lb. bag noodles

While cooking noodles, mix other ingredients together except cheese. Then stir in cooked noodles. Pour 1/2 in a 9 x 13 inch casserole dish. Cover with 1/2 the cheese, then repeat. Bake at 350 degress for 1 hour. Serves 6-8

Frances Blough (Waitress)

Sandwiches

They that have no other meat
Bread and butter are glad to eat.

TWICE BAKED POTATOES

2 med. baking potatoes
vegetable oil
2 T. butter or margarine, softened
1 T. chopped chives
1/8 t. pepper

1/2 c. cream style cottagecheese
1 T. mayonnaise
1/4 t. salt
2 T. shredded cheddar cheese
paprika

Scrub potatoes throughly and rub skins with oil. Bake at 400 degrees for 1 hour or until done. Allow potatoes to cool to touch. Cut potatoes in half lengthwise. Carefully scoop out pulp, leaving shells intact. Mash pulp. Combine potato pulp with next 6 ingredients. Mix well. Stuff potato skins with potato mixture. Sprinkle with cheese and paprika. Place in shallow baking dish. Bake at 375 degrees for 15 - 20 minutes or until thoroughly heated. Makes 2 servings

Mary Arlene Bontrager (Waitress)

UPSIDE-DOWN PIZZA

2 lbs. hamburger   1 T. onion

Brown and season hamburger with salt and pepper; drain. Add 2 c. pizza sauce. Put in 9 x 13 pan. Layer mushroom, pepperoni, and green peppers. Bake at 350 degrees for 15 minutes. Add 8 to 10 oz. of sour cream and mozzarella cheese. Then top with 8 un-rolled crescent rolls. Bake at 400 degrees for 20 minutes or until brown.

Glenda Yoder (Waitress)

Lord, fill my mouth with worthwhile stuff,
And nudge me when I've said enough.

VARIETY BAKED BEANS

2-14 oz. cans baked beans
1-1 lb. can green lima beans
1-15 oz. can butter beans
1-1 lb. can dark red kidney beans
8-10 slices of bacon
1/2 c. brown sugar

2 small onions, chopped
1 t. salt
1/2 c. vinegar
1/4 t. garlic salt
1 t. dry mustard

Drain all beans and mix together. Fry bacon and set aside. Simmer the remaining ingredients in the bacon grease. Pour over the beans and add broken bacon bits. Bake for 1 1/2 hours in 350 degree oven.

Betti Kauffman (Hostess)

The ladder of life is full of splinters. But we never realize it until we begin to slide down.

VEGETABLE PIZZA BARS

Spread 2 packages of 8 oz. cresent rolls on a large cookie sheet. Bake at 350 degrees for 7-8 minutes. Let cool 10 minutes. Spread on this crust a mixture of 2-8 oz. packages of cream cheese, 1 package of ranch dressing, 1 c. mayonnaise, 1 1/2 c. green peppers, 1 1/2 c. cauliflower, 1 1/2 c. broccoli, 1 1/2 c. tomatoes. Top with 1 large package of shredded cheddar cheese. Gently press vegetables down into cream cheese mixture. Refrigerate. Cut into bars.

Wanda Sue Bontrager (Grill Cook)

WAN Q CHOW MEIN

2 T. peanut oil
1 clove garlic, minced
6 oz. thinly sliced beef,
tenderloin, or chicken breast
1 1/2 c. celery, sliced
1/2 water chestnuts, sliced thin
1/2 c. Chinese pea pods, sliced
thin, lengthwise
1/2 c. carrots, shredded

1 c. bamboo shoots, shredded
1 t. salt
2 T. soy sauce
1 t. sherry
1 c. chicken broth
1 T. cornstarch
1/2 c. water
hot cooked rice

Heat oil in skillet or wok. Add garlic and meat and quickly brown.
Remove meat and set aside. Add celery, water chestnuts, peas, carrots,
bamboo shoots, salt and soy sauce. Cook and stir until vegetables are
tender but crisp. Add sherry and broth. Cover and bring to a boil. Mix
cornstarch with water and add to broth. Cook until slightly thickened.
Serve with rice. 4 servings

Mary Arlene Bontrager (Waitress)

WET BURRITOS

1 lb. hamburger
3/4 c. onions

mushrooms (to taste)

Brown hamburger with onions; drain. Add 1 pkg. taco mix , mushrooms,
1 med. can refried beans. Mix 1 c. sour cream, 1 c. mushroom soup. Put
1/2 mixture in bottom of cake pan. Wrap meat mixture in tortilla and put
in cake pan. Put rest of soup mixture on top of tortillas. Add shredded
cheese. Bake until cheese is melted. Lettuce and tomatoes can also be
wrapped in tortillas with meat mixture. Makes 5 shells

Mrs. John Hochstetler
(Mother-Lynn Hochstetler/Dishwasher)

Nothing great or good can ever be accomplished without labor or toil.

WHOLE WHEAT PIZZA CRUST

1 pkg. dry yeast
1/2 t. sugar or honey
1/2 c. warm water
5 c. whole wheat flour *

1/2 t. salt
1 3/4 c. water
1 T. oil

Dissolve yeast , then sugar in warm water. Let stand for 10 minutes. Stir in 4 c. flour, salt, water, and oil. Mix well. Sprinkle remaining cup of flour on board. Pour dough onto board and knead for 10 minutes. Shape into a ball and cover with a towel. Let rise double, about 1 hour. Remove towel and punch down. Divide into 2 equal parts. The extra dough can be frozen for later use. Flatten onto pizza pan. Top with favorite pizza toppings. A blend of mozzarella, colby, monterey jack cheeses is very good. Bake at 350 degrees for 20 minutes.

*Very good with half amount of flour, either white or oat blend.

Carlene Miller (Restaurant Reservations)

WIGLER'S CASSEROLE

3 lb. hamburger
3 medium onions, chopped
3 c. cooked macaroni or spaghetti
2 cans peas
3 c. carrots, chopped

3 c. potatoes, chopped
3 c. celery, chopped
9 slices bacon
1 qt. tomato juice
2 cans cream of mushroom soup
1 lb. Velveeta cheese slices

Brown hamburger and onion together; drain. Put in roaster, mix with spaghetti or macaroni and add cooked vegetables and peas. Fry bacon and lay over the top. Pour tomato juice and mushroom soup over all. Put cheese slices on top. Bake for 1 hour at 350 degrees.

Agnes Cross (Bakery)
Anna Marie Slabaugh (Bakery)

What is worth doing at all, is worth doing well.

ZIPPY ZUCCHINI CASSEROLE

4 medium zucchini	1/2 t. thyme
1 lb. bulk sausage	2 cloves garlic, crushed
1/2 c. onion, chopped	1 c. saltines, crushed fine
4 eggs, beaten	1 c. grated parmesan cheese

Wash zucchini and trim ends. Cook whole zucchini in boiling salted water for 12 minutes. Drain and chop coarsely. In the meantime, cook the sausage and onion over medium heat until brown. Drain and combine sausage and zucchini and rest of ingredients except 1/4 c. cheese. Spoon into 3 qt. casserole. Sprinkle with remaining cheese. Bake at 350 degrees for 1 hour.

Alice Risser (Dutch Country Gifts)

ZUCCHINI FRITTERS

1 c. grated zucchini	1 carrot, shredded
2 T. onion	1 egg
1/8 t. green onion or garlic	1/4 t. Lawry's salt
1/8 t. accent	1/2 c. flour

Mix together and fry 1 T. at a time in vegetable oil. This will give patties.

Variations: Can be browned in butter and topped with cheese.

Mrs. John Hochstetler (Mother-Lynn Hochstetler/Dishwasher)
Variations by Freda Yutzy (Waitress)

ZUCCHINI FRITTERS

3 c. shredded zucchini	1 egg, beaten
1 c. Bisquick	1 t. salt
1 clove garlic, finely minced	1/2 c. shredded mozzarella cheese
pepper and parsley, to taste	

Mix all together. Drop by teaspoonful in hot oil. Fry slowly.

Jan Bontrager (Waitress)

Cookies
& Cupcakes

EQUIVALENTS

3 teaspoons	1 tablespoon
4 tablespoons	1/4 cup
5 1/3 tablespoons	1/3 cup
8 tablespoons	1/2 cup
10 2/3 tablespoons	2/3 cup
12 tablespoons	3/4 cup
16 tablespoons	1 cup
1/2 cup	1 gill
2 cups	1 pint
4 cups	1 quart
4 quarts	1 gallon
8 quarts	1 peck
4 pecks	1 bushel
16 ounces	1 pound
32 ounces	1 quart
8 ounces liquid	1 cup
1 ounce liquid	2 tablespoons

(For liquid and dry measurements use standard measuring spoons and cups. All measurements are level.)

Cookies & Cupcakes

AMISH COOKIES

5 lbs. sugar
2 1/2 lbs. lard
1 dozen eggs
2 lbs. oatmeal

1 small bottle molasses
6 lbs. flour
8 T. baking powder
1 qt. buttermilk

Grind together 2 lbs. of raisins and 1 lb. of Spanish peanuts.
Cream sugar and lard. Stir in eggs and your choice of spices. Add oatmeal and molasses. Beat well. Add peanuts and raisins. Stir in flour, baking powder, and buttermilk. Roll out about 3 c. on well floured board and cut out with large cookie cutter. Beat 2 eggs and brush on uncooked cookies. Bake at 350 degrees for 12 to 15 minutes. Cookies can be frozen. Yield: 20 dozen

Frances Blough (Waitress)

You can live without music;
You can live without books;
But show me the one
Who can live without cooks.

149

APPLE COOKIES

1 t. soda
1 t. cinnamon
1 t. cloves
1/2 t. nutmeg
1/2 t. salt
2 1/2 c. flour

1/2 c. shortening
1 1/2 c. brown sugar
1 egg
1 c. applesauce
1 c. chopped nuts

Add soda and spices to the flour. Cream shortening and sugar; add egg. Add flour mixture and applesauce alternately to sugar and shortening. Add nuts last. Drop from spoon to cookie sheet. Bake at 375 degrees for 10 to 14 minutes. While still hot, frost with the following frosting:

1 1/2 c. powdered sugar
1 t. butter

1/2 t. vanilla
2 T. cream

Barbara Miller (Maintenance)

APPLESAUCE COOKIES

2 eggs
1 t. vanilla
2 c. applesauce
1 c. whole wheat flour
2 c. quick oats
1 t. soda

1/2 t. nutmeg
1/2 t. salt
1 t. cinnamon
1/2 c. chopped nuts, optional
1 c. dates, chopped

Mix together eggs, vanilla, applesauce. Set aside. Mix together dry ingredients, stir in the applesauce mixture. Mix until smooth. Add dates and nuts. Drop onto cookie sheet and bake at 325 degrees for 15 to 20 minutes.

Lena Miller (Meatroom)

 Living without faith is like driving in a fog.

APPLESAUCE SPICE BARS

1 c. flour	2/3 c. brown sugar, packed
1 t. soda	1/2 t. salt
1 t. pumpkin pie spice	1 c. applesauce
1/4 c. shortening	1 egg
1/2 c. raisins (optional)	

Heat oven to 350 degrees. Grease 13 x 9 inch pan. Mix all ingredients thoroughly. Spread in pan. Bake 25 minutes. Cool and frost with Browned Butter Frosting. Cut into bars.

Browned Butter Frosting

3 T. butter or margarine	1 t. vanilla
1 1/2 c. powdered sugar	1 T. milk

Heat butter in saucepan until delicate brown. Blend in remaining ingredients and beat until frosting is smooth. Spread on cake.

Betti Kauffman (Hostess)

BANANA BARS

1/2 c. shortening	1 t. vanilla
1 c. sugar	2 c. flour
2 eggs	2 t. baking powder
1 c. mashed bananas	1/2 t. salt

Heat oven to 350 degrees. Grease a 15 1/2 x 10 1/2 x 1 inch jelly roll pan. Mix shortening, sugar, eggs, bananas, and vanilla thoroughly. Blend dry ingredients and stir into banana mixture. Spread in prepared pan. Bake 20 to 25 minutes or until golden brown. Frost immediately with frosting below:

1 stick oleo	1 t. vanilla
6 T. milk	1 c. nuts
1 lb. box powdered sugar	

Bring to boil the oleo and milk. Remove from heat and add powdered sugar, vanilla, and nuts.

Susanna Miller (Cook)

BILLY GOAT COOKIES

1 c. butter
2 c. white sugar
3 eggs
1/2 c. sour cream
1 t. vanilla

4 c. flour
4 t. baking powder
1/2 t. soda
2 c. chopped dates

Mix all ingredients and drop on un-greased cookie sheet. Bake at 350 degrees for 12 to 15 minutes.

Martha Coblentz (Bakery)

BUTTERMILK SUGAR COOKIES

8 c. sugar (1/2 brown sugar)
2 c. (scant) lard, melted, + 1 stick oleo
8 eggs

2 T. vanilla
4 c. buttermilk with 4 T. soda
dissolved in it

Beat these ingredients well, then add 8 c. flour and beat. Then add 3/4 c. sweet cream with 1 T. salt and 7 t. baking powder dissolved in it. Add 8 more c. flour. Let set in refrigerator overnight. Roll out or drop and press with sugar. Bake at 350 degrees.

Frosting

1 box butter brickle frosting mix
1 lb. powdered sugar

1 stick oleo
2 t. vanilla
a little milk

Mix well and frost cookies.

Treva Lehman (Waitress)

 Manners are the happy way of doing things.

BUTTERSCOTCH BROWNIES

1/4 c. butter	1 c. flour
1 c. brown sugar	1 t. vanilla
1 egg, beaten	1/2 t. salt
1 t. baking soda	1/2 c. butterscotch chips
	or nuts

Melt butter in pan then stir in sugar. Heat until sugar has melted. Cool. Add beaten eggs, flour, vanilla, salt, and baking powder. Add chips or nuts last. Bake at 350 degrees for 30 minutes. Cut in squares while warm.

Ruth Beachy (Restaurant Gifts)

If you are thick and tired...cut out the rich food and late hours.

CARAMEL COOKIES

1 c. oleo	2 t. vanilla
1 c. shortening	3 3/4 c. flour
1/2 c. brown sugar	1 t. salt
2 beaten eggs	1/2 t. soda
1 c. white sugar	

Cream shortening and oleo; add sugars, gradually, thoroughly. Add beaten eggs and vanilla. Add flour, salt, and soda to creamed mixture. Put dough in cookie press and form fancy designs. Place on un-greased pans. Bake for 10-12 minutes at 350 degrees.
Yield 6 doz.

Freda Yutzy (Waitress)

CARAMELECIOUS FUDGE BROWNIES

Prepare and bake 21 1/2 oz. package of fudge brownie mix according to package directions. Meanwhile, in a small saucepan over low heat melt 20 caramels with 3 T. milk, stirring until smooth. Immediately after removing brownies from the oven, sprinkle with 1/2 c. semi-sweet chocolate chips and 1/2 c. chopped pecans. Drizzle with caramels. Cool completely before cutting. Yield: 24 bars

Treva Yoder (Miller's Housekeeper)

CARAMEL CHOCOLATE SQUARES

Caramel mixture

1-14 oz. pkg. caramels   1/4 of a 5 oz. can of evaporated
                                   milk

Heat caramel and 1/4 c. milk in saucepan over medium heat, stirring constantly.

Cake

1 pkg. Betty Crocker Supermoist   evaporated milk
German Chocolate cake mix   3/4 c. pecans, coarsely chopped
2/3 c. margarine, melted   1 c. coconut, optional
3/4 c. or the remaining   1-6 oz. pkg. chocolate chips

Mix cake mix (dry), margarine, remaining milk, and pecans. Spread half of the dough in un-greased 13 x 9 x 2 pan. Bake 6 minutes at 350 degrees. Remove from oven. Sprinkle chocolate chips and coconut over baked layer. Drizzle caramel mixture over chocolate chips and coconut. Drop remaining dough by teaspoonful on caramel layer. Bake 15 to 20 minutes at 350 degrees. Cool.

Glenda Yoder (Waitress)
Tina Bobeck (Busser/Cashier)

CAKE MIX BROWNIES

1 white or yellow cake mix
1/4 c. brown sugar
1/4 c. water

2 eggs
1/4 c. oleo

Spread on cookie sheet. Put chocolate chips on top. Bake at 350 degrees for 20 to 25 minutes.

Delores Wagler (Maintenance)
Irene Bontrager (Cashier/Bakery)

CANDY CANE COOKIES

Mix together:

1 c. soft shortening (half butter)
1 1/2 t. almond extract
1 t. vanilla

1 c. powdered sugar
1 egg

Sift together and stir in the above mixture:

2 1/2 c. flour

1 t. salt

Divide the dough. To half of the dough, add 1/2 t. red food coloring. Take a small piece of dough and roll into a 4 inch strip. Place one of each color of strips side by side and twist like a rope. Place on un-greased cookie sheet. Curve top down to form handle of cane. Bake about 9 minutes or until lightly browned at 375 degrees.

Rosetta Miller (Bakery)

Diner: Do you serve crabs here?
Waiter: We serve anyone. Sit down.

CEREAL COOKIES

1 c. shortening	1/2 t. salt
1 c. sugar	2 t. baking powder
1 c. brown sugar	2 c. flour
2 eggs	2 c. rice krispies
1/2 t. vanilla	2 c. coconut
1 t. soda	

Cream shortening and sugars. Beat in eggs. Mix in remaining ingredients. Drop on greased cookie sheet. Bake for 15 minutes at 350 degrees.

Leola Kauffman(Laundry

CHOCOLATE CHIP COOKIES WITH SNAP! CRACKLE! POP!

1 3/4 c. flour	2 eggs
1 t. soda	1 t.vanilla
1/2 t. salt	3/4 c. sugar
1 c. butter	2 c. rice krispies
2/3 c. brown sugar	1 pkg. (6 oz.) chocolate chips

Stir together flour, soda, and salt. Set aside. Blend together butter and sugar. Add eggs, vanilla, and dry ingredients. Mix until combined. Stir in rice krispies and chocolate chips. Drop onto greased cookie sheet. Bake at 350 degrees for 10 minutes. Makes 6 dozen.

Judy Beachy (Kitchen Manager)

People who complain about the way the ball bounces are usually the ones who dropped it.

CHOCOLATE CHIP REFRESHER BARS

1 1/4 c. flour
3/4 t. baking soda
1 t. salt
3/4 c. brown sugar
1/2 c. water
1/2 c. butter

1 1/4 c. chopped dates
2 eggs
1/2 c. fresh orange juice
1/2 c. milk
1 c. chopped nuts
1 c. semi-sweet chocolate chips

Stir together flour, baking soda, and salt. In heavy saucepan combine brown sugar, water, butter, and nuts. Bring to a boil. Boil for 5 minutes, stirring constantly. Cool completely. Add eggs, orange juice, and milk. Mix well. Gradually add dry ingredients. Stir in chocolate chips and nuts. Place in greased 15 x 10 x 1 jelly roll pan. Bake at 350 degrees for 30 to 35 minutes.

Icing

1 1/2 c. powdered sugar
2 t. grated orange rind

2 T. butter, soft
2 to 3 T. orange juice

Combine all ingredients, using enough orange juice to reach a spreading consitency. For a thicker frosting, add 1/2 c. more powdered sugar.

Dorothy Slabaugh (Bakery)

COCONUT OATMEAL COOKIES

2 c. flour
1 c. sugar
1 t. baking powder
1 t. soda
1 c. shortening
1 c. brown sugar

2 eggs
1/2 t. vanilla
1 1/2 c. quick cooking oats
1 c. chopped walnuts
1 c. flaked coconut

Sift together flour, granulated sugar, baking powder, soda and salt. Add brown sugar, shortening, eggs, and vanilla. Beat well. Stir in oats, walnuts, and coconut. Roll dough in small balls. Dip in sugar. Place on cookie sheet and bake at 375 degrees for 12 to 14 minutes.

Rosalie Bontrager (Inn Keeper)

COWBOY COOKIES

1 c. butter	1 t. salt
1 c. brown sugar	1 t. soda
1 c. white sugar	1/2 t. quick oats
1 c. whole wheat flour	1 c. coconut
1 c. wheat germ	1 c. chopped nuts
2 eggs	6 oz. carob or chocolate chips
1 t. vanilla	

Blend all ingredients in the above order, adding coconut, nuts, and carob or chocolate chips last, by folding them in. Drop by tablespoon on un-greased cookie sheet. Bake at 350 degrees for 12 to 15 minutes.

Option: Raisins may be added.

Vyvyan Dunlap (Decorating Department)

CREAM CHEESE SUGAR COOKIES

4 c. flour	1/2 t. shortening
1 t. baking soda	1-8 oz. pkg. cream cheese
1/4 t. salt	1 1/3 c. sugar
1/4 t. nutmeg	1 egg
1/2 t. butter	1/2 t. vanilla

Combine flour, baking soda, salt, and nutmeg. Set aside. Cream together butter and shortening. Add cream cheese and sugar, beat until fluffy. Add eggs and vanilla and beat well. Gradually beat in flour mixture. Divide dough in half. Cover and chill 1 to 2 hours. On lightly floured surface, roll dough 1/8 inch thick. Cut with cookie cutters. Place on un-greased cookie sheets. Bake at 375 degrees for 8 to 10 minutes. Cool and frost.

Ruthann Wagler (Kitchen/Bakery)

Lost time is like a run in a stocking. It always gets worse.

CREAM FILLED OATMEAL COOKIES

1 1/2 c. oleo or shortening
2 c. flour
1 t. salt
1/2 t. nutmeg
2 t. vanilla

4 eggs
3 c. brown sugar
1 1/2 t. soda
4 c. quick oats
2 t. cinnamon

Mix all ingredients together. Roll in balls and flatten on cookie sheet. After baking, use filling recipe below and put between 2 cookies.

Filling

1 egg white
1 t. vanilla

2 c. powdered sugar

Alma Hershberger (Cashier/Restaurant Gifts)
Erma Yoder (Maintenance)

CRUNCH COOKIES

2 c. shortening
2 c. brown sugar
2 c. white sugar
4 eggs
2 t. vanilla

4 c. sifted flour
2 t. soda
1 t. salt
4 c. rice krispies
2 c. coconut
4 c. oatmeal

Cream shortening and sugars together. Add eggs and vanilla. Sift dry ingredients and add to creamed mixture. Mix well. Add cereal, coconut and oatmeal. Drop by teaspoon on un-greased cookie sheet. Bake at 350 degrees for 8 to 10 minutes. Do not over-bake!

Anna Marie Slabaugh (Bakery)

Never put off until tomorrow the hug you can give today.

CRUNCHY BARS

1 c. crunchy peanut butter
1/2 c. sugar
2 eggs

2 c. rice krispies
6 oz. (1c) semi-sweet
chocolate bits

Thoroughly beat together the peanut butter and sugar. Beat in the eggs well, one at a time. Stir in the rice krispies, 1 cup at a time. Press into a buttered 9" square baking pan. Bake in a preheated 325 degree oven for 20 minutes. Sprinkle chocolate bits over the top. Tightly cover the pan with foil and let stand at room temperature until chocolate melts, about 5 minutes. Spread chocolate evenly over the top. Cut into bars.

Alma Hershberger (Bakery)

Don't discourage the other man's plans unless you have better ones to offer.

DATE BALLS

1 1/2 stick oleo
1 egg, beaten
1 c. sugar
1-8 oz. pkg. dates

4 c. rice krispies
1 t. vanilla
dash of salt

Slowly cook the oleo, egg, sugar, and dates until sugar is dissolved. Cook slowly for 10 minutes more. Remove from the heat and add rice krispies, vanilla, and salt. Let cool. Mix and form into balls. Roll in powdered sugar.

Fannie Yoder (Van Driver)

DATE FILLED OATMEAL COOKIES

2 c. sugar
2 c. water

2 c. ground dates

Cook for 15 minutes. After cooking, stir in 2 T. flour and cool.

2 lbs. oleo or butter
6 c. brown sugar
8 eggs, beaten
4 t. vanilla
8 c. sifted flour

4 t. baking powder
4 t. salt
2 t. soda
10 c. quick oats

Cream butter and sugar well. Add eggs and vanilla. Mix well. Add dry ingredients. Mix well. Chill at least one hour. Roll out on floured surface. Put filling on one cookie and top with another and seal the edges. Bake at 375 degrees. Cut a small hole in the top so cookie won't explode.

Becky Helmuth (Waitress)

DOUBLE CRUMBLE CHOCOLATE BARS

1/2 c. butter
3/4 c. sugar
2 eggs
1 t. vanilla
3/4 c. flour

1/2 c. pecans, chopped
2 T. cocoa
1/4 t. baking powder
1/4 t. salt

Cream together sugar and butter. Beat in eggs and vanilla. Set aside. Stir together flour, nuts, cocoa, baking powder and salt. Stir into egg mixture. Spread in bottom of 9 x 13 x 2 cake pan. Bake at 350 degrees for 15 minutes or until bars test done.

Topping:
2 c. miniature marshmallows
1 c. chocolate chips

1 c. peanut butter
1 1/2 c. rice cereal

Sprinkle marshmallows evenly on top. Bake 3 minutes and then cool. Combine chocolate chips and peanut butter. Cook and stir over low heat until chocolate is melted. Stir in cereal. Spread mixture on top of cooled bars. Chill and cut into bars.

Erma Yoder (Maintenance)

DOUBLE TREAT COOKIES

1 c. white sugar
1 c. brown sugar
1 c. shortening
2 eggs
1 t. vanilla
1/2 t. salt

3 c. oatmeal
2 c. flour
2 t. soda
3/4 c. peanut butter
1 c. chocolate chips
1 c. chopped nuts, optional

Cream together white sugar, brown sugar, shortening, eggs, and vanilla. Stir in remaining ingredients. Drop onto cookie sheet. Bake at 350 degrees for 8 to 10 minutes.

Freda Yutzy (Waitress)

DROP SUGAR COOKIES

2 c. sugar (scant)
4 eggs
1 c. buttermilk
2 t. baking powder in 4 c. flour

1 c. shortening
1 t. soda
1 t. vanilla

Mix all ingredients and drop by teaspoonful on greased cookie sheet. Bake 10 minutes at 350 degrees. Frost with powdered sugar frosting.

Powdered Sugar Frosting

Melt 1 stick of butter. Add 2 c. powdered sugar. Add milk to desired consistency. Spread on cookies.

Wilma Weaver (Waitress)

You are only young once but you can stay immature indefinitely.

EAGLE BRAND BARS

2 c. melted oleo
4 c. brown sugar
4 eggs
2 T. vanilla

5 c. flour
2 t. soda
2 t. salt
6 c. oatmeal

Filling
1-12 oz. pkg. chocolate chips
2 T. oleo
1 c. chopped nuts

1 can Eagle Brand milk
1/2 t. salt
2 t. vanilla

Cream together oleo and sugar. Add eggs and vanilla and mix well. Add flour, soda, salt, and mix well. Add oatmeal and set aside. Mix together the filling in a double boiler until melted. Spread part of cookie dough in two 9 x 13 cookie sheets. Spread filling on top. Spread the rest of cookie dough on top of the filling mixture. Bake at 350 degrees until golden brown, approximately 25 minutes.

Irene Bontrager (Cashier/Bakery)

EASY CHOCOLATE CHIP BARS

1 c. brown sugar
1/2 c. shortening
1 egg
1 t. vanilla
1 3/4 c. flour

1/2 t. soda
1/2 t. salt
1/2 c. buttermilk
1 1/2 c. chocolate chips

Cream together sugar, shortening, egg, and vanilla. Mix with dry ingredients and buttermilk, alternately. Add chips. Pour into greased and floured 15 x 10 cookie sheet. Bake at 350 degrees for 20 minutes. Do not over-bake! When cool, frost with powdered sugar icing. They freeze well.

Powdered Sugar Icing
1 stick oleo, melted
6 T. milk
1 lb. powdered sugar

1 t. vanilla
1 c. nuts, optional

Mix together until smooth.

Susanna Miller (Kitchen)

EDITH BARS

1 c. butter
2 c. sugar
1 t. vanilla
4 eggs

4 squares unsweetened chocolate
1 c. flour
1 1/2 c. chopped nuts

Cream butter, sugar, and vanilla. Add eggs and beat well. Blend in melted chocolate and nuts. Stir in flour. Pour into 9 x 13 inch pan. Bake at 325 degrees for 30 minutes. Take out and cover with small marshmallows and return to oven. When marshmallows are melted, remove from oven. Melt and add 1 c. chocolate chips, 1 c. peanut butter, and 1 c. rice cereal. Spread on top of marshmallows.

Martha Coblentz (Bakery

GINGERSNAPS

1 c. sugar
1/4. c. molasses, light

3/4 c. shortening or margarine

Beat thoroughly.

1 egg
2 t. soda
1/2 t. cinnamon
1/2 t. ginger

2 c. flour
1/2 t. salt
1/2 t. cloves

Mix well and add to the above mixture. Chill dough for easier handling. Roll into balls the size of walnuts and roll into saucer of sugar. Bake on greased cookie sheet at 375 degrees for 9 to 10 minutes.

Vada Whetstone (Bakery)

Footprints in the sand of time were not made by sitting down.

GRANDMA'S COOKIES

3 c. sugar (2 white & 1 brown)
1 c. lard
1 c. shortening
4 eggs
2 c. milk
1 t. lemon extract

1 t. vanilla
6-7 c. flour
1 t. salt
4 t. baking powder
3 t. soda

Cream together sugar, lard, and shortening. Add eggs and beat. Add milk and flavorings. Add dry ingredients and mix well. Drop on baking sheets and bake at 350 degrees for 5-7 minutes.

Frosting

1 lb. powdered sugar
2 T. butter

1 t. lemon extract
milk

Mix ingredients together and add enough milk to spread nicely. Makes 9 doz. soft sugar cookies. Freezes well.

Susanna Miller (Cook)

Some people are like blisters - they don't show up until the work is done.

GUMDROP SQUARES

1 1/3 c. applesauce
1-6 oz. pkg. jello, any flavor
1 t. lemon juice, bottled

2 pkg. unflavored gelatin
2 c. sugar

Mix all ingredients together and heat to boiling for 1 minute, stirring frequently. Rinse loaf pan with cold water. Pour mixture into wet pan. Refrigerate for 3 hours. Cut into squares and put on ungreased cookie sheet. Let stand for 8 hours. Roll in sugar and serve.

Amanda Miller (Bakery)

HONEY, OATMEAL, CHOCOLATE CHIP COOKIES

1 c. honey
1/2 c. shortening
1/2 c. butter or margarine
2 eggs
1 t. vanilla
2 c. flour

1 c. quick oats
2 t. baking powder
1/2 t. baking soda
1/4 t. salt
1 c. semi-sweet chocolate chips
1/2 c. chopped nuts

Cream honey, shortening, and butter until smooth. Beat in eggs, one at a time, and add vanilla. Combine flour, oats, baking powder, soda and salt. Mix well. Add flour mixture to honey mixture and mix well. Stir in chocolate chips and nuts. Drop by heaping teaspoonful onto greased baking sheet. Bake at 350 degrees for 12 to 16 minutes or until lightly browned. Yield: 5 doz.

Delores Wagler (Maintenance)
Fannie Lehman (Meat Room)

JAM BARS

2 c. uncooked oatmeal
1 c. butter
1/2 c. chopped nuts
3/4 t. salt
3/4 c. jam (your choice)

1 3/4 c. flour
1 c. brown sugar
1 t. cinnamon
1/2 t. soda

Combine all ingredients, except jam. Beat until crumbly. Reserve 2 c. of mixture. Press rest of mixture into greased 9 x 13 pan. Spread jam over mixture. Sprinkle rest of crumbs over jam. Bake in 350 degree oven for 35 to 40 minutes.

Lena Miller (Meat Room)

We all know someone with a waterproof voice. No one can drown them out.

JUMBO RAISIN COOKIES

2 c. raisins
1 c. water
3 1/2 c. flour
1 t. baking powder
1 t. baking soda
1 t. salt
1/2 c. chopped nuts

1/2 t. cinnamon
1/2 t. nutmeg
1 c. shortening
1 3/4 c. sugar
2 eggs, beaten
1 t. vanilla

Boil raisins and water for 3 minutes. Cool, do not drain. Mix dry ingredients. Cream shortening and sugar. Add raisin mixture and dry mixture alternately with creamed mixture until blended thoroughly. Add nuts. Drop 2" apart on greased cookie sheet. Bake at 375 degrees for 12 minutes.

Marilyn Kehr (Cashier/Restaurant Gifts)

LEMON CHEESE BARS

1 box yellow cake mix
2 eggs
1/3 c. vegetable oil

1-8 oz. cream cheese, soft
1/3 c. sugar
1 t. lemon juice

Mix dry cake mix, 1 egg, and oil until crumbly. Reserve one cup. Pat remaining mixture in an un-greased cake pan. Bake 15 minutes at 350 degrees. Beat cream cheese, sugar, lemon juice, and 1 egg until light and smooth. Spread over baked layer. Sprinkle with reserve crumb mixture. Bake 15 minutes longer. Cool. Cut into bars.

Cecelia Berkey (Office)

Most of us are umpires at heart; we like to call balls and strikes on somebody else.

167

LUSCIOUS LEMON BARS

Crust

1 c. margarine, softened   dash of salt
1/2 c. powdered sugar   2 c. flour

Mix together and press into a cake pan. Bake for 15 minutes or until done at 350 degrees.

Filling

4 eggs   2 c. sugar
1/2 c. flour   6 T. lemon juice

Beat ingredients together and pour into crust. Bake at 350 degrees for 25 minutes or until set. Cool and sprinkle with powdered sugar. Cut in small squares. Best when set overnight.

Freda Yutzy (Waitress)

MALTED MILK SQUARES

1 envelope Knox gelatin   1 t. vanilla
1/3 c. brown sugar   1 c. coarsely crushed malted
3 T. cocoa   milk candy (reserve small
2 eggs, separated   amount for topping)
1 c. milk

In saucepan, mix gelatin, sugar, and cocoa. Blend in egg yolks beaten with milk. Let stand for 1 minutes. Stir over heat until gelatin is dissolved. Stir in vanilla. Pour into bowl and chill, stirring occasionally until mixture mounds slightly when dropped from a spoon. Beat egg whites until stiff. Fold egg whites and crushed candy into mixture. Pour into graham cracker crumb crust.

Crust

1 c. crushed graham cracker   2 T. melted butter
2 T. sugar

Combine and press into 9" square baking dish. Bake at 350 degrees for 10 minutes. Chill.

Clara Yoder (Kitchen)

MAPLE PUFFS

2 c. brown sugar
2 eggs
2/3 c. margarine
1 t. vanilla
1 t. maple flavoring

3 1/2 c. all-purpose flour
3 t. baking powder
1 t. baking soda
1/2 t. salt
2 c. sour cream

Preheat oven to 375 degrees. Lightly butter cookie sheet. Beat sugar, eggs, and margarine until well blended. Stir in flavorings. Add dry ingredients alternately with sour cream. Mix lightly after each addition. Drop by teaspoon on prepared cookie sheets. Bake 7 to 8 minutes or until springs back when touched lightly in the center. Do not overbake! Cool. Put together like sandwich cookies with filling. Yield: 6 dozen

Filling

1 c. soft butter
2 egg yolks
1 t. maple extract

2 t. vanilla
3 c. powdered sugar

Mix well.

Anna M. Slabaugh (Bakery)

MELTING MOMENTS

1 c. flour
2 T. cornstarch
1/2 c. powdered sugar

1 c. butter or oleo, soft
1 1/2 c. coconut

Mix flour, cornstarch, and sugar in a bowl. Blend in butter until soft dough is formed. If dough is too soft to handle, cover and chill. Shape into 3/4 inch balls and roll in coconut. Place 1 1/2 inches apart on ungreased cookie sheet. Bake at 300 degrees for 20 to 25 minutes or until lightly browned.

Ellen Mishler Hostess/Cashier)

169

MOCK PINEAPPLE BARS

1 c. oil
4 eggs
2 t. baking powder
1 t. soda
2 c. sugar

2 c. flour
1/2 t. salt
2 t. cinnamon
2 c. mock pineapple mixture *

Mix together and bake at 350 degrees until done.   Ice with Cream Cheese Icing.

Cream Cheese Icing

2 c. powdered sugar
1 T. butter

1-8 oz. pkg. cream cheese
1 t. vanilla

Cream and spread over bars.

* Mock Pineapple

1 gal. ground up zucchini,
peeled and seeded
3 c. sugar

1 1/2 c. Realemon
1-46 oz. can pineapple juice

Bring to a good boil. Simmer for 20 minutes. Pack into pint jars. Cold pack for 30 minutes.

Mary Lehman (Bakery)

FOR PERFECT ROLLED COOKIES

Cookie dough that is to be rolled is much easier to handle after it has been in a cold place 10 to 30 minutes. This keeps the dough from sticking, even though it may be soft. If not cooled, the soft dough may require more flour, and too much flour makes cookies hard and brittle. When rolling, take out on a floured board only as much dough as can be managed easily. Flour the rolling pin slightly and roll dough lightly to desired thickness. Cut shapes close together and keep all trimmings for last. Place pans or sheets of cookies in upper third of oven. Watch cookies carefully while baking to avoid burning edges. When sprinkling sugar on cookies, try putting it into a salt shaker. It saves time.

MOM'S OATMEAL COOKIES

1 lb. raisins
1/2 lb. peanuts
1 1/4 c. lard (half oleo)
2 1/2 lb. sugar
6 eggs
2 t. vanilla
9 t. baking soda
1 pt. whole milk

9 t. baking powder
3 lbs. flour
1 1/2 t. nutmeg
1 1/2 t. cinnamon
1 t. salt, level
1/2 c. dark corn syrup
1 lb. oatmeal

Grind raisins and peanuts together and set aside. Put lard and oleo in large bowl. Add sugar and cream well. Add eggs and vanilla. Put soda in milk and stir well. Add to lard mixture. Add baking powder, flour, nutmeg, cinnamon, and salt together and set aside. Stir dark corn syrup with egg mixture, then add oatmeal/raisin mixture and flour last. Roll out on floured board. You can cut with cookie cutter or roll out and cut. Bake at 325 degrees for 12 to 15 minutes.

Walter Lehman (Essenhaus Foods)

MONSTER COOKIES

1 stick oleo
1 c. brown sugar
1 c. white sugar
1 t. vanilla
2 t. soda
1 3/4 c. flour

3 eggs
1 1/2 c. peanut butter
1 t. light corn syrup
3 c. quick oatmeal
1/4 lb. chocolate chips
1/4 lb. M & M's

Mix in order given. Bake at 350 degrees.

Mrs. Noah (Amanda) Lehman

Before you give someone a piece of your mind - make sure you can spare it.

MOUND COOKIE BAR

Crust

18 squares (1 1/2 c.) crushed
graham crackers

4 T. sugar
1/3 c. melted butter

Press into 9 x 13 pan and bake 10 minutes at 350 degrees.

Filling

3 c. coconut
1 t. vanilla

1 can sweetened condensed milk
1/4 t. salt

Spread on crust and bake at 350 degrees for 12 minutes.

Topping

1 1/3 c. chocolate chips

1 T. peanut butter

Melt together, spread on top, chill and cut.

Marilyn Stautz (Bakery)

NEIMAN MARCUS BARS

1 box german chocolate cake mix
1 c. coconut

1 stick butter
1 c. chopped pecans
2 eggs

Mix all ingredients and put into 11 x 14 greased pan.

Topping

1 lb. powdered sugar
8 oz. cream cheese, room temp.

1 stick butter

Put on top of other mixture and bake at 350 degrees for 30 to 35 minutes
or until top caramelizes.

Charlotte Miller (Waitress)

172

NUTRITIOUS POPPIN' FRESH COOKIES

2 1/4 c. flour
1 t. soda
1 c. margarine or butter
2 eggs
1 c. chocolate chips

2 c. firmly packed brown sugar
1 t. salt
2 t. vanilla
2 c. quick cooking oats
1/2 c. chopped nuts or
sunflower seeds

Stir ingredients together like regular cookies. May add 1 of the following to the dough if desired:

1 c. peanut butter
1 c. flaked coconut

1 c. wheat germ
1 c. non-fat dry milk

Bake at 350 degrees until golden brown.

Lorene Schlabach (Cashier/Dutch Country Gifts)

Swallowing angry words is much easier than having to eat them.

OATMEAL CARAMELITAS

50 caramels
1/2 c. canned milk
2 c. flour
2 c. quick rolled oats
1 1/2 c. brown sugar

1 t. soda
1/2 t. salt
1 c. oleo, melted
1 c. chopped pecans
1 c. chocolate chips

Melt caramels and canned milk in saucepan. Cool slightly. Combine remaining ingredients, except chocolate chips and nuts. Press half of crumbs in bottom of 9 x 13 cake pan. Bake at 350 degrees for 10 minutes. Remove from oven. Sprinkle with chocolate chips and nuts. Spread carefully with caramel mixture. Sprinkle with remaining crumb mixture. Bake another 15 to 20 minutes. Chill for 1 to 2 hours. Cut into bars.

Clara Yoder (Kitchen)

OATMEAL CHOCOLATE CHIP COOKIES

3/4 c. brown sugar
3/4 c. white sugar
1 c. oleo
2 c. oatmeal
2 c. flour

2 eggs
1 t. vanilla
1 t. soda
1 T. water
1 c. chocolate chips

Mix all ingredients together. Drop on cookie sheet and bake at 350 degrees for 12-15 minutes.

Ruthann Wagler (Kitchen/Bakery)

Salt dissolved in alcohol will remove grease spots from clothing.

OATMEAL COOKIES

3 lb. margarine
1 qt. + 3 c. brown sugar
2 1/2 c. sugar
2 T. + 2 t. vanilla
2 1/2 c. eggs
2 qt. + 1 1/4 c. flour

1 T. + 2 t. soda
2 1/2 t. salt
2 T. + 1 t. cinnamon
1 gallon + 1 c. oatmeal
3 3/4 c. nuts

Cream together margarine, brown sugar, white sugar, vanilla, and eggs. Mix together dry ingredients. Stir in sugar mixture. Add raisins and chocolate chips if desired. Bake at 350 degrees for 12 to 15 minutes.

Becky Helmuth (Waitress)

OATMEAL COOKIES

2 c. margarine   1 1/2 c. sugar

Cream together.

1 t. vanilla   4 eggs

Add to creamed mixture.

4 c. flour   1 1/2 c. brown sugar
1/4 t. salt   2 t. soda
4 c. oatmeal

Add to above mixture.

May add chocolate chips or nuts. Bake at 350 degrees for 10 minutes.

Randi Yoder (Shift Supervisor)

OATMEAL COOKIES

2 c. brown sugar   1 t. soda
1 c. butter and lard, melted   2 c. flour
2 eggs, beaten   2 c. oatmeal
1 1/2 t. vanilla   1 c. coconut

Mix sugar and butter. Add well beaten eggs and vanilla. Mix in soda, flour, oats, and coconut. Form in 2 rolls and put in refrigerator overnight. Cut in 1/2 inch slices and bake at 375 degrees.

Fannie Yutzy (Bakery)

Thou shalt the Sabbath not misuse, nor come to church to take thy snooze.

OATMEAL SCOTCHIES

1 c. softened butter	1 1/2 c. packed brown sugar
2 eggs	1 T. water

Mix well.

2 c. flour	2 t. baking powder
1 t. baking soda	1 t. salt

Blend and combine with butter mixture. Mix in 1 1/2 c. quick oats, (uncooked), 12 oz. butterscotch morsels, and 1/2 t. orange extract. Drop slightly rounded tablespoons onto cookie sheet. Bake at 375 degrees for 10 to 12 minutes. Yield: 48 cookies

Linda Wenger (Laundry)
Irene Schrock (Kitchen)

OVERNIGHT CHOCOLATE CHIP COOKIES

1 c. shortening (or 1 stick butter and 1 stick oleo), room temperature	3 1/2 c. flour
	1/2 t. salt
	1 t. soda
2 c. brown sugar, packed	1 c. miniature chocolate chips
2 eggs, well beaten	1/2 c. finely chopped nuts

Cream shortening and sugar. Add eggs and then all dry ingredients. Add chips and nuts last. Batter will be stiff. Shape in two rolls, 2 inches across, wrap in wax paper, and chill overnight. Slice and bake 8 to 10 minutes at 400 degrees. Yield: 4 doz.

These can be stored in refrigerator a week before baking. If storing for any length of time, wrap in plastic wrap.

Mary Ann Schlabach (Waitress)

Treat arguments like weeds; nip them in the bud.

OVERNIGHT COOKIES

4 c. flour	1 c. white sugar
1 t. soda	1/2 c. brown sugar
1 t. salt	1 c. shortening
1 t. cinnamon	1/2 c. milk
2 eggs	1 c. nuts or coconut

Mix ingredients well. Form into rolls and wrap in waxed paper. Place in refrigerator. Can be refrigerated several days. Slice and bake for 8 to 10 minutes at 375 degrees.

Cecelia Berkey (Office)

PARK PLAZA SQUARES

1 box Duncan Hines butter recipe cake mix	1 stick butter/margarine, room temperature
1 egg	1 c. chopped pecans

Mix all ingredients by hand. Press into greased 9 x 13 Pyrex dish.

Filling

1 box powdered sugar	1-8 oz. pkg. cream cheese, room temperature
1 egg	

Beat with mixer and spread over top of other ingredients. Bake at 350 degrees for 35 to 40 minutes. Let cool completely. Cut into squares.

Rosanna Beachy (Essenhaus Foods)

 Middle age is when your narrow waist and broad mind begin to change places.

PECAN BARS

1 pkg. yellow cake mix   1/2 c. butter
1 egg   1 c. chopped pecans

Grease 13 x 9 pan. In large bowl place 1/3 c. cake mix, butter and egg. Mix until crumbly. Press into cake pan and bake at 350 degrees for 10 to 15 minutes. Prepare filling and pour over baked crust. Sprinkle with chopped pecans. Return to oven and bake for 30 to 35 minutes. Cool. Cut into bars. Yield: 3 dozen

Filling

2/3 c. reserved cake mix   1 t. vanilla
1/2 c. brown sugar   3 eggs
1 1/2 c. dark corn syrup

Clet Miller (Maintenance)

PECAN SANDIES

1 c. butter   2 t. water
1/2 c. sugar   2 c. flour
2 t. vanilla   1 c. chopped pecans

Cream butter and sugar. Add vanilla and water. Mix well. Blend in flour and nuts. Chill several hours. Shape in balls and place on greased cookie sheet and flatten. Bake at 350 degrees for 15 to 20 minutes. Cool slightly and roll in powdered sugar.

Betty Troyer (Kitchen)

If your troubles are deep-seated and of long-standing, try kneeling.

PEANUT BUTTER OATMEAL COOKIES

3/4 c. butter flavored shortening
1 c. peanut butter
1 1/2 c. firmly packed brown sugar
1/2 c. water
1 egg

1 t. vanilla
1 1/2 c. all purpose flour
1/2 t. baking soda
3 c. oatmeal (quick old fashioned)
granulated sugar

Beat shortening, peanut butter, and brown sugar until creamy. Beat in water, egg, and vanilla. Add combined dry ingredients. Mix well. Cover and chill about 2 hours. Heat oven 350 degrees. Shape into 1 inch balls. Place on un-greased cookie sheet and flatten with tines of fork dipped in granulated sugar to form a criss-cross pattern. Bake for 9 to 11 minutes or until edges golden brown. Cool 1 minute on cookie sheet. Cool completely. Store tightly covered. Yield: 7 doz.

Barbara Miller (Maintenance)

When God measures men, he puts the tape around the heart, not the head.

PEANUTTY BARS

1 pkg. yellow cake mix
3/4 c. quick oatmeal
1/2 c. margarine

1/4 c. peanut butter
1 egg

Combine all ingredients until crumbly. Press mixture into a pan. Bake until golden brown. Cool. Make your favorite Chocolate Fudge frosting and add 1/4 c. peanut butter. Blend well. Spread on cooled bars. Sprinkle with nuts. Yield: 36 bars

Barb Weaver (Cashier/Restaurant Gifts)

PINEAPPLE BARS

2 eggs, beaten
2 c. sugar
1/2 t. salt

2 t. baking powder
2 c. flour
1 can crushed pineapple, drain

Mix and bake at 350 degrees for 30 minutes.

Frosting
1 stick oleo
1-8 oz. pkg. cream cheese

1 t. vanilla
2 c. powdered sugar

Sprinkle nuts on top if desired.

Erma Yoder (Maintenance)

PINEAPPLE COOKIES

1 c. shortening
2 c. brown sugar
2 eggs, beaten
4 c. sifted flour

1 t. salt
2 t. soda
1 t. vanilla
1 c. crushed pineapple, drained

Mix shortening and brown sugar. Mix in eggs and other ingredients. Bake for 10 to 12 minutes at 350 degrees. Yield: 60 cookies

Fannie Yutzy (Bakery)

A smart wife always has the pork chops ready when her husband comes home from a fishing trip.

POUND COOKIES

8 T. baking powder
6 lb. flour
4 T. soda
1 qt. buttermilk
2 lbs. oatmeal
1 lb. peanuts, chopped
pinch of nutmeg

2 lbs. raisins
pinch of cinnamon
1 c. molasses
2 1/2 lb. lard
5 lbs. sugar
2 dozen eggs

Put baking powder in flour and soda in milk. Mix oatmeal, nuts, and raisins together. Mix well. Add remaining ingredients. Roll, cut and brush each cookie with beaten egg before baking. Yield: 300 cookies

Agnes Cross (Bakery)

PUMPKIN COOKIES

1 c. lard
1 c. brown sugar
1 c. pumpkin or squash
1 egg
1 t. cinnamon

1 t. baking powder
2 c. flour
1 t. soda
1/2 t. salt

Mix lard, brown sugar, and pumpkin together. Beat eggs and add to mixture. Combine cinnamon, baking powder, flour, soda, and salt. Add to pumpkin mixture. Bake at 350 degrees for 10 to 12 minutes.

Frosting

3 egg whites, beaten stiff
vanilla
creamed shortening

milk
powdered sugar

Beat 3 egg whites. Add vanilla and some milk. Make a paste with creamed shortening and powdered sugar. Add other ingredients. Add enough powdered sugar to make creamy.

Marietta Helmuth (Waitress)

When a man has a "pet peeve," it's amazing how often he pets it.

PUMPKIN WHOOPIE PIES

2 c. sugar
1 c. shortening
1 c. margarine
2 eggs
2 t. vanilla
2 c. pumpkin (cooked)

4 c. flour
2 t. baking powder
2 t. soda
2 t. cinnamon
1 t. salt
3/4 to 1 c. oatmeal

Cream sugar, shortening, and margarine. Add eggs, vanilla, and pumpkin. Blend well. Add flour, baking powder, soda, cinnamon, and salt. Stir in oatmeal. Drop by teaspoonful on un-greased cookie sheet. Bake at 350 degrees for 12 to 14 minutes.

Filling

1 egg white, beaten
1 T. vanilla
2 T. milk

2 c. powdered sugar
3/4 c. shortening

Beat until smooth. Spread this on bottom of cookie and place on top of another cookie. Yield: 30 cookies

Betti Kauffman (Cashier/Hostess)

The true test of humility is whether you can say grace before eating crow.

PUMPKIN WHOOPIE PIES

2 c. brown sugar	1 t. baking powder
1 c. vegetable oil	1 t. soda
1 1/2 c. pumpkin	1 t. vanilla
2 eggs	1 1/2 T. cinnamon
3 c. flour	1/2 T. cloves
1 t. salt	1/2 T. ginger

Cream sugar and oil. Add pumpkin and eggs. Add flour, salt, baking powder, soda, vanilla, and spices. Mix well. Drop by heaping teaspoons onto greased cookie sheet. Bake at 350 degrees for 10 to 12 minutes. When cool, put cookies together with cream cheese frosting in the middle.

Cream Cheese Frosting

1 t. margarine	3 oz. cream cheese, softened
2 t. vanilla	1 box powdered sugar

Mix together.

Karen Hochstedler (Bakery)

Find your joy in something finished and not in a thousand things begun.

ROLLED SUGAR COOKIES

Beginning with 6 eggs, beat 2 eggs at a time, putting them in a cup with 3 c. melted lard, (you will do this a total of 3 times). Add 3 c. brown sugar and 3 c. white sugar. Beat. Add 3 c. milk, 6 t. baking soda, 6 t. baking powder, 2 t. lemon flavoring, 1 1/2 t. salt, 4 T. vanilla, and 14 or 15 c. pastry flour . Roll out and sprinkle with sugar. Bake at 350 degrees for 10 to 12 minutes.

Mary K. Schmucker (Kitchen)

SANDWICH COOKIES

Vanilla Part

1/2 c. oleo or butter	1 c. sugar
1 egg	1 t. vanilla
1 1/2 t. soda	1/2 t. salt
3 T. cream	2 3/4 c. sifted flour

Chocolate Part

3/4 c. oleo	1 c. sugar
1 egg	2 c. sifted flour
1 t. baking powder	1/2 t. salt
2/3 c. cocoa	1/4 c. milk
1/2 t. vanilla	

Mix in separate bowls, each part in order given. Chill a few hours. Roll out and cut the size of sandwich cookies. Bake at 400 degrees for 8-10 minutes. When cold, put 1 vanilla and 1 chocolate together with frosting below.

Frosting

5 T. butter	3 or 4 T. cream
1 t. vanilla	1/4 t. salt
3 c. powdered sugar	

Mix well.

Bertha Miller (Shop Supervisor)

Marriage is the only union that can't be organized. Both sides think they're management.

7 LAYER BARS

1 stick margarine
1 1/2 c. graham cracker crumbs
1 1/3 c. coconut
1 c. chocolate chips

2 c. peanut butter chips
1 c. nuts and raisins, optional
1 1/3 c. sweetened condensed milk

Melt margarine in 9 x 13 pan. Sprinkle cracker crumbs and press down with fork. Place remaining ingredients in layers and drizzle condensed milk over the top. Bake in 350 degree oven for 20 minutes or until golden brown.

Mary Arlene Bontrager (Waitress)

SOFT CHOCOLATE COOKIES

1 c. butter or lard
1/2 c. white sugar
1 1/2 c. brown sugar
2 eggs
4 1/2 c. flour
2 t. baking powder

2 t. baking soda
1/2 t. salt
1 T. vanilla
1 c. buttermilk
1 c. chocolate chips

Cream butter or lard and white sugar. Beat well and add brown sugar. Beat well and add eggs. Mix well before adding dry ingredients, vanilla, buttermilk, and chips. Drop by teaspoon on cookie sheet. Bake at 350 degrees for 10 to 12 minutes.

Lena Miller (Meatroom)

SORGHUM COOKIES

5 c. sugar
3 c. shortening
4 eggs
8 t. soda, dissolved in 1 c. buttermilk

1 c. sorghum
2 t. baking powder
4 t. salt
12 c. flour

Mix in order given. Chill dough, then roll in small balls. Dip in sugar. Do not press flat. Bake at 400 degrees for 10 to 12 minutes.

Wilma Weaver (Waitress)
Linda Wenger (Laundry)

TIGER COOKIES

1 c. (6 oz.) semi-sweet
chocolate morsels
3 c. sugar frosted flakes cereal
2 c. sifted all-purpose flour
1 t. baking soda

1/2 t. salt
1 c. margarine
1 c. sugar
2 eggs
1 t. vanilla

Melt chocolate in double boiler, stirring occasionally. Crush 1 1/2 c. of sugar frosted flakes and set aside. Stir together flour, soda, and salt and set aside. Measure margarine and sugar into mixing bowl and beat until light and fluffy. Add eggs and vanilla and beat well. Add dry ingredients and mix thoroughly. Fold in flakes and chocolate, leaving streaks in bater. Drop by level teaspoonful on ungreased cookie sheet. Bake at 375 degrees for 12 minutes.

Marna Schlabach (Kitchen)

ULTIMATE CHOCOLATE CHIP COOKIES

3/4 c. Crisco
1 1/4 c. firmly packed brown sugar
2 T. milk
1 T. vanilla
1 egg
1 c. pecan pieces

1 3/4 c. all purpose flour
1 t. salt
3/4 t. baking soda
1 c. semi-sweet chocolate chips
1 c. Reeses peanut butter chips

Heat oven to 375 degrees. Cream Crisco, brown sugar, milk, and vanilla in large bowl. Blend until creamy. Blend in egg. Combine flour, salt, and baking soda. Add to creamed mixture, gradually. Stir in chocolate pieces, peanut butter pieces, and nuts. Drop rounded tablespoons of dough 3 inches apart on ungreased baking sheet. Bake at 375 degrees for 8 to 10 minutes.

Lori Miller (Waitress)

VERMONT MAPLE COOKIES

1/2 c. shortening
1 c. brown sugar
1/2 c. sugar
2 eggs
1 c. sour cream

1 T. maple flavoring
2 3/4 c. flour
1/2 t. soda
1 t. salt
1 c. pecans

Mix shortening, sugars, and eggs. Stir in sour cream and maple flavoring. Stir dry ingredients together. Blend into cream mixture and mix well. Add nuts and mix. Chill dough if soft. Heat oven to 375 degrees. Drop by rounded teaspoons about 2" apart onto greased baking sheets. Bake for 10 minutes. Spread cooled cookies with maple glaze below.

Maple Glaze

Heat 1/2 c. butter until golden brown. Blend in 2 c. sifted powdered sugar. Add 2 t. maple flavoring. Stir in 2-4 T. hot water until icing is smooth.

Tina Bobeck (Busser/Cashier)

WYOMING WHOPPER COOKIES

2/3 c. butter
3/4 c. sugar
1 1/4 c. brown sugar
3 beaten eggs
1 1/2 c. chunky style peanut butter

6 c. old fashioned oats, not quick
2 t. soda
1 1/2 c. raisins
1-12 oz. pkg. chocolate chips

Melt butter over low heat. Blend in sugars, eggs, and peanut butter. Mix until smooth. Add oats, soda, raisins, and chocolate chips. Mixture will be sticky. Drop on greased baking sheet with an ice cream dipper or large spoon. Flatten slightly. Bake at 350 degrees for about 15 minutes for large cookies 3" in diameter. Yield: 2 dozen

Mattie Diener (Waitress)

BLACK BOTTOM CUPCAKES

Cream and mix well with mixer:

8 oz. cream cheese	1 egg
1/3 c. sugar	

Stir in 6 oz. chocolate chips. Set aside.

Cake mixture:

1 1/2 c. flour	1 t. vanilla
1 c. sugar	1 T. vinegar
1/4 c. cocoa	1 c. water
1 t. baking soda	1/2 c. vegetable oil
1 t. salt	

Mix all ingredients in order. Fill cupcake papers 1/3 full with cake mixture. Put 1 heaping T. of cream cheese mixture on top. Bake at 350 degrees for 20 to 25 minutes.

Tina Bobeck (Cashier)

 The person who is always blowing his own horn is usually off key.

CHEESECAKE CUPCAKES

24 vanilla wafers	1 t. vanilla
1 c. sugar	2 eggs
2-8 oz. cream cheese, softened	1 can cherry pie filling

Put one wafer in each paper muffin cup (24 in all). Cream sugar and cream cheese with mixer. Blend in vanilla and eggs. Pour over wafers. Bake at 350 degrees for 20 minutes. Cool well. Top with cherry pie filling. Refrigerate or freeze.

Amanda Miller (Bakery)
Norma Velleman (Cashier, Restaurant Gifts)

CHOCOLATE CUPCAKES WITH FILLING

2 c. sugar
3 c. flour
1 t. salt
6 T. cocoa
2 t. soda, rounded

1 T. vinegar
3/4 c. vegetable oil
1 T. vanilla
2 c. cold water

Mix sugar, flour, salt, and cocoa. Dissolve soda in vinegar and add to sugar and flour mixture with the remaining ingredients. Beat with mixer. Batter will be thin. Bake for 20 minutes at 350 degrees. Yield: 30 cupcakes

Filling

1 c. milk
3 T. flour
1/4 c. margarine

1/2 c. shortening
3/4 c. sugar
1 1/2 t. vanilla

Cook the flour and milk until it boils, using wire wisk to mix. Let mixture cool. In seperate bowl, beat together margarine and shortening until fluffy. Add sugar and vanilla and beat until fluffy. Add the cooked mixture. Cut out a circle cone shape in each cupcake and fill with 1 T. filling. Place cone cut-out back in cupcake.

Marilyn Bontrager (Waitress)

5 T. flour
1/4 t. margarine

Madlyn Bontrager (Mantress)

Cakes
& Frostings

Cakes & Frostings

ANGEL FOOD CAKE

2 1/4 c. sugar
1 1/4 c. cake flour
1/4 t. salt

1 1/2 t. cream of tartar
2 c. egg whites
1/4 t. vanilla

Put all dry ingredients in a bowl. Mix well with wire whip. Use a bigger bowl and beat egg whites with cream of tartar and vanilla until stiff. Then mix with dry ingredients. This makes a large cake. Start oven at 275 degrees and bake for 1 hour, increasing heat every 15 minutes. Increase 30 degrees the first 15 minutes, 15 degrees every 15 minutes thereafter.

Mattie Marie Diener (Waitress)

Influence

Drop a pebble in the water
and its ripples reach out far;
And the sunbeams dancing on them
May reflect then to a star.
Give a smile to someone passing
Thereby making his morning glad;
It may greet you in the evening
When your own heart may be sad.
Do a deed of simple kindness
Though its end you may not see;
It may reach, like widening ripples
Down a long eternity.

When trying to get black heel marks off of your vinyl floor, try a damp cloth and baking soda, or rub a little nongel toothpaste on the mark.

APPLE BUTTER SPICE CAKE

2 1/2 c. flour
1 t. baking powder
1/2 t. salt
1 c. sugar
1 t. soda

3/4 c. apple butter
2 eggs
1 c. sour cream
1 t. vanilla
1/2 c. oleo

Put all ingredients in large bowl. Blend on low speed until moistened, then 2 minutes on medium speed. Pour 1/2 batter in greased 13 x 9 cake pan. Sprinkle with 1/2 of topping. Spoon remainder of batter on top of topping. Cover with remaining topping. Bake at 350 degrees for 40 to 45 minutes.

Topping

1/2 c. brown sugar
1 t. cinnamon

1/2 t. nutmeg
1/2 c. chopped nuts

Ellen Mishler (Hostess/Cashier)

I am my neighbor's Bible,
He reads me when we meet,
Today he reads me in the house,
Tomorrow in the street.

He may be relative or friend,
Or slight acquaintance be,
He may not even know my name,
Yet he is reading me.

APPLE CAKE

1 c. vegetable oil	1/2 t. salt
1 1/2 c. sugar	2 t. cinnamon
2 eggs + 1 egg white	3 large apples, peeled,
1 t. vanilla	cored & finely diced
2 c. flour	1 c. chopped nuts
1 t. soda	

In a large bowl, beat oil and sugar until smooth. Beat in egg, egg white, and vanilla. Stir in flour, soda, salt, and cinnamon. Beat well. Stir in apples and nuts. Bake in greased 9 x 13 pan for 45 minutes or until center springs back when pressed gently. Bake in 350 degrees oven. Cool.

Frosting

1/2 c. softened oleo	1 t. vanilla
1 egg yolk	1 1/2 c. powdered sugar

Beat oleo in bowl. Add remaining ingredients and beat until smooth. Spread on cooled cake.

Ellen Mishler (Hostess/Cashier)

Here are several ways to put the shine back on your stainless flatware. Soak the flatware in hot water and a little ammonia; rinse and dry. Soaking in vinegar and water does a super job as well.

APPLE PUDDING CAKE

Cream:

1/4 c. oleo   1 beaten egg
1 c. sugar

Add:

1 c. flour   1/2 t. nutmeg
1 t. cinnamon   1 t. soda
dash of salt

Mix in:

3 medium apples, peeled   1/2 c. nuts
and diced

Batter will be thick. Bake for 30 minutes in 350 degree oven.

Sauce

1/2 c. brown sugar   1/2 c. half & half
1/2 c. white sugar   1/2 c. butter

Boil until thick. Add 1 t. vanilla.

Pamela Frey (Bakery)

Elephant Stew

1 elephant   salt
2 rabbits (optional)   pepper

Cut up the elephant in bite size pieces. This will take about 2 weeks. Salt and pepper to taste. Cook over kerosene fire at 475 degrees for 8 days. This will serve 1,360 people. If more people are expected, add 2 rabbits. Do this only if necessary, as most people don't like to find hare in their stew.

To keep rolls hot longer in your basket line the basket with aluminum foil.

APPLE NUT COFFEE CAKE

1/2 c. shortening
1 c. sugar
2 eggs
1 t. vanilla
2 c. flour

1 t. baking powder
1 t. baking soda
1/4 t. salt
1 c. sour cream
2 c. finely chopped apples

Cream shortening and sugar. Add eggs and vanilla. Beat well. Stir together flour, baking powder, soda, and salt. Add to creamed mixture alternately with sour cream. Fold in chopped apples. Spread batter in greased 13 x 9 baking pan. Combine topping ingredients and sprinkle mixture evenly over batter. Bake for 35 minutes at 350 degrees.

Topping

1/2 c. brown sugar
2 T. melted butter

1 t. cinnamon
1/2 c. chopped nuts

Sharon Boley (Waitress)

When having trouble with burning your fingers when lighting your candles, try using a piece of spaghetti to light them. You can get down into the holders when the candle is burned down.

APPLESAUCE CAKE

Creamed mixture

1 c. butter   3 t. vanilla
2 c. sugar

Flour mixture

4 c. flour, sifted 5 times   3 t. soda
and your choice of spices

Liquid mixture

2 1/2 c. stewed apples   1 c. chopped nuts
1 c. grape juice or 2 eggs   1 c. raisins

Cream butter and sugar. Add alternately with flour and liquid mixtures until well mixed. Bake in tube pan at 350 degrees for approximately an hour. Best served after 2 days.

Frances Blough (Waitress)

BANANA CAKE

1 c. oil   1 t. salt
2 c. sugar   2 t. baking powder
3 eggs   1 t. cream of tartar
2 c. mashed bananas   2 t. vanilla
3 c. flour   chopped nuts, to taste
1 t. soda

Cream sugar and oil. Add eggs and beat well. Stir in bananas. Add the remaining ingredients. Bake for 30 to 35 minutes at 350 degrees.

Rosanna Miller (Kitchen)

198

BANANA CAKE

3/4 c. shortening
2 c. sugar
1 t. vanilla
2 eggs
1 c. sour milk

1 c. bananas
3 c. flour
1 t. baking powder
1 t. soda
1/2 t. salt

Cream shortening and sugar. Add eggs, sour milk, and bananas. Add flour, baking powder, soda, and salt. Bake at 350 degrees for 30 minutes.

Mary K. Schrock (Kitchen)

BANANA CAKE WITH PEANUT BUTTER ICING

2 1/4 c. flour
1 1/4 t. baking powder
1 t. baking soda
1 t. salt
1 c. ripe, mashed bananas
1 t. vanilla

1 c. buttermilk, room temperature
2/3 c. shortening
1 1/2 c. sugar
2
2 eggs, room temperature

Combine flour, baking powder, baking soda, and salt and set aside. In separate bowl combine bananas and buttermilk and set aside. Cream together shortening and sugar in large bowl, beating until light and fluffy. Add eggs, one at a time, beating well after each addition; add vanilla. Alternately add flour mixture and banana mixture, beginning and ending with flour. Beat well. Bake in greased and floured 9 x 13 pan at 350 degrees for 30 to 35 minutes or until toothpick comes out clean. Cool cake completely.

Icing

1-8 oz. pkg. cream cheese, soft
1/2 c. light corn syrup

1/2 c. creamy peanut butter
1 c. chopped unsalted peanuts

Mix cream cheese and corn syrup until smooth. Add peanut butter and beat well. Spread on cooled cake. Garnish with chopped peanuts. Refrigerate cake until serving time.

Diane Beachy (Waitress)

BLACK WALNUT CAKE

2 c. sugar
1 c. butter
1 c. cold water
3 c. cake flour*

2 t. baking powder
1 c. chopped walnuts
1 t. vanilla
white of 4 eggs

Cream together sugar and butter. Add water gradually. Sift flour and baking powder; coat nuts in some of this mixture. Add to butter mixture. Add vanilla. Beat egg whites until stiff and fold into mixture last. Bake in 2-9" layer pans.

Filling between layers:

1/2 c. milk
1 T. flour

3 egg yolks
1 c. chopped nuts

Mix and boil until thick. Put between layers. Put the nuts in after removing from the heat.

* Homemade cake flour: Fill 1 cup half full of flour and add 3 T. cornstarch. Finish filling the cup with flour until it is full; sift 3 times.

Walter Lehman (Essenhaus Foods)

BUTTERMILK CAKE

4 c. flour
2 c. white sugar

3/4 c. butter or lard

Mix together until crumbly. Set aside 1 c.

1 t. soda
1 t. cinnamon

1 3/4 c. buttermilk

Mix and add to the above mixture. Put reserved crumbs on top and bake at 350 degrees for 35 to 40 minutes.

Ruth Beachy (Bakery)

CHOCOLATE ZUCCHINI CAKE

3 squares unsweetened chocolate	4 eggs
3 c. unsifted flour	3 c. sugar
1 t. baking soda	1 1/2 c. oil
1 1/2 t. baking powder	3 c. shredded zucchini
1 t. salt	1 c. chopped nuts

Melt and cool chocolate. Sift together dry ingredients. Beat eggs until thick and creamy. Add sugar, oil, chocolate, zucchini, and nuts. Bake in greased 9 x 13 pan at 350 degrees for 1 hour and 15 minutes.

Alice Risser (Cashier/ Dutch Country Gifts)

Slip your hand into a waxed sandwich bag and you have a perfect mitt for greasing your baking pan or casserole dishes.

CHOCOLATE ANGEL FOOD CAKE

2 c. egg whites	1 c. + 5 T. cake flour
2 t. cream of tartar	1/2 t. salt
2 c. sugar	3 T. cocoa
2 t. vanilla	

Put egg whites and cream of tartar in a large bowl and beat until foamy. Add 1 c. sugar, 2 T. at a time. After all sugar added, beat until stiff. Fold in vanilla. Sift cake flour, sugar, salt, and cocoa. Fold into the stiff egg whites. Bake at 375 degrees for 45 to 50 minutes.

Frosting

1/2 c. margarine	1/3 c. buttermilk
1/4 c. cocoa	1/2 t. vanilla

Mix and bring to a boil: margarine, cocoa, and buttermilk. Add vanilla and powdered sugar, enough to spread.

Mattie Diener (Waitress)

COCA COLA CAKE

1/2 c. butter
3 T. cocoa

1/2 c. vegetable oil
1 c. cola drink

Bring to a rapid boil. Add this to a mixture of 2 c. sugar and 2 c. flour.
Add to this mixture:

2 eggs
1 t. cola drink

1/2 c. buttermilk
1 1/2 c. miniature marshmallows

Put in buttered 10 x 14 1/2 pan. Bake at 350 degrees for 30 minutes.

Icing

1/2 c. butter
3 T. cocoa

6 T. cola drink
1 t. vanilla

Bring to boil. Add 1 c. nuts and 1 lb. box of powdered sugar. Put on hot
cake.

Gayle Martin (Bakery)

COTTAGE PUDDING CAKE

2 c. flour
3 t. baking powder
3/4 c. sugar
pinch of salt

1/4 c. softened butter
1 egg
1 c. milk

Mix first 5 ingredients. Beat egg and mix to milk. Add to flour mixture.
Grease 8 x 8 pan. Bake in 350 degree oven until golden brown or
toothpick comes out clean. Add any fresh fruit or milk.

Marietta Helmuth (Waitress)

202

CREAM CHEESE YELLOW CAKE

1 box yellow cake mix   1 stick oleo, softened
2 eggs, beaten

Mix and pour into cake pan. Batter will be very thick.

Topping

1-3 oz. cream cheese   2 eggs, beaten
3 1/2 c. powdered sugar

Mix and put on top of cake mixture. Bake at 350 degrees for 30 to 35 minutes.

Walter Lehman (Essenhaus Foods)

CREAM FILLED CHOCOLATE CAKE

Prepare 1 chocolate cake mix as directed on the box. Bake in a
10 1/2 x 15 1/2 pan. Cook 1 1/4 c. milk and 5 T. flour until thick. Allow
to cool. Cream together 1 c. sugar, 1/2 c. shortening, and 1 stick oleo.
Add to cooled flour mixture and spread over warm cake.

6 T. cocoa   1 stick oleo, melted
3 C. powdered sugar   1 egg
2 1/2 T. hot water   1 t. vanilla

Combine above ingredients and mix well. Spread over cooled cake.

Rosanna Miller (Kitchen)

Some people are like a wheel barrow; they have to be pushed for everything they do.

203

CREME DE MENTHE CAKE

1 box white cake mix

1/3 c. creme de menthe syrup or use 1/3 c. water as substitute

Mix as directed. Bake in 9 x 13 pan. Cool cake completely.

Topping

1 can Hershey's Fudge
1-8 oz. Cool Whip

1/4 c. creme de menthe syrup
green food coloring

Spread fudge over cooled cake. Mix Cool Whip, syrup, and a few drops of food coloring. Spread over fudge. Store cake in the refrigerator.

Malinda Eash (Loom Creations)

 A tactful person is one who can build a fire under someone without making his blood boil.

CRUMB CAKE

2 c. flour
1 1/2 c. sugar

2 t. baking powder
1/2 c. butter or lard

Mix all ingredients together with hands. Reserve 1/2 c. crumbs. Break 2 eggs into the remaining mixture. Add 2/3 c. milk. Beat until smooth. Pour into pan and sprinkle with crumbs. Bake at 350 degrees for 35 minutes.

Sophia Helmuth —Becky Helmuth's Mother (Waitress)

DELICIOUS COFFEE CAKE

2 c. flour
1 c. sugar
1 t. salt
4 eggs

1 c. oil
1 can pie filling—
cherry, blueberry, or raisin

Mix all above ingredients, except pie filling. Pour 1/2 batter into greased 9 x 13 cake pan. Cover with pie filling. Cover this with remaining batter. Sprinkle with topping consisting of 1/2 c. brown sugar, 1 T. oleo, 1/2 t. cinnamon, and nuts, if desired. Bake at 350 degrees for 30 minutes. Cool. Drizzle with powdered sugar glaze (1 c. powdered sugar and enough milk to make runny).

Ellen Mishler (Hostess/Cashier)

DEPRESSION CAKE

2 c. sugar
1 1/2 c. strong coffee
1/2 c. lard
1 c. raisins
1 apple, peeled and grated
1 t. allspice

2 c. flour
1 t. baking soda
1 t. baking powder
1 t. cinnamon
1 t. nutmeg
1/2 c. chopped walnuts

Simmer the first five ingredients for 10 minutes, stirring occasionally. Cool 10 minutes. Blend the dry ingredients together and stir into the raisin mixture. Pour batter into greased and floured 9 x 13 pan. Bake at 350 degrees for 25 to 30 minutes.

James Teall (Kitchen)

You grow up the day you have the first real laugh--at yourself.

DOUBLE PISTACHIO CAKE

1 box white or yellow cake mix   1 c. water
1 pkg. instant pistachio pudding   4 eggs
1/2 c. chopped nuts   1/4 c. oil

Combine all ingredients in large mixing bowl. Bake in 9 x 13 pan for 40 to 45 minutes at 350 degrees.

Frosting

Pour 1 1/2 c. cold milk into deep bowl. Add 1 envelope Dream Whip; whip. Add 1 pkg. pistachio instant pudding. Beat at low speed until blended. Increase beating to high and whip until soft peaks are formed. Yield: 3 c.

Freda Yutzy (Waitress)

DUTCH APPLE CAKE

2 c. sugar   2 eggs, beaten
1 c. butter   3 c. flour, scant
2 t. soda   pinch salt
1 1/2 t. cinnamon   6 apples, diced

Mix all ingredients, except apples, adding apples after all other is mixed. Mix and bake at 350 degrees for 45 minutes.

Topping

1/2 c. butter   2 T. flour
1 c. sugar   1 c. milk
3 t. vanilla

Cook until thick and pour over cake. Serve warm with ice cream.

Lena Lehman

EASY CARROT CAKE

1 yellow cake mix
1 1/4 c. Miracle Whip
4 eggs
1/4 c. cold water

2 t. cinnamon
2 c. shredded carrots
1/2 c. chopped walnuts

Mix cake, Miracle Whip, eggs, water, and cinnamon. Mix until blended. Stir in carrots and walnuts. Bake at 350 degrees for 35 minutes in a 13 x 9 baking pan. Cool. Spread with Cream Cheese ready to spread frosting.(Betty Crocker or Pillsbury cream cheese)

Sharon Boley (Waitress)

FILLED COFFEE CAKE

Dissolve 1 1/2 t. yeast in 1/2 c. warm water. Heat 3/4 c. milk. Add 1/2 c. oleo, 1 1/4 t. salt, and 1/2 c. sugar. Beat 2 eggs and add to milk mixture. After it's lukewarm, add yeast. Add 4 to 5 c. flour, as needed. Let rise until doubled and divide into 4 parts. Spread in greased pie pans. Put crumbs on top and let rise until double.

Crumbs

1/2 c. brown sugar
1 t. cinnamon

1/4 c. flour
1 T. oleo

Bake at 400 degrees until golden brown. When cool, cut tops off and fill.

Filling

Beat 2 egg whites until stiff. Add at least 3 c. powdered sugar. Add 1/3 c. Crisco and a little milk. Add more powdered sugar if needed.

Mrs. John Hochstetler

Kissin' wears out; cookin' don't.

FRESH APPLE CAKE

2 c. sugar
3 eggs
3/4 c. oil
3 c. all-purpose flour
1 1/2 t. soda
1 1/2 t. nutmeg

1/2 t. salt
1 t. cinnamon
1 t. vanilla
3 c. apples, chopped
1 c. nuts, chopped

Preheat oven 350 degrees. Mix sugar, eggs, oil, and beat. Sift flour, soda, nutmeg, salt, and cinnamon. Add to egg mixture gradually. Add apples and nuts. Grease and flour tube pan or sheet cake pan. Bake for 55 minutes. Before putting in oven, sprinkle with 1 c. butterscotch chips or after cake is baked.

Glaze

1/2 c. margarine
1 c. brown sugar

1/4 c. orange juice or milk

Boil over slow heat for 5 minutes. Pour over cake. Return to oven for 5 minutes.

Frances Blough (Waitress)

GOOEY BUTTER CAKE

1 butter recipe cake mix
4 eggs
1 stick butter, melted
8 oz. pkg. cream cheese

1 lb. powdered sugar,
reserve 1/2 c.
1 c. nuts, optional

Mix cake mix, 2 eggs, and melted butter. Pour into 9 x 13 cake pan. Mix cream cheese, 2 eggs, and sifted powdered sugar. Pour over cake layer. Sprinkle with nuts. Bake at 350 degrees for 35 to 40 minutes or until lightly brown. Sprinkle with remaining powdered sugar when cooled slightly.

Rosanne Bontrager (Busser)

LEMON CHEESECAKE

Mix 1 lemon cake mix and 1 stick butter to consistency of pie dough. Add 2 beaten eggs and spread evenly in 9 x 13 pan. Cream together 1-8 oz. cream cheese and 3 c. powdered sugar. Add 2 beaten eggs and spread on first mixture. Bake at 350 degrees for 30 to 40 minutes.

Edna Borntrager (Essenhaus Foods)

NO FROST OATMEAL CAKE

Pour 1 1/2 c. boiling water over 1 c. oatmeal. Add:

1 c. brown sugar	1 c. sugar
1/2 c. shortening	2 eggs
1 t. soda	1/2 t. salt
1 T. cocoa	1 1/2 c. flour

Stir in 1/2 c. chocolate chips. Pour in 9" square pan and top with 1/2 c. chocolate chips and 1/2 c. nuts. Bake at 350 degrees for 35 to 40 minutes.

Carol Wiggins (Cashier/Restaurant Gifts)

MILLIONAIRE CAKE

2 c. white sugar	20 oz. crushed pineapple
2 eggs	1 c. nuts
2 t. soda	2 c. flour
1 c. coconut	

Mix sugar, eggs, and soda. Add coconut, pineapple, nuts, and flour. Pour into 9 x 13 pan. Bake at 350 degrees for 35 to 40 minutes.

Delores Wagler (Maintenance)

Build a reservoir of good will by placing the interests of other people above your own.

OATMEAL CAKE

1 c. quick oatmeal   1 1/2 c. boiling water

Combine and let set for 20 minutes.

1/2 c. margarine   1 1/2 c. flour
1 c. white sugar   1 t. soda
1 c. brown sugar   1/2 t. salt
2 eggs   1 t. cinnamon

Cream margarine and sugars. Add eggs and beat well. Add dry ingredients and mix well. Add oatmeal.

Topping

1 c. brown sugar   1/2 c. nuts
4 T. butter   1 c. coconut
1/2 c. evaporated milk or cream

Mix ingredients. Have topping ready and when cake is done put on top of cake and put under broiler until brown.

Rosalie Bontrager (Manager/Inn)
Ruth Beachy (Restaurant Gifts)

Watch out when you stretch the truth; it could snap back at you.

PECAN CAKE

6 eggs	3 T. flour
1 c. sugar	4 t. baking powder
2 1/2 c. pecans	

Mix eggs and sugar in blender. Gradually add pecans. Add remaining ingredients. Mix until batter is smooth. Bake for 30 minutes at 350 degrees in 2 well greased round cake pans. When cool, split each layer in half. Divide filling in thirds and spread each half with filling. Ice with your favorite icing.

Filling

8 oz. cream cheese	1/4 c. margarine
1/2 c. brown sugar	1 t. vanilla or orange peel

Anne Yoder (Restaurant Manager)

PINEAPPLE CAKE

2 c. flour	2 eggs
2 c. sugar	20 oz. can crushed pineapple,
1 t. soda	reserve juice

Mix all ingredients, including reserved pineapple juice, together. Bake in 13 x 9 greased and floured pan for 30 minutes at 375 degrees.

Frosting

8 oz. cream cheese	1/2 t. vanilla
1/2 c. butter	1 box powdered sugar

Mix and frost cake.

Tina Bobeck (Busser/Cashier)
Betti Kauffman (Hostess/Cashier)
Susanna Miller (Kitchen)

211

"PRUNE KUCHEN"

1/3 c. shortening or lard
1 c. scalded milk
1/2 c. sugar
1 pkg. yeast, dissolved in
1/4 c. warm water & 1 t. sugar
4 c. flour

1 egg
1/2 t. salt
1 pkg. prunes, soaked, cooked, cooled, pitted & drained
1/4 c. mashed potatoes

Melt lard in milk. Cool milk to just warm and add rest of ingredients, except prunes, to make a soft dough. Knead well. Let rise for 2 hours. Punch down and let rest for 15 minutes. Divide dough in half and roll each half out to 1/2" thick. Fit in a greased 9 x 13 pans. Let rise about 1/2 hour and brush with melted butter. Sift a little flour over the top. Arrange prunes, skin side down, on the top of dough.

Combine 1 c. sour cream, 1 T. flour, and 2 T. sugar. Pour over prunes and sprinkle with a brown sugar and cinnamon mixture (1/2 c. brown sugar and 1/4 t. cinnamon). Bake until brown and cream is set, about 15 minutes at 400 degrees.

Bill Burns (Bakery)

PUMPKIN CAKE

1 2/3 c. sugar
4 eggs

1 c. oil
1-16 oz. can pumpkin

Mix together. Then add:

2 c. flour
2 t. cinnamon

2 t. baking powder
1 t. salt

Bake in 9 x 13 pan at 350 degrees for 35 to 40 minutes.

Frosting

1-8 oz. cream cheese
1/2 c. oleo, melted

2 c. powdered sugar
1 t. vanilla

Wilma Weaver (Waitress)

212

RAINBOW CAKE

1 pkg. white cake mix   1/2 c. cold water
1-3 oz. pkg. strawberry jello   2 c. Cool Whip
1 c. boiling water

Prepare cake mix as directed on package, baking in 9 x 13 cake pan. Cool cake for 15 minutes. Prick cake with utility fork at 1/2 inch intervals. Meanwhile, dissolve jello in boiling water. Add cold water and carefully pour over warm cake. Chill for 3 to 4 hours. Top with Cool Whip. Cut into squares and garnish with strawberries, if desired.

Rosanne Bontrager (Busser)

 Nowadays you'll find almost everything in the average American home except the family.

7-UP CAKE

1 box yellow cake mix   1/4 c. vegetable oil
1 box vanilla pudding   1-10 oz. bottle 7 Up
4 eggs

Bake in two layer pans or 9 x 13 pan at 325 degrees for 30 to 35 minutes.

Icing

Boil 4 beaten eggs, 1 1/2 c. sugar, and 1 T. flour together. Remove from heat and add 1-16 oz. can coconut and 1-20 oz. can drained crushed pineapple. Cool and spread on cake.

Ellen Mishler (Hostess/Cashier)

SCRUMPTIOUS COFFEE CAKE

2 c. flour   1 t. soda
1 c. sugar   1/4 t. nutmeg
1/2 t. salt   1 t. cinnamon
1 t. baking powder

Mix together. Add and mix until just blended:

1/4 c. orange juice   1 c. milk
1 egg   1/2 c. oil

Pour batter into greased and floured 9 x 13 pan. Crumble together and sprinkle over batter before baking:

1 c. brown sugar   1 c. chopped nuts, optional
1/2 stick margarine

Bake at 350 degrees for 30 minutes. When slightly cool, drizzle the following over the top:

3/4 c. powdered sugar   1/2 t. vanilla
1 T. milk

Ruth Ann Yoder (Bakery)

"Good Samaritan Oil" for bruises, aches, pains: Blend into 1 quart of raw linseed oil the following: 1/4 oz. oregano oil, 1/4 oz. oil of hemlock, 1/2 oz. oil of sassafras, 1/4 oz. oil of wintergreen, 1/4 oz. oil of lavender, 1 oz. gum camphor. Gently rub in.

SOUR CREAM COFFEE CAKE

Topping

1/3 c. brown sugar
1/4 c. sugar

2 t. cinnamon
1/2 c. chopped nuts

Combine and set aside.

1/2 c. butter, soft
1 c. sugar
2 eggs
1-8 oz. pkg. sour cream
1 t. vanilla

2 c. all-purpose flour
1 t. baking powder
1 t. soda
1/4 t. salt

Cream butter and sugar in a bowl. Add eggs, sour cream, and vanilla. Mix well. Combine flour, baking powder, soda, and salt. Add to butter and egg mixture. Beat until combined. Pour 1/2 the batter into greased 9 x 13 pan. Sprinkle with 1/2 the topping mixture. Add remaining batter and then topping. Bake at 325 degreees for 40 minutes or until done. Yield: 12-15 servings

Ida Weaver (Waitress)

SPICE CAKE

2 c. flour
1 t. soda
2 c. brown sugar
1 t. cinnamon
1/4 t. allspice

1/4 t. cloves
2 eggs
1/2 c. butter & lard mixture
1 c. sour milk *

Mix all ingredients together. Bake at 350 degrees for 35 minutes.

* Mix 1 1/2 t. vinegar with milk to sour.

Ida Weaver (Waitress)

215

WALNUT - APPLE CAKE

2 eggs   4 c. diced apples, peeled

Mix well. Mix the following ingredients:

2 c. sugar   1 c. chopped walnuts
2 t. cinnamon   1 t. vanilla

Mix with eggs and apples. Sift together:

2 c. flour   3/4 t. salt
2 t. soda

Mix with the above mixture. Pour into greased and floured pan. Bake at
350 degrees for 45 to 55 minutes.

Judy Beachy (Manager/Kitchen)

WATERGATE CAKE

1 box white cake mix   3 eggs
1 box pistachio pudding   1 c. ginger ale
1 c. vegetable oil   1/2 c. chopped nuts

Mix these ingredients together and bake in a 9 x 13 pan at 350 degrees
for 40 minutes.

Impeachment Icing

1 1/2 c. milk   1 box pistachio pudding mix
3 envelopes powdered topping

Put milk and Dream Whip in bowl. Gradually add dry pudding to this
and beat until stiff. Spread on cooled cake.

Ellen Mishler (Hostess/Cashier)

216

BUTTER CREAM ICING

9 c. sifted powdered sugar
1/2 t. salt
1 1/2 c. shortening

1/4 c. water
vanilla or favorite flavor,
to taste

Mix in large bowl. Beat until all lumps are out. Add 1/2 c. butter. Continue beating until icing is fairly light and fluffy. In hot weather, use less water. In cold weather, use more water. Will ice a 9" cake.

Wanda Yoder (Bakery)

CARAMEL FROSTING

4 T. butter

1/2 c. brown sugar

Cook slowly for 5 minutes. Let cool. Add 1/4 c. cream and boil 5 more minutes or to a rolling boil. Cool and add powdered sugar until creamy.

Erma Yoder (Maintenance)

COCONUT PECAN FROSTING

1 c. sugar
1/2 c. butter or oleo
3 egg yolks

1 c. evaporated milk
1 t. vanilla

Cook and stir over medium heat until thickened, about 12 minutes. Add 1 1/3 c. coconut and 1 c. chopped pecans. Beat until thick enough to spread. Yield: 2 1/2 c.

Ruthann Wagler (Kitchen)

People are lonely because they build walls instead of bridges.

CREAMY MAPLE FROSTING

1/2 c. butter flavored Crisco   4 T. milk
1 box powdered sugar   2 t. vanilla
1/3 c. maple blend syrup

Mix all ingredients. Add more sugar to thicken or milk to thin, if needed, for good spreading consistency. Top with pecans. Excellent on spice cake or chocolate cake. Frosts on 9 x 13 cake.

Norma Velleman (Cashier/Restaurant Gifts)

MELTED CANDY BAR FROSTING

Melt a Milky Way candy bar and 1/4 c. of hot water in a sauce pan over medium heat. Add 1 c. brown sugar and stir well or until mixture comes to a boil. Remove from stove and stir in milk and powdered sugar. The amount of powdered sugar and milk depends on the size of cake to be iced. Delicious for chocolate or spice cake.

Walter Lehman(Essenhaus Foods)

NEVER FAIL CARAMEL ICING

6 T. brown sugar   3 T. butter
6 T. white sugar   1/2 c. milk or cream

Bring this to a boil and boil hard for 2 minutes. Remove from heat and add 9 large marshmallows. Stir until they are melted. Add 1 1/2 t. caramel flavoring and 1 1/2 c. powdered sugar. Beat until thick enough to spread on cake.

Ida Weaver (Waitress)

Pies
& Candies

Pies & Candies

APPLE PAN DOWDY

2-8" pie crusts
1-20 oz. can apple slices, drained
1/2 c. brown sugar, packed

3 T. butter or margarine, melted
6 T. maple flavored syrup

Heat oven to 425 degrees. Stir together apple slices and brown sugar. Turn into pastry lined pie pan. Top with butter and 3 T. of the syrup. Cover with top crust, that has slits, seal and flute. Bake 15 minutes. Remove from oven. Make criss-cross cuts about 1" apart through crust and filling. Drizzle remaining syrup on top. Cover edge with 2 or 3 strips of aluminum foil to prevent excess browning. Bake 25 minutes longer. Serve warm. Can serve with syrup.

Irene Schrock (Kitchen)

BAKED COCONUT CREAM PIE

2 eggs, beaten
1 c. corn syrup
1 c. milk
1 t. vanilla

1/4 c. white sugar
1 T. flour
2 t. melted butter
1 c. coconut

Mix ingredients well. Put in 9" pie crust and bake at 350 degrees for 45 minutes to 1 hour.

Mary Esther Miller (Manager/Restaurant Gifts)

221

BERRIED TREASURE PIE

1 large banana, sliced
1 graham cracker pie crust
2 T. sugar
1-8 oz. cream cheese, softened
1 c. milk

1 qt. strawberries, rinsed, drained & sliced
1 small package instant vanilla pudding
1 small tub Cool Whip

Put the sliced banana in the bottom of the pie crust. Mix 2 T. sugar into softened cream cheese and spread on top of banana slices. Put sliced strawberries on top of cream cheese mixture. If strawberries are not very sweet, sprinkle with 1 or 2 T. sugar. Mix vanilla pudding with 1 c. milk. Pudding will be stiff. Stir in about 2/3 of Cool Whip, saving rest for the top of the pie. Spread the pudding mixture on top of strawberries. Top with remaining Cool Whip. Garnish with several whole strawberries.

Carol Detweiler (Waitress)

BLUEBERRY LEMON PIE

2 1/2 c. water
2 c. sugar
1 c. fresh blueberries
3 T. clear jel
1/2 t. salt
1/2 c. water

1/2 c. sugar
3 oz. pkg. lemon jello
4 c. fresh blueberries
1 c. whipped cream
1-8 oz. cream cheese
1 c. powdered sugar

Mix 2 1/2 c. water, 2 c. sugar, and 1 c. fresh blueberries together in a saucepan and bring to a boil. Mix 3 T. clear jel, 1/2 t. salt, 1/2 c. water, and 1/2 c. sugar together and add to boiling mixture. Cook until clear. Add jello and then cool mixture. Add 4 c. fresh blueberries. Beat 1 c. whipped cream. Add cream cheese and powdered sugar. Beat until smooth. Line baked pie shell with whipped cream, cream cheese and powdered sugar mixture, saving enough for the top. Add blueberry filling and then top with the whipped cream mixture.
Yield: 2 pies

Mary Arlene Bontrager (Waitress)

BOB ANDY PIE

3 eggs, separated
1/2 t. cream of tartar
3 1/2 c. brown sugar
2 c. milk

1/2 c. white sugar
2 T. flour
1 T. butter

Beat egg whites until stiff. Put 1/2 t. cream of tartar in egg whites. Add remaining ingredients. Put in unbaked pie shell. Sprinkle cinnamon over the top of pie. Bake 10 minutes at 400 degree, then at 350 degrees until done, about 1/2 hour.

Katie Miller (Bakery)

BROWN BAG APPLE PIE

2 T. lemon juice
1/2 c. sugar
2 T. flour

1/2 t. cinnamon
1 stick margarine

Preheat oven 425 degrees. Mix and add enough quartered apples to fill a heaping 9" pie shell. Sprinkle with 2 T. lemon juice. Mix 1/2 c. sugar and 1/2 c. flour and sprinkle over the top of the apples. Cut up 1 stick of margarine and place on top. Place pie in large brown paper bag and fold several times to seal. Place on cookie sheet and bake for one hour.

Dana Graber (Decorating Department)

BROWN SUGAR CUSTARD PIE

2 eggs, separated
2 c. milk (1/2 cream is best)
1 t. vanilla

1 T. flour, rounded
1 c. brown sugar

Mix all ingredients but egg whites and put in unbaked pie shell. Beat egg whites and put in last. Bake at 400 degrees for 10 minutes, then 350 degrees until done.

Freda Yutzy (Waitress)

223

CARAMEL RAISIN PIE

6 c. raisins
4 1/2 c. brown sugar
9 heaping T. clear jel
2 cans Milnot

2-3 c. whole milk
pinch of salt
4 T. butter

In a 6 quart sauce pan, boil raisins and 6 c. water. In another pan, cook brown sugar and 1 c. water for about 7 minutes. Add to raisins with an additional 4 c. water. Bring to a boil. Stir in clear jel immediately. Add Milnot and whole milk. Boil just a few more minutes and then add salt and butter. Makes enough filling for 6 pies. Top with whipped cream. Add additional sugar to taste. Another can of Milnot can be added for a richer pie.

Walter Lehman (Essenhaus Foods)

CHOCOLATE MALT SHOPPE PIE

1 1/2 c. chocolate cookie crumbs
1/4 c. melted butter
1 pt. vanilla ice cream, soft
1/2 c. crushed malted milk balls
2 T. milk, divided

3 T. instant chocolate malted milk powder
3 T. marshmallow cream topping
1 c. Rich's whipping cream, additional whipped cream and malted milk balls for garnish

Combine cookie crumbs and butter and put in a 9" pie pan. Freeze while preparing filling. In a bowl, blend ice cream, crushed malted milk balls, and 1 T. milk. Spoon into crust. Freeze for 1 hour. Meanwhile, blend malted milk powder, marshmallow cream, and remaining milk. Stir in whipping cream. Whip until soft peaks form. Spread over ice cream layer. Freeze several hours or overnight. Before serving, garnish with whipped cream and malted milk balls.

Mattie Marie Diener (Waitress)

 Too many people quit looking for work when they find a job.

224

CHOCOLATE PEANUT BUTTER PIE

3/4 c. butter   1/2 c. brown sugar, firm pack
3/4 c. peanut butter   5 1/4 c. Cool Whip, thawed

Beat margarine, peanut butter, and sugar until well blended. Reserve 1/4 c. of the whipped topping for garnish. Gently stir in the remaining 5 cups of whipped topping until mixture is smooth and creamy. Spoon into chocolate nut crust.

Chocolate Nut Crust

6 squares Bakers semi-sweet chocolate   1 T. butter
1 1/2 c. toasted, finely chopped nuts

Melt chocolate and butter together until completely melted. Stir in nuts. Press mixture into bottom and up the sides of prepared pie plate. Refrigerate until firm, about 1 hour. Spoon pie mixture into chocolate nut crust. Refrigerate until firm, about 4 hours. Garnish with reserved whipped topping. Sprinkle on peanuts and drizzle with melted chocolate, if desired.

Lori Miller (Waitress)

CHOCOLATE PEANUT BUTTER PIE

Mix together:

1 c. powdered sugar   1/3 c. peanut butter

Form small crumbs. Line a baked pie shell with crumbs and add 1 quart of chocolate pudding.* Top with whipped cream and sprinkle a few crumbs on top.

*Can use chocolate pudding made from scratch or a mix may be used.

Sue Miller (Manager)

COCONUT CREAM PIE

2/3 c. sugar
1/2 t. salt
2 1/2 T. cornstarch
1 T. flour
3/4 c. coconut

3 c. milk
3 egg yolks
1 T. butter
1 1/2 t. vanilla

Mix ingredients and cook over a medium heat, stirring constantly, until mixture begins to thicken. Pour into baked pie shell. Top with meringue or Cool Whip.

Ruth Ann Wagler (Kitchen & Bakery)

COCONUT CREAM PIE

3 c. cold water
2 cans sweetened condensed milk

2 pkgs. instant coconut cream pudding

Mix together and add 3 c. whipped topping. Set in refrigerator until set. Top with 8 oz. Cool Whip or Rich's Topping.

Martha Coblentz (Bakery)

COCONUT MACAROON PIE

2 eggs
1 1/2 c. sugar
1/2 t. salt
1/2 c. butter or oleo, soft

1/4 c. flour
1/2 c. milk
1 1/2 c. shredded coconut

Beat eggs, sugar, and salt until mixture is lemon colored. Add butter and flour and blend well. Add milk and fold in 1 c. coconut. Pour into unbaked 9" pie shell. Top with 1/2 c. coconut. Bake in slow oven at 325 degrees for about 60 minutes.

Esther Nisley (Bakery)

CREAM PIE

3/4 c. white sugar
1/3 c. brown sugar
1 T. flour
pinch of salt

1 c. cream
1 t. vanilla
1 c. scalded milk
2 eggs, separated

Mix together in order given, adding beaten egg whites last. Pour into unbaked pie shell. Bake at 400 degrees for 10 minutes then reduce heat to 350 degrees until done.

Erma Yoder (Maintenance)

CREAM PIE DELUXE

1 1/2 c. brown sugar
2 T. butter
1 c. cream
pinch of salt

1 1/2 c. whole milk
1/2 t. cinnamon
2 T. flour

Mix all together and put in unbaked pie shell. Bake until golden brown or until done at 350 degrees.

Ellen Mishler (Hostess/Cashier)

CUSTARD PIE

2 egg yolks, beaten
1/4 c. brown sugar
1/2 c. white sugar
1 heaping T. flour or cornstarch

pinch of salt
1 pt. milk, heated to scalding
1 t. vanilla

Mix together egg yolks, sugars, flour, and salt. Add to heated milk. Beat egg whites until stiff. Fold into first mixture. Add vanilla. Bake in hot oven (425 degrees) for 10 minutes. Reduce heat to 300 degrees until done.

Katie Miller (Shop Director)

227

DUTCH APPLE PIE

Preheat oven to 400 degrees. Prepare pie shell. Refrigerate until ready to use.

Filling

2 lbs. apples
1 T. lemon juice
2 T. flour

3/4 c. sugar
dash of salt
1 t. cinnamon

Core apples and pare. Slice thin and put into large bowl. Sprinkle with lemon juice. Combine flour, sugar, salt, and cinnamon. Mix well. Toss lightly with apples. Put in shell. Sprinkle on topping. Bake at 400 degrees for 40 to 45 minutes.

Topping

2/3 c. sifted flour
1/3 c. light brown sugar,
firm pack

1/3 c. margarine

Combine flour and sugar in medium bowl. Cut in margarine with pastry blender until mixture is the consistency of coarse corn meal. Refrigerate until use.

Wilma Weaver (Waitress)

PIE HINTS

A pie crust will be more easily made and better if all ingredients are cool.

If you want to make a pecan pie and haven't any pecans, substitute cornflakes. They will rise to the top the same as nuts and give a delicious flavor and crunchy surface.

To prevent a cream pie crust from becoming soggy, sprinkle with powdered sugar.

Cut drinking straws into short lengths and insert through slits in pie crust to prevent juices from running over in the oven and permit steam to escape.

FRENCH RHUBARB PIE

1 egg
1 t. vanilla
2 T. flour

1 c. sugar
2 1/2 c. diced rhubarb

Mix well. Put rhubarb mixture into an unbaked pie shell. Cover with topping. Bake at 400 degrees for 10 minutes, then 350 degrees for 30 minutes.

Topping

3/4 c. flour
1/3 c. oleo

1/4 c. brown sugar

Ellen Mishler (Hostess/Cashier)

FRESH GLAZED STRAWBERRY PIE

1 c. crushed strawberries
1 c. water
1/2 c. sugar
2 1/2 T. clear jel
3 oz. pkg. cream cheese

1/2 c. powdered sugar
1/2 t. vanilla
1/4 t. almond flavoring
1/2 c. whipped cream

Mix 1 c. crushed strawberries and 1 c. water. Bring to a boil and cook for 2 minutes. Strain (do not stir while straining). Add 1/2 c. sugar and 2 1/2 T. clear jel. Moisten with small amount of water. Bring to a boil and set aside. Mix 3 oz. cream cheese, 1/2 c. powdered sugar, 1/2 t. vanilla, 1/4 t. almond flavoring, and 1/2 c. whipped cream. Put cream cheese mixture in baked pie shell and spoon strawberry glaze on top. Can also be used with fresh peaches.

Walter Lehman (Essenhaus Foods)

A gossiper is like an old shoe; its tongue never stays in place.

FUDGE SUNDAE PIE

1/4 c. corn syrup
2 T. firmly packed brown sugar
3 T. margarine
2 1/2 c. rice cereal
1/4 c. peanut butter

1/4 c. fudge sauce (for ice cream)
3 T. corn syrup
1 qt. vanilla ice cream

Combine the 1/4 c. corn syrup, brown sugar, and margarine in medium sized sauce pan. Cook over low heat, stirring occasionally until mixture begins to boil. Remove from heat and add rice cereal. Stir until well coated. Press evenly into 9 inch pie pan to form crust. Stir together peanut butter, fudge sauce, and the 3 T. corn syrup. Spread half the mixture over the crust. Freeze until firm. Allow ice cream to soften slightly. Spoon into frozen crust, spreading evenly. Freeze until firm. Let stand at room temperature about 10 minutes before cutting. Warm remaining peanut butter mixture and drizzle over the top.

Betti Kauffman (Cashier/Hostess)

 For every minute you are angry, you lose 60 seconds of happiness.

GROUND CHERRY PIE

5 heaping c. ground cherries
6 c. water
pinch of salt

2 1/2 c. sugar
2 T. and 1 t. Realemon
1 T. butter

Put in saucepan and bring to a boil. Make a thickening of 5 heaping T. of clear jel and a little water. Add to cherries and water. Make double crust and bake as fruit pies.

Rosanna Miller (Cook)

GROUND CHERRY PIE

2 1/2 c. ripe,ground cherries   2 T. water
1/2 c. brown sugar   1 T. flour

Wash ground cherries and place in unbaked pie shell. Mix sugar and flour and sprinkle over cherries. Sprinkle water on top. Cover with top crust. Seal edges securely. For variation, crumbs consisting of 3 T. flour, 3 T. sugar, and 2 T. butter, may be used instead of top crust. Bake at 425 degrees for 15 minutes and then reduce heat to 375 degrees for 25 minutes.

Viola Miller (Ned Miller's wife-Essenhaus Foods)

HOLIDAY PIE

1/3 c. butter   3 c. milk
1/3 c. packed brown sugar   1 envelope Dream Whip
1/2 c. chopped pecans   or other whipped topping
1 baked 9" pie shell
1-5 oz. pkg. vanilla pie filling

Heat butter, brown sugar, and nuts in saucepan until butter is melted. Spread on bottom of pie shell and bake at 450 degrees for 5 minutes. Cool. Prepare pie filling mix with milk, as directed on box. Cool 5 minutes, stirring occasionally. Measure 1 c. and cover with wax paper and chill. Pour remainder into pie shell and chill. Fold whipped topping into the cup of chilled pie filling and spread over filling in pie shell. Chill.

Erma Swartzendruber (Office)

All that you do, do with your might.
Things done by halves are never done right.

LEMON CAKE PIE

1 c. sugar
pinch salt
2 egg yolks

2 T. melted oleo
2 T. flour, heaping

Beat ingredients until creamy. Add grated rind of 1 large or 2 small lemons. Add 1 c. whole milk and the whites of 2 eggs, beaten stiff. Pour into an unbaked pie shell. Bake for 30 minutes in a slow oven, 325 degrees.

Mary K. Schmucker (Kitchen)
Karen Hochstedler (Bakery)

MARSHMALLOW CREAM PEACH PIE

20 marshmallows
1/4 c. milk
2 c. whipped cream

3 c. diced peaches (5-6 medium)
9" graham cracker pie crust

Melt marshmallows in milk. Cool until set. Beat smooth and fold in whipped cream and peaches. Pour into crust. Chill several hours.

Leola Kauffman (Laundry)

MOTHER'S PIE CRUST

3/4 c. Crisco
2 1/4 c. sifted flour
1/2 t. baking powder, if desired

1 t. salt
5 T. cold water

Add half of Crisco to dry ingredients and mix , using pastry blender, until like fine meal. Cut in remaining Crisco until dough is the size of peas. Sprinkle water over flour mixture and make into balls with hands. Roll out on pastry board. Yield: 3 crusts

Marilyn M. Kehr (Cashier/Restaurant Gifts)

NO BAKE CREAM PIE

2 1/4 c. milk
3/4 c. sugar
1/4 c. cornstarch

1 stick margarine
1 baked pie shell

Cook 2 c. milk. Mix 1/4 c. milk with sugar and cornstarch. Add to hot milk. Boil until thickened. Remove from heat and add margarine. Pour in pie shell and sprinkle with cinnamon. Chill.

Rosanne Bontrager (Busser)

OATMEAL PIE

3 eggs, beaten
2/3 c. brown sugar
2/3 c. coconut
3 T. melted butter
1 unbaked pie shell

2/3 c. sugar
2/3 c. quick oatmeal
1 t. vanilla
1/2 c. chopped nuts

Mix all ingredients and pour into an unbaked pie shell. Bake at 350 degrees for 45 minutes. Serve with whipped cream.

Leola Kauffman (Laundry)

OATMEAL PIE

2 eggs, beaten
3/4 c. maple syrup
3/4 c. quick oatmeal

3/4 c. sugar
1 stick oleo, melted
1 unbaked pie shell

Stir together in order given and pour into an unbaked pie shell. Bake at 350 degrees for about 40 minutes.

Joann Bontrager (Busser)

Use your used wrapping paper from gifts to line your dresser drawers.

PEACH CREAM PIE

1-9" unbaked pie shell
4-5 large fresh peaches, sliced
1 egg
1 c. sugar

1/4 c. flour
1/2 t. vanilla
1 c. cream

Spread peach slices over the bottom of unbaked pie shell. Beat egg. Add sugar and flour. Beat and blend in vanilla and cream. Pour over peaches and sprinkle with cinnamon, if desired. Bake 10 minutes at 400 degrees then 350 degrees until done.

Katie Miller (Bakery)

PEAR PIE

1/2-3/4 c. sugar
4 T. flour, heaping
pinch of salt

2-3 medium pears, peeled, sliced
2 c. cream

Mix sugar, flour, and salt together. Put 1 heaping T. of mixture in bottom of 9 inch pie shell. Add pears. Mix 2 c. cream and rest of mixture. Mix well and pour over pie. Bake at 350 degrees for 1/2 to 3/4 of an hour. Should be bubbly and get brown on top.

Viola Miller (Ned Miller's wife-Essenhaus Foods)

PISTACHIO PIE

1 small box instant pistachio
pudding
1-8 oz. container sour cream

1 small can crushed pineapple,
drained
1 small container Cool Whip

Mix together and pour into prepared chocolate graham cracker pie crust. Put in refrigerator and let set.

Wilma Weaver (Waitress)

234

PUMPKIN (SQUASH) PIE

3 eggs
2 c. squash or 1 1/2 c. pumpkin
1 c. sugar
1/2 t. salt
1 t. ginger
1 t. cinnamon

1/2 t. cloves
1/2 t. nutmeg
1 1/2 c. milk, heated
1 can evaporated milk
1 T. flour

Beat eggs. Add squash or pumpkin, sugar, salt, and spices. Add the heated milk and evaporated milk. Add the flour. Bake for 15 minutes in 400 degrees. Turn down heat to 350 degrees for 45 minutes.

Linda Wenger (Laundry)

Charity begins anywhere and should have no end.

SHOESTRING APPLE PIE

4 eggs
1 3/4 to 2 c. white sugar
2 T. flour

1/2 t. salt
1 c. milk or 3 T. cream + 1 t. water
5 c. shredded apples

Mix all together and put in unbaked pie shells. Sprinkle with cinnamon and bake at 325 degrees until done. Test like custard pie.

Esther Nisley (Bakery)
Ruth Ann Yoder (Bakery)

STRAWBERRY SATIN PIE

Creamy Satin Filling

1/2 c. sugar	2 c. milk
3 T. cornstarch	1 egg
3 T. flour	whipping cream
1/2 t. salt	1 t. vanilla

Glaze

1/2 c. strawberries	1/2 c. water
1/4 c. sugar	1 T. cornstarch

Combine sugar, cornstarch, flour, and salt in a saucepan. Add milk gradually, stirring until smooth. Cook, stirring constantly, until mixture is very thick and bubbly. Stir a little hot mixture into slightly beaten egg. Return to remaining hot mixture. Cook until just bubbly again. Cool. Chill thoroughly (mixture will be thick). Beat until smooth. Whip 1/2 pint of whipping cream until stiff and fold into filling mixture. Add vanilla. Put into a 9" baked pie shell and chill at least 3 hours.

Slice 1 1/2 c. strawberries, reserving 1/4 c., arrange slices on top of filling. Crush remaining 1/4 c. strawberries and add to 1/2 c. water and cook 3 minutes. Strain. Combine 1/4 c. sugar and 1 T. cornstarch and stir into berry juice. Cook mixture, stirring constantly, until thick and clear. Cool then spoon carefully over strawberries. Refrigerate 1 hour.

Luella Yoder (Kitchen)

I asked, "Why doesn't somebody do something?" Then I realized I was somebody.

SUGAR FREE FRUIT PIE

3 lb. fruit
3 1/2 c. water

1 T. lemon juice

Mix and bring to a boil. Add:

6 oz. jell-starch
1 1/3 c. water

3/4 t. salt

Mix well. Cook until clear. Turn off heat and add 2 1/2 T. Equal. (If using cherries add 1/2 T. more Equal). This is enough filling for 2-9" pies. Bake at 350 degreees until nice and brown, approximately 45 minutes.

Mary Esther Miller/Manager Restaurant Gifts

VANILLA CRUMB PIE

1/2 c. brown sugar
1 egg
1 T. flour, heaping

1/2 c. white sugar
1 1/2 c. water
1 t. vanilla

Cook over low heat until thick. Pour into pie crust. Top with crumbs consisting of 1 c. flour, 1/2 c. brown sugar, 1/4 c. shortening, and 1/2 t. baking soda. Bake for 1 hour at 350 degrees.

Rosie Eash (Waitress)

VANILLA CRUMB PIE

2 pts. milk
1 c. brown sugar
1 c. sugar
2 c. corn syrup

1 T. vanilla
2 eggs
1 c. flour
1 t. salt

Cook until thick. Put into 3 pie shells. Top with crumbs consisting of 4 c. flour, 1 c. sugar, 2 t. soda, 2 t. cream of tartar and 3/4 c. lard and pinch of salt. Bake at 400 degrees for 10 minutes then at 350 degrees until done.

Katie Miller (Bakery)

VANILLA TART PIE

1 egg, beaten
1 T. vanilla

1 c. light corn syrup
1 c. sugar

Mix and put in unbaked pie shell.

2 c. sugar
1/2 c. lard or shortening, soft
2 c. flour

1 c. sour milk
1 egg
1 t. soda

Mix this and drop by spoonful on top of first mixture in pie shell. Bake
for 35 to 45 minutes at 350 degrees.

Ellen Mishler (Cashier/Hostess)

VELVETY CUSTARD PIE

4 slightly beaten eggs
3/4 c. sugar
1/4 t. salt

1 t. vanilla
2 1/2 c. milk, scalded
1-9" unbaked pie shell

Thoroughly mix eggs, sugar, salt, and vanilla. Slowly stir in hot milk. At
once pour into unbaked pie shells. Sprinkle with nutmeg and cinnamon.
Bake in a very hot oven at 475 degrees for 5 minutes; reduce heat to 425
degrees and bake for 10 minutes. Cool on a rack.

Sophia Helmuth (Becky Helmuth's, Waitress, mother)

 An ulcer is something you get when you mountain climb
over mole hills.

Candy

CHERRY CHOCOLATE CANDY

2 lb. powdered sugar
1/2 c. Crisco
2 T. butter
1/4 c. cream

1 T. vanilla
3-10 oz. maraschino cherries
1/2 pkg. chocolate chips

Mix like pie dough. This will take a while. Add a little cream to make handling easier. Make into balls with a cherry in the center. Let cool for 1 hour. Melt together chocolate chips and a little paraffin. Stick a toothpick in the ball and dip in chocolate. Put on waxed paper on a cookie sheet to cool.

Anna Marie Slabaugh (Bakery)

CHOCOLATE FUDGE

2 c. sugar
3 heaping T. Nestles Quik mix

1/2 c. butter
1 c. milk

Cook together until a 1/2 teaspoon of mixture forms a hard ball when dropped in a cup of cold water. Stir while cooking. Add nuts and put on buttered plate.

Delores Wagler (Maintenance)

CLARK BAR CANDY

2 1/2 c. powdered sugar
1 c. oleo, room temperature
1 lb. crunchy peanut butter

3 t. vanilla
1 lb. graham crackers, crushed

Mix ingredients with hands. Roll into bon bon size balls and dip in dipping chocolate.

Clara Yoder (Kitchen)

239

ENGLISH WALNUT CANDY

3 lbs. white sugar
1 pt. light corn syrup
1/2 lb. butter

1 large & 1 small can
Carnation condensed milk
1 lb. English walnut meats

Put all ingredients in large kettle and cook until thick, stirring all the time. Beat until creamy. Pour into a buttered pan and cool. Cut in squares.

Susanna Miller (Kitchen)

FUDGE

4 c. sugar
1 stick butter

1 large can Milnot

Mix above items. Stir and cook until hard ball is formed when 1/2 teaspoon is dropped into a cup of cold water. Reduce heat and mix in 7 oz. jar marshmallow creme. Mix in 12 oz. bag chocolate chips and 1 teaspoon. vanilla. Beat until slightly stiff. Add 1 c. English walnuts, if desired. Pour into buttered pan. Cut in squares when cold.

Sharon Boley (Waitress)

GOOF BALLS

1 stick oleo
1 pkg. unwrapped caramels
1 can Eagle Brand milk

1 bag large marshmallows
crushed rice krispies

Melt oleo and caramels in milk over medium heat . Dip marshmallows in mixture and then roll them in crushed rice krispies.

Jan Bontrager (Waitress)

 Do I push, or do I ride and drag my feet?

HARD MINT CANDY

1 c.corn syrup　　　　　　　　2 c. sugar
1 c. water　　　　　　　　　　1/4 t. peppermint oil
1 t. coloring

Put everything , except oil, in 3 qt. kettle and boil it together. To check, put a teaspoonful in cup of cold water and if it hardens before it sinks to the bottom, it's ready. Cool for 5 minutes and add oil. Stir thoroughly and put on cookie sheet. Sprinkle with powdered sugar. Cut into pieces while warm or break into pieces when cool. You can use another kind of flavoring.

Alma L. Hershberger (Restaurant Gifts Cashier)

MAPLE CREAMS

3 lb. powdered sugar, 3 c. = 1 lb.　　8 oz. pkg. cream cheese
2 sticks oleo, melted　　　　　　　1 T. maple flavor

Mix and form into patties. Dip in chocolate. Mix peanuts and chocolate and put dabs on top of patties.

Ruth Beachy (Cashier/Restaurant Gifts)
Freda Yutzy (Waitress)

MILLION DOLLAR FUDGE

4 1/2 c. white sugar　　　　　　　1 can Carnation condensed milk

Boil together 7 minutes at medium heat. Remove from heat. Add 2-9 oz. Hershey bars with almonds, shredded , 1 large package chocolate chips (should be shredded before you put milk on stove), and 10 oz. marshmallow cream. Stir all ingredients together until thick. Pour on a waxed cookie sheet. Cool completely and cut.

Marietta Helmuth (Waitress)

NAPOLEON CREAMS

1/2 c. soft butter
1/4 c. sugar
1/4 c. cocoa
1 t. vanilla
1 egg, beaten
2 c. graham cracker crumbs
1 c. flaked coconut
1/2 c. soft butter

3 T. milk
1-3 3/4 oz. box instant vanilla
pudding
2 c. powdered sugar
1 c. chocolate chips
2 T. butter
1 T. paraffin

Combine 1/2 c. butter, sugar, cocoa, and vanilla in top of double boiler.
Cook over simmering water until butter melts. Stir in 1 egg and continue
to stir and cook until mixture is thick. Blend in graham cracker crumbs
and coconut. Press into a 9" square buttered pan. Cream 1/2 c. butter
well. Stir in milk, pudding mix, and powdered sugar. Beat until light and
fluffy. Spread evenly over crust. Chill until firm. Melt chocolate chips, 2
T. butter, and paraffin over simmering water. Spread on top of second
layer. Chill and cut into squares.

Clara Yoder (Kitchen)

PEANUT BRITTLE (MICROWAVE)

1 c. sugar
1/2 c. white corn syrup
1 c. dry roasted salted peanuts

1 t. butter
1 t. vanilla
1 t. baking soda

In 1 1/2 qt casserole, stir together sugar and syrup. Microwave on high
for 4 minutes. Stir in peanuts and microwave on high until light brown
(3-5 minutes). Add butter and vanilla to syrup, blending well. Microwave
on high for 1 to 2 minutes. Peanuts will be lightly browned and syrup
very hot. Add baking soda and gently stir until light and foamy. Quickly
pour mixture onto lightly greased cookie sheet or un-buttered non-stick
coated cookie sheet. Let cool for 1/2 hour. When cool, break into small
pieces and store in airtight container. This brittle can be made with
pecans or cashews.

Erma Swartzendruber (Office)

PRALINE PECAN CRUNCH

1/2 c. light corn syrup
1/2 c. firmly packed brown sugar
1/4 c. margarine

1 t. vanilla
1/2 t. baking soda
10 c. pecan halves

Combine corn syrup, brown sugar and margarine. Microwave on high for 1 1/2 minutes. Stir and microwave another 1/2 to 1 1/2 minutes or until boiling. Add vanilla and baking soda; pour over pecans. Stir until coated evenly. Spread on baking sheet and bake at 250 degrees for 1 hour. Stir every 20 minutes. Cool before storing in container.

Sue Miller (Owner/Manager)

SADIE'S CORNFLAKES CANDY

1 c. white sugar

1 c. light corn syrup

Bring to a boil. Add 1 c. peanut butter. Pour over 6 c. corn flakes and 1 c. peanuts. Stir well and press into a 9 x 13 pan. Cut into squares after 5 minutes.

Ruth Beachy (Cashier/Restaurant Gifts)

TAFFY TAN FUDGE

2 c. sugar
1 c. milk
2 c. marshmallow cream

1-12 oz. jar crunchy peanut butter
1 t. vanilla

Combine sugar and milk and bring to a boil. Stir 5 minutes over medium heat to soft boil stage (238 degrees). Remove from heat. Stir in marshmallow cream, peanut butter, and vanilla. Beat until well blended. Pour into greased 9" square pan. Cool and cut into squares.

Leona Yutzy (Essenhaus Foods)

Desserts & Ice Cream

CHEESE GUIDE

American, Cheddar

Favorite all-around cheese. Flavor varies from mild to sharp. Color ranges from natural to yellow-orange: texture firm to crumbly.

Serve in sandwiches, casseroles, souffles, and creamy sauces; or with fruit pie or crisp crackers, on a snack or dessert tray with fruit.

Blue, Gorgonzola, Roquefort

Compact, creamy cheeses with blue or blue-green mold. Sometimes crumbly. Mild to sharp flavor. (Stilton is similar, but like a blue-veined Cheddar).

Crumble in salads, salad dressings. dips. Delicious with fresh pears or apples for dessert. Blend with butter for steak topper. Spread on crackers or on crusty French or Italian bread.

Brick

Medium firm; creamy yellow color, tiny holes. Flavor very mild to medium sharp.

Good for appetizers, sandwiches, or desserts. Great with fresh peaches, cherries, or melons.

Cottage

Soft, mild, unripened cheese; large or small curd. May have cream added.

Used in salads, dips, main dishes. Popular with fresh and canned fruit.

Cream

Very mild-flavored soft cheese with buttery texture. Rich and smooth. Available whipped and in flavored spreads.

Adds richness and body to molded and frozen salads, cheesecake, dips, frostings, sandwich spreads. Serve whipped with dessert.

Swiss

Firm, pale yellow cheese, with large round holes. Sweet nutty flavor.

First choice for ham and cheese sandwiches, fondue. Good in salads, sauces, as a snack.

Process Cheeses

A blend of fresh and aged natural cheeses, pasteurized and packaged. Smooth and creamy, melts easily. May be flavored.

Ideal for cheese sauces, souffles, grilled sandwiches, in casseroles. Handy for the snack tray.

Mozzarella, Scamorze

Unripened. Mild-flavored and slightly firm. Creamy white to pale yellow.

Cooking cheese. A "must" for pizza, lasagna; good in toasted sandwiches, hot snacks.

Desserts & Ice Cream

APPLE CRUNCH

Place 3 c. of diced apples in a 9″ square pan and add 1/4 c. water.
Combine and sprinkle over apples and water:

3/4 c. dry rolled oats	1/4 t. baking powder
3/4 c. flour	1/4 t. salt
3/4 c. brown sugar	1/4 c. chopped nuts (walnuts)
1/4 t. soda	1/3 c. melted butter

Bake about 30 minutes at 375 degrees. Cool and serve in squares with
Cool Whip or ice cream.

Keith Miller (Busser)

A laugh at your own expense costs you nothing.

APPLE CRUNCH

1/2 c. sugar
2 T. shortening
1 egg
1/2 t. vanilla
1/2 t. soda

1/2 c. sour milk (or buttermilk)
1 c. flour
1/2 t. salt
1 t. baking powder
1 1/2 c. sliced apples

Cream sugar and shortening together. Add egg and beat. Add soda to sour milk and stir into mixture. Add sifted, dry ingredients and stir thoroughly. Add sliced apples and blend into mixture. Rub together the following for crumbs:

6 T. brown sugar
1/2 t. cinnamon

1 1/2 t. flour
1 1/2 T. butter

Sprinkle over top of apple mixture. Bake at 375 degrees for 35 to 40 minutes. Serve hot with rich milk.

Laura Bontrager (Bakery)

APPLE DESSERT

3 c. diced apples
1 1/2 c. sugar
2 eggs, beaten
1 1/2 c. flour

1 1/2 t. soda
2 1/4 t. cinnamon
3/4 c. chopped nuts

Mix all ingredients together. Pour into a 9 x 9 inch baking pan. Bake at 350 degrees for 35 minutes. While cake is baking, mix together in a pan to cook on top of the stove:

3/4 c. brown sugar
1/2 c. white sugar

3 T. flour
1 1/2 c. water

Boil until smooth and thick. Remove from heat and add 1/4 c. margarine and 1 1/2 t. vanilla. Stir well and pour over hot cake and let cool. Before serving cut into squares and serve with whipped topping.

Mary K. Schmucker (Kitchen)

APPLE DUMPLINGS

2 c. flour   2 t. baking powder
1 t. salt

Work this into 2 T. lard and 1 T. softened butter. Add 1 1/3 c. milk. Put 1/2 dough in 9 x 9 greased pan. Spread with chopped apples. Sprinkle with brown sugar and cinnamon. Cover with the remaining dough. Bake for 1 hour or when golden brown in 350 degree oven. When about half done, cover with 1/2 sauce.

Sauce
1 c. sugar   1 T. flour
1 t. salt   1 t. cinnamon

Add 1 c. hot water and boil for 3 minutes.

Use remaining sauce to add with milk at the table.

Marietta Helmuth (Waitress)

APPLE DUMPLINGS

2 T. lard   2 t. baking powder
1 T. butter or margarine   7/8 c. milk
2 c. flour

Work lard and butter in flour and baking powder. Add 7/8 c. milk. Mix well. Roll out and spread with margarine. Sprinkle with brown sugar. Slice apples and put on dough. Sprinkle with cinnamon. Roll up and cut in slices. Place in pan as you would cinnamon rolls. Cover with sauce and bake.

Sauce
1 c. sugar   1 c. water
1 T. flour

Mix sugar and flour. Add water and boil for 3 minutes. Pour over dumplings. Bake at 375 degrees for 1 hour.

Lena Miller (Meatroom)

APPLE RINGS

1 c. baking mix
1 egg

1/2 c. milk
2 medium apples, pared and cored

Beat baking mix, egg, and milk with rotary beater until smooth. Slice apples crosswise into 1/8 inch rings. Dip rings into batter. Bake on hot greased griddle until golden brown, turning once. Serve immediately. May serve with syrup or jelly or sprinkle with powdered sugar. Yield: 2 doz.

Treva Yoder (Miller's Housekeeper)

APPLE SLICES

2 1/2 c. sifted flour
1 T. sugar
1 t. salt
1 c. shortening
1 egg, separated

milk
5 c. apples, sliced/peeled
1 1/2 c. sugar
1 t. cinnamon

Sift together flour, 1 T. sugar, and salt. Cut in shortening with pastry blender. Put egg yolk in measuring cup and add enough milk to make 2/3 c. Add to dry mixture and mix just enough to make dough shape into a ball. Roll out half of dough to fit 15 x 11 baking sheet. Cover dough with apples and mix 1 1/2 c. sugar and the cinnamon. Sprinkle over apples. Roll out other half of dough for top crust. Place over top of apples. Beat egg white until stiff and spread over top crust. Bake at 375 degrees for 40 minutes. Top with glaze if desired. Cut in squares.

Glaze

1 1/2 c. powdered sugar
2 1/2 T. apple juice or milk

1 T. butter
1 t. vanilla

Mix together until smooth.

Viola Miller (Ned Miller's wife Essenhaus Foods)

BABY PEARL TAPIOCA

2/3 c. baby pearl tapioca   2 eggs, beaten
Soak in water until all soaked up.   2/3 c. water
4 c. milk   1 1/2 c. sugar

Put all ingredients in double boiler and cook until tapioca looks light colored and thick. When cold, add Cool Whip.

Pamela Frey (Bakery)

BAKED CUSTARD

Beat slightly to mix:

2 large eggs   1/3 c. sugar
1/4 t. salt

Scald 2 c. milk and pour into egg mixture. Add 1 t. vanilla, if desired. Pour into custard cups and sprinkle nutmeg on top to flavor. Bake at 350 degrees for 30 to 35 minutes. Set custard cups in pan with water. Makes 6 servings. Can also be used for Custard pie.

Walter Lehman (Essenhaus Foods)

 One thing you can give and still keep is your word.

BUTTERFINGER CANDY DESSERT

Crust:

3 med. frozen Butterfinger bars   1 c. crushed graham crackers
1 c. crushed soda crackers

Mix together with 1/4 c. butter. Put in bottom of 9 x 13 pan, reserving 1 cup crumbs for top.

Filling:

3 boxes (4 oz.) vanilla pudding   3 c. milk
2 c. vanilla ice cream

Mix and put on top of crust. Top with whipped cream and 1 cup crumbs.

Ruth Peshina (Waitress)

BROKEN GLASS DESSERT

Dissolve 1 small box of each (red, green, and orange) jello in 1/2 c. hot water and put each mixture in separate pans. Let set until cool. Cut in cubes. Dissolve 2 T. plain gelatin in 1/2 c. cold water. Add 1 c. boiling water and 1 c. crushed pineapple. Let cool. Whip 1 pint cream and 1/2 c. sugar in bowl. To this add gelatin mixture and colored jello cubes. Pour in pan lined with graham cracker crust.

Graham Cracker Crust:

Crush 24 crackers. Mix in 1/2 c. sugar and 1/4 c. melted butter. Save some to put on top.

Lorene Schlabach (Dutch Country Gifts)

Most folks are about as happy as they make up their minds to be.

CARAMEL CHOCOLATE SQUARES

1 pkg. (14 oz.) caramels
1 can (5 oz.) evaporated milk
1 pkg. German chocolate
cake mix

2/3 c. margarine, melted
3/4 c. pecans, coarsely chopped
1 pkg. (6 oz.) chocolate chips
1 c. coconut, optional

Heat caramels and 1/4 c. milk in saucepan over medium heat, stirring constantly. Mix cake mix (dry), margarine, remaining milk, and pecans. Spread half the dough in un-greased 13 x 9 x 2 pan. Bake 6 minutes at 350 degrees. Remove from oven. Sprinkle chocolate chips and coconut over baked layer. Drizzle caramel mixture over chocolate chips and coconut. Drop remaining dough by teaspoon on caramel layer. Bake 15 to 20 minutes at 350 degrees. Cool.

Glenda Yoder (Waitress)
Tina Bobeck (Busser/Cashier)

I had no shoes and complained, until I met a man who had no feet.

CAKE MIX BROWNIES

1 white or yellow cake mix
1/4 c. brown sugar
1/4 c. water

2 eggs
1/4 c. oleo
chocolate chips, to taste

Spread on cookie sheet. Sprinkle desired amount of chocolate chips on top. Bake at 350 degrees for 20 to 25 minutes.

Delores Wagler (Maintenance)
Irene Bontrager (Cashier/Bakery)

CHERRY BERRIES ON A CLOUD

Shell

Heat oven 275 degrees. Cover baking sheet with paper bag. Beat 3 egg whites (1/3 or 1/2 c.) and 1/4 t. cream of tartar until foamy. Beat in 3/4 c. sugar (1 T. at a time). Continue beating until stiff, glossy. On paper bag, shape meringue , building up sides. Bake 1 1/2 hour. Turn off oven, leave meringue in oven with door closed 1 hour. Remove from oven. Finish cooling away from draft.

Pudding

1-3 oz. pkg. soft cream cheese
1/2 c. sugar
1/2 t. vanilla

1 c. whipped topping
1 c. mini marshmallows

Blend cream cheese, sugar, and vanilla. Gently fold topping and marshmallows into cheese mixture. Pile into shell. Chill. Before serving top with strawberry or cherry filling.

Ruth Ann Yoder (Bakery)

CHERRY TOPPED ICEBOX CAKE

20 whole graham crackers
2 c. cold milk
1-6 oz. pkg. vanilla or chocolate
instant pudding

1 3/4 c. thawed Cool Whip
2-21 oz. cans cherry pie filling

Line 9 x 13 pan with some of the graham crackers, breaking may be necessary. Pour cold milk into a bowl. Add pudding mix. With electric mixer at slow speed, beat until well blended, 1 to 2 minutes. Let stand 5 minutes. Blend in whipped topping. Spread half of the pudding mixture over the crackers. Add another layer of crackers. Top with remaining pudding mixture and remaining crackers. Spread cherry pie filling over crackers. Chill for about 3 hours. Yield: 12 servings

Wanita Yoder (Kitchen)

CHOCOLATE CHIP PUDDING

24 large marshmallows or
240 small marshmallows
1/2 c. milk
1 c. cream, whipped

1/2 t. vanilla
1/2 large bag of chocolate
chips, grind w/ nut chopper
graham cracker crust

Heat marshmallows with milk in top of double boiler until dissolved. Cool. Fold in cream, vanilla, and ground chocolate. Pour into graham cracker crust and chill. Can be chilled, not frozen.

Bertha Miller (Shop Supervisor)

If you meet someone without a smile, give him one of yours.

CHOCOLATE CREAM CHEESE PUDDING

1-6 oz. bag chocolate chips
1-8 oz. pkg. cream cheese
3/4 c. brown sugar
1/2 t. salt

1 t. vanilla
2 eggs, separated
2 c. heavy cream, whipped
graham cracker crust

Melt chocolate over hot, not boiling, water, Cool 10 minutes. Blend cheese, 1/2 c. sugar, salt, and vanilla. Beat egg whites until stiff, not dry. Slowly beat in 1/4 c. sugar. Beat until very stiff. Fold chocolate mixture into beaten egg whites and fold in whipped cream. Pour into pie crust and chill overnight.

Millie Whetsone (Kitchen)

255

CHOCOLATE DELIGHT

1 c. flour
1/2 c. butter

1/2 c. chopped nuts

Mix and press into cake pan. Bake at 350 degrees for 15 minutes. Cool.

8 oz. pkg. cream cheese
1/3 c. peanut butter

1/2 c. powdered sugar
3/4 c. whipped topping

Whip topping and pour into the rest of the ingredients. Pour mixture on top of baked crust.

1 pkg. vanilla instant pudding
4 c. milk

1 pkg. choc. instant pudding

Beat together and pour on top of cream cheese mixture. Beat 1 1/2 c. whipped topping and spread on top. Sprinkle with nuts and chocolate chips.

Erma Yoder (Maintenance)

CHOCOLATE ECLAIR

3 c. milk
2 small boxes vanilla pudding
1-8 oz. pkg. cream cheese

1 c. whipped topping, thawed
graham crackers

Heat milk to touch. Add pudding, then cream cheese. Cool. Add whipped topping. Put a layer of graham crackers in a pan. Add half of pudding mixture, another layer crackers, then the rest of pudding, add another layer crackers, topped by frosting.

Frosting
3 T. butter
4 T. cocoa
2 T. corn syrup

1 c. powdered sugar
2 T. vegetable oil
3 T. milk

Mix well.

Fannie Lehman (Meatroom)

CHOCOLATE SUNDAE DESSERT

20 Oreo cookies   1/4 c. melted oleo

Crush cookies and add butter. Blend well. Reserve 1/2 c. for topping. Press remaining crumbs in 9 x 13 pan. Freeze until firm. Combine and bring to boil 1 c. sugar, 1-5 1/2 oz. can evaporated milk, and 2 oz. unsweetened baking chocolate. Cool. Layer softened vanilla ice cream over frozen crust. Pour cooled chocolate mixture over ice cream. Freeze. Top with 1 c. Cool Whip, 1/2 c. crumb mixture, and nuts (pecans). Cover tightly and freeze until 10-15 minutes before serving.

Tina Bobeck (Busser/Cashier)

CINNAMON FLOP

1 1/2 c. sugar   2 T. melted butter
1 beaten egg   2 c. flour
2 t. baking powder   1 c. milk

Mix and pour into well greased 13 x 9 pan (not glass). Mix the following and sprinkle on mixture:

1 c. brown sugar   4 T. melted butter
1 t. cinnamon
Bake 20 minutes at 425 degrees.

Hope Miller (Kitchen Supervisor)

CORNSTARCH PUDDING

3 c. milk   1 T. flour
1 c. sugar   2 eggs
1 T. cornstarch, heaping

Mix together in saucepan and cook, stirring constantly, until it thickens. Add 1 t. vanilla. Serve with bananas and graham crackers or just plain.

Delores Wagler (Maintenance)

DATE PUDDING

1 c. brown sugar
dash of salt
1 1/2 c. flour

1 c. dates
1 t. soda
1 c. boiling water

Mix brown sugar, salt, and flour. Chop dates. Add soda and boiling water to dates. Mix with dry ingredients. Bake at 350 degrees for 45 minutes.

Sauce

2 c. brown sugar
4 T. oleo

2 c. water
2 T. flour

Cook together for 3 to 4 minutes or until thick. Drizzle between layers of date pudding when putting together before serving.

Carolyn Hershberger (Bakery)

DEATH BY CHOCOLATE

1-9 x 13 pan of brownies,
baked, cooled, crumbled &
divided in half
2 pkgs. mousse mix, prepare as
package directs & divide

1-16 oz. pkg. Cool Whip,
8 chocolate toffee bars-regular size,
crushed and divided
1 c. pecans, divided

Layer in pan or dish in order given. Repeat. Fits well in 13 x 9 pan. Cover dessert and refrigerate overnight.

Dick Carpenter (Material Handling)

 Will Power: The ability to eat just one piece of chocolate or one cookie.

DIRT PUDDING

1-12 oz. pkg. Oreo cookies, crushed
1-8 oz. pkg. Cool Whip
1-8 oz. pkg. cream cheese, softened
1 c. powdered sugar
1/2 stick margarine, softened
2 pkg. French Vanilla instant pudding
3 1/2 c. milk

Spread crushed cookies on bottom of 9 x 13 pan, reserving 1/2 c. crumbs for later use. Mix whipped topping, cream cheese, powdered sugar, and margarine. In separate bowl mix 2 pkg. vanilla pudding with 3 1/2 c. milk. Then mix with cream cheese mixture and spread over the cookies. Top with the 1/2 c. crumbs. Chill well.

Wilma Weaver (Waitress)

ECLAIR CAKE

1 lb. box of graham crackers
2 small pkg. instant vanilla pudding
3 1/2 c. milk
1-9 oz. pkg. Cool Whip

Butter bottom of 9 x 13 pan. Line with graham crackers. Mix pudding with milk. Beat at medium speed for 2 minutes. Blend in Cool Whip. Pour 1/2 mixture of pudding over crackers, layer again with crackers and pudding.

Frosting

6 T. cocoa
2 t. vanilla
1 1/2 c. powdered sugar
2 T. oil, optional
2 T. soft butter
3 T. milk

Mix all ingredients and frost pudding mixture. Refrigerate for 24 hours.

Betti Kauffman (Hostess/Cashier)

 Too busy to laugh? Smile, it adds to your face value.

FLUFFY TAPIOCA PUDDING

3 T. minute tapioca
1/8 t. salt
3 T. sugar
2 c. milk

1 egg yolk
2 T. sugar
1 egg white
3/4 t. vanilla

Mix tapioca, salt, 3 T. sugar, milk, and egg yolk in pan. Let set 5 minutes. Beat egg white until foamy. Beat in 2 T. sugar. Beat until forms soft peaks and then set aside. Cook tapioca mixture over medium heat to a full boil, stirring occasionally, for 6 to 8 minutes. Gradually add to beaten egg white, stirring quickly until blended. Stir in vanilla. Pineapple and nuts or Snicker Bar bits can be added.

Mary K. Schmucker (Kitchen)

 When a person begins to throw dirt, he begins to lose ground.

FRUIT DELIGHT

2 sm. cans Eagle Brand milk
1/3 c. lemon juice
12 oz. Cool Whip
1 c. coconut

16 graham crackers
1/4 c. sugar
1/2 stick margarine
frozen blueberries & strawberries

Beat together Eagle Brand milk and lemon juice. Fold in Cool Whip and coconut. Crush graham crackers. Melt oleo and mix with crackers. Press into bottom of 9 x 14 pan. Pour milk mixture on top and chill. Press frozen blueberries and strawberries into chilled milk mixture and top with crushed walnuts.

Carlene Miller (Restaurant Reservations)

GRAHAM CRACKER ECLAIR DESSERT

Put a layer of graham cracker squares in a 9x13 pan. Mix together:

2 boxes instant French vanilla   3 1/2 c. milk
pudding   8 oz. container whipped topping

Pour half mixture over the crackers in pan. Add another layer of crackers and then the rest of the pudding. Put another layer of crackers on top.

Topping

Heat together the following:

3 T. milk   4 T. butter
3 T. cocoa

Add 1 1/3 c. powdered sugar. Spread topping on last layer of graham crackers.

Sue Miller (Manager)

GRANDMA CLARK'S RICE PUDDING

1 c. rice   2 c. water
1 T. margarine   1 t. salt

Bring to a boil. Cook 14 minutes. Let sit until dry looking. Add 1 egg beaten in 1 c. milk, 1 t. vanilla, and 1/2 c. raisins. Cook on low until thickened. Put in serving dish. Brown 2 to 3 t. butter. Sprinkle brown sugar over rice and pour butter over. Serve.

Bill Burns (Bakery)

 Good character, like soup, is usually homemade.

HEATH BLIZZARD CRUNCH

1/4 c. melted butter
2 c. vanilla wafer crumbs
1 c. chocolate syrup
2-8 oz. pkgs. Cool Whip

1/2 gallon vanilla ice cream, softened
12 crushed Heath Bars

Pour melted butter over cookie crumbs and mix well. Press in bottom of 9 x 13 pan. Mix ice cream and chocolate syrup. Add 10 crushed Heath Bars. Fold in one pkg. 8 oz. Cool Whip. Pour ice cream mixture over cookie crumbs. Freeze. When serving, put a spoonful of Cool Whip on each piece and sprinkle remaining 2 Heath Bars on top.

Treva Yoder (Miller's Housekeeper)

ICEBOX DESSERT

10 chocolate sandwich cookies
20 large marshmallows
1/2 c. milk

2 c. heavy cream
1 t. vanilla
1/2 c. nuts

Roll cookies to fine crumbs and place half in bottom of pan and freeze. Heat marshmallows and milk in top of double boiler until marshmallows are melted. Cool. Whip cream. Add vanilla and nuts. Add to pan. Put the rest of the crumbs on top. Freeze.

Ruth Ann Schrock (Kitchen)

ICE CREAM PUDDING

3 c. milk
1 box any flavor instant pudding
1 medium container Cool Whip

1 box vanilla instant pudding
1 qt. vanilla ice cream, soft

Mix milk and puddings. Add softened ice cream and mix. Add whipped topping and pour into pan lined with 1 1/2 pkg. crushed graham crackers, 1/4 c. sugar, and 1 stick melted oleo or butter. Save some crumbs to put on top.

Mary K. Schrock (Kitchen)

LEMON DELIGHT

1 stick oleo
1 c. flour
1/2 c. nuts
8 oz. cream cheese

1 c. Cool Whip (9 oz. size)
3 c. milk
2 pkg. lemon instant pudding
1 c. powdered sugar

Mix oleo, flour and nuts. Put into 9 x 13 pan. Bake at 375 degrees for 15 minutes. Mix cream cheese, powdered sugar, and 1 c. Cool Whip together. Put this layer on crust and cool. Beat milk and pudding until thick. Put on top of cream cheese mixture. Top with remaining Cool Whip.

Agnes Cross (Bakery)

LEMON TORTE

Meringue

4 egg whites
1/4 t. cream of tartar

1 c. sugar
1 t. vanilla

Custard

4 egg yolks
2 T. lemon juice

2 T. to 1/2 c. sugar
2 T. lemon rind

Topping

1 pt. whipping cream, whipped

Beat egg whites and cream of tartar until stiff and glossy. Gradually beat in sugar and vanilla. Spread in well buttered 9 x 13 pan or large tart pan with removable bottom. Bake at 300 degrees for 1 hour. Remove from the oven to a draft free spot. Cool thoroughly. Beat egg yolks until lemon colored. add sugar, lemon juice and rind. Cook in double boiler over low heat, stirring occasionally until thick. Cool thoroughly. Spread half of whipped cream on cooled meringue shell. Cover with custard layer. Spread whipped cream over top. Refrigerate, covered. Best if made a day ahead. Yield: 16 servings

Walter Lehamn (Essenhaus Foods)

LOLLIPOPS

Use favorite white bread recipe. After final kneading take a small amount of dough and form 1″ balls. Arrange in baking dish so that balls do not quite touch. Allow balls to raise to desired size and add syrup until balls are almost covered. Sprinkle tops of balls with a cinnamon and sugar mixture and bake at 350 degrees for 30 to 35 minutes. Best if eaten warm.

Syrup for lollipops

2 c. milk
2 1/2 c. white sugar

2 c. cream
1 stick butter or oleo

Heat slowly until sugar is dissolved, but do not make syrup hot.

Mary Esther Miller (Manager/Restaurant Gifts)

NORMA'S DESSERT

graham crackers
2 pkgs. French vanilla instant pudding
2 1/2 c. milk

1 large container Cool Whip
1 can chocolate frosting

Line 9 x 13 pan with graham crackers. Mix pudding and milk with mixer. Fold in Cool Whip. Pour 1/2 on crackers. Add another layer of crackers. Add remaining pudding mixture. Add another layer of crackers. Frost with chocolate frosting. Cover and refrigerate at least 2 hours before serving.

Norma Velleman (Cashier/Restaurant Gifts)

 Experience is a wonderful thing. It enables you to recognize a mistake when you make it again.

OREO COOKIE DESSERT

1 lb. Oreo cookies, crushed   1/2 stick butter, melted

Mix butter and cookies. Press in the bottom of a 9x13 pan, reserving some crumbs for the top. Cool and add 3 qt. chocolate chip mint ice cream. Top with remaining crumbs and freeze.

Sue Miller (Manager)

OREO PUDDING

6 c. milk   2 c. Rich's Topping
3 small boxes vanilla pudding   20 Oreo cookies
1-8 oz. pkg. cream cheese

Heat milk. Put pudding in milk and cook for 1 to 2 minutes. Add cream cheese while hot. Cool. Add 2 c. topping, whipped, and 20 crushed Oreo cookies.

Treva Yoder (Miller's Housekeeper)

ORANGE SHERBET

2 small boxes orange jello   1 c. pineapple chunks, well
1/4 c. white sugar   drained
2 c. boiling water   1 pt. orange sherbet ice cream
1 c. whipping cream

Mix jello and sugar with water. When jello starts to set, fold in whipping cream and pineapple. Then add orange sherbet.

Carolyn Hershberger (Bakery)

265

PEACH CRUNCH

1 qt. can sliced peaches
1 pkg. yellow cake mix (dry)
1 stick margarine, melted

1-6 oz. pkg. Bits O' Brickle
1 c. chopped pecans, optional

Pour peaches, with juice, in 9 x 13 cake pan. Sprinkle dry cake mix on top. Drizzle melted margarine on top of cake mix. Sprinkle Bits O' Brickle on top and nuts, if desired. Bake at 350 degrees for 35 to 45 minutes or until cake is golden brown. Serve warm with ice cream.

Carol Detweiler (Waitress)

PEACH DELIGHT

Crust

1 c. flour
1/2 c. pecans

1/2 c. margarine

Mix and press into 9 x 13 pan. Bake for 15 minutes at 350 degrees. Cool.

Cream cheese layer

1-8 oz. pkg. cream cheese
1 c. powdered sugar

1 1/2 c. whipped cream

Mix and put on top of crust.

Peach filling

2 c. water
2 c. sugar
pinch of salt

1/2 c. corn syrup
1/2 c. cornstarch or clear jel

Cook all ingredients except cornstarch and clear jel. When boiling, thicken with cornstarch (mixed with a little water). If using clear jel, add jel and cool. Add 2 qts. fresh peaches. Pour over cream cheese mixture. Top with whipped cream. You can add a little yellow food coloring to peach filling.

Ruth Peshina (Waitress)

266

PEANUT BUTTER PUDDING

2 1/2 c. flour   2 sticks oleo
1 c. pecan pieces

Mix and press into bottom of cake pan and bake for 15 to 20 minutes. Mix 1 c. peanut butter with 2 c. powdered sugar. Put some of these crumbs on top of the crust and save the rest for the top. Add 2 boxes vanilla instant pudding mixed with 2 c. milk and 4 c. soft vanilla ice cream. Add a layer of whipped cream and the remaining crumbs.

Rosetta Miller (Bakery)

PEPPERMINT DELIGHT

1/2 box vanilla wafers   1/2 pkg. mini marshmallows
6 peppermint candy sticks   1 pt. whipping cream

Crush wafers and line 9 x 13 pan with half the crumbs. Crush candy sticks and blend with whipped cream and marshmallow mixture. Pour into crumb lined pan. Top with remaining crumbs. Refrigerate for 24 hours before eating.

Ellen Mishler (Hostess/Cashier)

PEPPERMINT CHEESECAKE

1 c. chocolate wafer crumbs   1/2 c. sugar
3 T. margarine, melted   1/2 c. milk
1 envelope unflavored gelatin 1/4 c. crushed peppermint candy
1/4 c. cold water   1 c. whipping cream, whipped
2-8 oz. pkg. cream cheese,   2-1.45 oz. milk chocolate bars,
softened   finely chopped

Combine crumbs and margarine. Press into bottom of 9 inch spring form pan. Bake at 350 degrees for 10 minutes. Cool. Soften gelatin in water. Stir over low heat until dissolved. Combine cream cheese and sugar, mixing at medium speed on electric mixer until well blended. Gradually add gelatin, milk, and peppermint candy. Mixing until blended. Chill until thickened, but not set. Fold in whipped cream and chocolate. Pour into crust. Garnish with additional whipped cream, combined with crushed peppermint candy, if desired. Yield: 10-12 servings

Susanna Miller (Kitchen)

PINEAPPLE FLUFF

20 graham crackers, crushed
1/4 c. butter or margarine, melted
1/2 c. pineapple juice

1 lb. marshmallows
1/2 c. crushed pineapple
2 c. cream

Mix graham crackers with butter or margarine and line bottom of dish with mixture (reserve small amount of graham crackers for top). Combine pineapple juice and marshmallows in double boiler. Heat until marshmallows are melted, stirring as needed to prevent scorching. Remove from heat and add crushed pineapple. Let cool until begins to thicken. Whip cream and mix into the mixture. Pour into dish with graham cracker. Put remaining crumbs on top.

Alma Hershberger (Bakery)

PLAIN CUSTARD

6 eggs
1/2 c. sugar

1 qt. milk
1 T. vanilla

Beat eggs . Add sugar and beat again. Add milk and vanilla. Pour into greased casserole or custard cups. Place in shallow pan of water while baking. Bake in slow oven at 350 degrees for 1 hour.

Mel Lambright (Dishwasher)

POPSICLES

1 pkg. jello
1 c. sugar

1 pkg. Kool Aid
2 c. hot water

Mix well. Add 2 c. cold water. Pour into popsicle trays and freeze.

Lorene Schlabach (Cashier/Dutch Country Gifts)

For instant energy, nothing beats having the boss walk in.

PRETZEL DESSERT

2 c. coarsely crushed pretzels
3/4 c. melted margarine
3 t. sugar
8 oz. cream cheese
1 c. sugar

8 oz. Cool Whip
6 oz. pkg. strawberry jello*
2 c. boiling water
2-10 oz. pkg. frozen
strawberries*

Mix pretzels, margarine, and 3 t. sugar. Press in a 9 x 13 pan. Bake at 400 degrees for 8 minutes. Cool. Combine cream cheese, sugar, and Cool Whip. Blend well and spread over cooled crust. Refrigerate. Combine jello, water, and strawberries. When slightly congealed, pour over the top of cheese mixture. Refrigerate.

* Use blueberry or black raspberry jello in place of strawberry.
* Use blueberries or black raspberries in place of strawberries.

Bill Burns (Bakery)

PUMPKIN DESSERT

1-16 oz. can pumpkin
4 eggs
1 can Milnot
1 1/2 c. sugar
1 t. salt

2 t. pumpkin pie spice
1 Duncan Hines butter recipe
yellow cake mix
2 sticks butter, melted
1 c. chopped nuts

Combine first six ingredients. Sprinkle with cake mix. Pour melted butter over all. Top with nuts. Bake for 1 hour at 350 degrees.

Rosie Eash (Waitress)

PUMPKIN PIE DESSERT

1 yellow cake mix, reserve 1 cup   1/2 c. margarine
1 egg

Combine and press in greased 9 x 13 pan.

2 eggs   1-16 oz. can pumpkin
2/3 c. milk   2/3 c. milk
2 1/2 t. pumpkin pie spice

Combine, stirring until smooth. Pour over crust.

1 c. cake mix   1/4 c. margarine, soft
1 t. cinnamon, optional

Crumble, sprinkle, or glob over filling. Bake at 350 degrees for 45 to 50 minutes, or until knife comes out clean. Serve with whipped topping. NOTE: Bottom tends to over-bake if done in glass pan.

Barb Weaver (Cashier/Restaurant Gifts)

RASPBERRY DELIGHT

1 c. flour   1/2 c. butter
1/2 c. crushed pecans or walnuts

Mix and press in a 9 x 9 pan. Bake at 375 degrees for 15 minutes.

1-8 oz. pkg. cream cheese   1 c. powdered sugar
2 c. Rich's whipped topping

Mix and pour into crust.

1 1/2 c. water   1 c. sugar
2 T. clear jel, heaping   lemon juice
pinch of salt

Cook until thick. Remove from heat and cool. Fold in 3 c. black raspberries.* Put on top of cream cheese mixture.
* May use strawberry glaze and strawberries.

Ruth Ann Yoder (Bakery)

RASPBERRY SWIRL

3/4 c. graham cracker crumbs	1 c. sugar
3 T. melted butter or oleo	1 c. heavy cream, whipped
2 T. sugar	8 oz. pkg. cream cheese
3 eggs, seperated	10 oz. pkg. frozen raspberries,
1/8 t. salt	partially thawed

Thoroughly combine crumbs, butter, and 2 T. sugar. Press mixture into well greased 11 x 17 x 1 1/2 inch baking dish. Bake in 375 degree oven about 8 minutes. Cool completely. Beat egg yolks in bowl with electric mixer high speed until smooth and light; add salt. Beat egg whites until stiff peaks form; add sugar and whip. Add whipped cream. Fold egg whites and whipped cream into softened cream cheese; mix. Puree raspberries in a mixer or blender. Gently swirl half of puree through cheese filling. Spread mixture in crust. Spoon remaining puree over top and swirl with a knife. Freeze, then cover and return to freezer. Yield: 6-8 servings

Mary Arlene Bontrager (Waitress)

OLD TIME REMEDIES

I sort of want to give a list
O' Mother's famous cures;
There'll be, of course, some that she missed
Which may be found in yours.

In spring we took our sassafras,
Molasses-sulphur mix,
To clean our blood, make us first class
When we got out of fix.

Her catnip and her boneset tea
Were taken 'stead of pills;
We didn't dare refuse this need
For curin' all our ills.

By rubbing goose grease on our chest
She'd cure most any cold
While mustard, lamp-oil 'n the rest
Might also be extolled.

Her poultices were mighty fine
O' flaxseed 'n o' bread,
'N fat-meat, onions, this whole line
Would bring things to a head.

But strikes me it was Mother love
That really made us well,
A healin' sent from heaven above
That worked her magic spell.

For when she'd tuck us snug in bed
And give that tender kiss,
Ain't nothing further need be said
'Bout such a cure as this!

Reprinted by permission from
S. Chupp's Herbs & Vitamins
27539 Londick
Burr Oak, MI 49030

271

RHUBARB CREAM DELIGHT DESSERT

Crust

1 c. flour   1/2 c. butter or margarine
1/4 c. sugar

Mix flour, sugar, and butter. Pour into 10" pie plate. Set aside.

Rhubarb layer

3 c. fresh rhubarb,in 1/2" pcs.   1 T. flour
1/2 c. sugar

Combine rhubarb, sugar, and flour. Toss lightly and pour into crust. Bake at 375 degrees for about 15 minutes.

Cream layer

12 oz. cream cheese, softened   2 eggs
1/2 sugar

Beat together cream cheese and sugar until fluffy. Beat in eggs one at a time. Pour over hot rhubarb layer. Bake at 350 degrees for about 30 minutes or until set.

Topping

8 oz. dairy sour cream   2 T. sugar
1 t. vanilla

Combine and spread over hot layers. Chill.

Karen Hochstedler (Bakery)

 If you keep in the rut too long, it will get so deep that it becomes your grave.

RICE KRISPIES TOPPING

4 c. rice krispies	1 c. coconut
1 c. nuts	1 stick melted butter

Mix together and bake at 400 degrees until light brown, about 15 to 20 minutes. Add 1/2 c. brown sugar and stir thoroughly. Let cool. Good on ice cream.

Edna Borntrager (Essenhaus Foods)

ROAD TO HEAVEN DESSERT

Mix 2 small boxes of jello and 1 1/2 c. hot water. Let cool until it's partly set. Add 1 c. whipped cream, 1 c. pineapple, 1 c. nuts, and 2 large bananas. Mix thoroughly and refrigerate.

Alma Hershberger (Cashier/Restaurant Gifts)

SALTED NUT ROLL

1-16 oz. jar dry roasted peanuts	2 1/2 T. butter
1-12 oz. pkg. peanut butter chips	2 c. mini marshmallows
	1 can Eagle Brand milk

Sprinkle 1/2 jar of the peanuts on the bottom of a 9 x 13 pan. Melt chips and butter together. Fold in the marshmallows and Eagle Brand milk. Press in the pan over the peanuts. Press the remaining peanuts on top. Can be kept in refrigerator or frozen. Good served with ice cream.

Betti Kauffman (Host/Cashier)

SNICKER DESSERT

2 c. flour
1 c. margarine
1/2 c. powdered sugar
5 chopped Snicker bars

6 oz. pkg. instant chocolate
pudding
12-16 oz. pkg. whipped topping

Mix first three ingredients. Sprinkle, do not press, into 9 x 13 inch pan. Bake at 350 degrees for 30 minutes or until light brown. Cool completely. Mix pudding according to package directions. Fold in thawed topping and chopped candy bars. Pour into crust and chill.

Mattie Diener (Waitress)

SQUASH PARFAIT SQUARES

1 1/2 c. graham cracker crumbs
1/4 c. margarine, melted
1/4 c. sugar
1/2 c. nuts, finely chopped
1 quart vanilla ice cream
pinch of salt

1 1/2 c. squash
1/2 c. brown sugar
1/2 t. cinnamon
1/4 t. ginger
1/8 t. cloves

Combine crumbs, margarine, sugar, and nuts. Press mixture firmly against sides and bottom of 9" square pan. Bake at 375 degrees for 8 minutes. Cool. Soften ice cream to custard consistency. Mix together squash, sugar, salt, and spices. Stir squash mixture into ice cream. Put into cool crust. Place in freezer until hard. Wrap with foil to store. Remove from freezer 20 minutes before serving.

Linda Wenger (Laundry)

STRAWBERRY FLUFF

1 egg white
3/4 c. sugar

3/4 c. strawberries

Beat egg whites until very stiff. Then beat in sugar and berries, 1 T. at a time. This is wonderful over angel food cake.

Dana Graber (Decorating Department)

STRAWBERRIES CHEESE CAKE TRIFLE

2-8 oz. pkgs. cream cheese	1 T. sugar
2 c. powdered sugar	1 angel food cake torn into
1 c. dairy sour cream	bite size pieces
1/2 t. vanilla	2 qt. fresh strawberries,
1/4 t. almond flavor	thinly sliced
1 c. whipping cream	3 T. sugar
1/2 t. vanilla	3 T. almond flavor

In large bowl, cream together cream cheese and powdered sugar. Add sour cream, vanilla, and almond flavoring. Set aside. In small bowl, mix whipping cream, vanilla, and sugar. Fold whipped cream into cream cheese mixture. Add cake pieces. Set aside. Combine strawberries, sugar, and almond flavoring. Layer together in large bowl, starting with strawberries then adding cake mixture. Continue layering, finish with strawberries. Cover with plastic wrap. Chill well. Yield: 24 servings

Walter Lehman (Essenhaus Foods)

STRAWBERRY DESSERT

Bottom layer

1 c. flour	1 c. chopped nuts
1/2 c. oleo	1 T. powdered sugar

Mix and put in a 9 x 13 pan. Bake at 375 degrees for 20 minutes. Cool.

Middle layer

1 pkg. cream cheese	1 c. powdered sugar
2 to 4 c. Cool Whip	

Mix together and put on top of the bottom layer.

Top layer

Prepare, following the directions, a box of Strawberry Danish Dessert. Fold in some strawberries right after the dessert is cooked. Chill and put on middle layer.

Clara Yoder (Kitchen)

THREE LAYER DESSERT

First layer
2 boxes jello, any flavor   1 c. chopped nuts
1-#2 can crushed pineapple, drained

Second layer
Mix large pkg. cream cheese and 1 c. whipped topping; sugar to taste.

Third layer
Cook 3 egg yolks, 1 c. sugar, 3 t. flour, and 1 c. pineapple juice. If mixture gets too thick, add more pineapple juice or water.

Mrs. John Hochstetler

TOFFEE PUDDING DELIGHT

6 oz. crushed vanilla wafers   1-7 oz. carton frozen whipped
1-3 oz. pkg. instant vanilla   topping
pudding (per pkg. direction)   7 oz. Heath bars, finely chopped

In 9 x 9 pan, layer 1/2 of crushed wafers, half of pudding, half of whipped topping, and half of chopped Heath bars. Repeat layers. Refrigerate overnight.

Clara Yoder (Kitchen)

FRENCH SILK ICE CREAM

6 egg yolks, beaten   1 c. semi-sweet chocolate chips
1 c. sugar   3 c. whipping cream
2 c. half & half   1 T. vanilla

Combine egg yolks, sugar, half & half, and chocolate bits. Heat until mixture is bubbly, stirring often. Stir in cream and vanilla. Chill. Freeze in a one gallon ice cream freezer.

Sharon Boley (Waitress)
Dick Carpenter (Material Handling)

HOMEMADE ICE CREAM

6 eggs	1 can sweetened condensed milk
2 1/2 c. sugar	1 qt. whipping cream
pinch of salt	3 T. vanilla

Beat eggs with electric mixer until well blended. Add sugar and salt slowly. Continue to mix and add sweetened condensed milk, whipping cream, and vanilla. Pour contents into freezer can and fill with whole milk. Be sure to stir well before freezing. Freeze immediately. Makes 1 1/2 gal.

Glenda Yoder (Waitstaff)
Pamela Frey (Bakery)

Some of us are like wheelbarrows -- only useful when pushed, and very easily upset.

ICE CREAM

Pudding

3 pt. milk	3 T. cornstarch
5 c. white sugar	1 T. vanilla
5 eggs	1 can Milnot

Cook ingredients until mixture is bubbly. Add 1 c. brown sugar and 1 package clear gelatin, which has been dissolved in a little cold milk. Add Milnot and enough milk to fill freezer. Yield: 1 1/2 gal.

Wilma Weaver (Waitress)

ICE CREAM

4 eggs
1 1/2 c. corn syrup
1 pt. whipping cream or
1 can evaporated milk
1 can Eagle Brand milk

pinch of salt
2 small boxes vanilla instant
pudding (mix as box directs)
1 T. vanilla
1/2 t. maple flavoring

Beat eggs. Add corn syrup and mix well. Add whipping cream or milk, Eagle Brand milk, salt, pudding, and flavorings. Pour into freezer can. Add enough milk to fill can to 2/3 full. Yield: 1 1/2 gal.

Martha Coblentz (Bakery)

QUICK PEPPERMINT ICE CREAM

20 marshmallows
1 c. hot milk
1/4 t. salt
1 c. whipped cream

1 c. peppermint candy, crushed
1 t. vanilla

Cut marshmallows into small pieces. Add hot milk and salt; stir until dissolved. Remove from heat. Cool and chill. Fold marshmallow mixture into whipped cream and beat until smooth. Fold in crushed candy and vanilla. (Candy may be also be dissolved in hot milk.) Pour into freezer tray and freeze. Yield: 1 qt.

Irene Schrock (Kitchen)

SNOW ICE CREAM

Fill a small pail with clean snow. In a large bowl beat 1 egg, slightly. Add 1/2 c. sugar, a pinch of salt, 1 t. vanilla, and 2 c. milk. Mix well. Stir in snow until it is as thick as desired. Eat at once, as it melts quickly.

Irene Schrock (Kitchen)

Canning,
Freezing &
Miscellaneous

BUYING GUIDE FOR FRESH FRUITS AND VEGETABLES

Experience is the best teacher in choosing quality, but here are a few pointers on buying some of the fruits and vegetables.

Asparagus: Stalks should be tender and firm. Tips should be close and compact. Choose the stalks with very little white, they are more tender. Use asparagus soon, it toughens rapidly.

Beans, Snap: Those with small seeds inside the pods are best. Avoid beans with dry-looking pods.

Berries: Select plump, solid berries with good color. Avoid stained containers, indicating wet or leaky berries. Berries such as blackberries and raspberries with clinging caps may be underripe. Strawberries without caps may be too ripe.

Broccoli, Brussels Sprouts, and Cauliflower: Flower clusters on broccoli and cauliflower should be tight and close together. Brussel sprouts should be firm and compact. Smudgy, dirty spots may indicate insects.

Cabbage and Head Lettuce: Choose heads heavy for size. Avoid cabbage with worm holes, lettuce with discoloration or soft rot.

Cucumbers: Choose long, slender cucumbers for best quality. May be dark or medium green. Yellowed cucumbers are undesirable.

Melons: In cantaloupes, thick close netting on the rind indicates best quality. Cantaloupes are ripe when the stem scar is smooth and space between the netting is yellow or yellow-green. They are best when fully ripe with fruity odor.

Honeydews are ripe when rind has creamy to yellowish color and velvety texture. Immature honeydews are whitish-green.

Ripe watermelons have some yellow color on one side. If melons are white or pale green on one side, they are not ripe.

Oranges, Grapefruit, and Lemons: Choose those heavy for their size. Smoother, thinner skins usually indicate more juice. Most skin markings do not affect quality. Orange with slight greenish tinge may be just as ripe as fully colored ones. Light or greenish-yellow lemons are more tart than deep yellow ones. Avoid citrus fruits showing withered, sunken, or soft areas.

Peas and Lima Beans: Select pods that are well-filled but not bulging. Avoid dried, spotted, yellowed, or flabby pods.

Canning, Freezing & Miscellaneous

APPLE PIE IN A JAR

Syrup

1 t. salt
10 c. water
1/4 t. nutmeg
3 T. lemon juice

4 1/2 c. sugar
2 t. cinnamon
1 c. cornstarch or clear jel

Peel and slice enough apples for 28 c. Fill quart jars with tightly packed apples and cover with syrup. Cook syrup until thick and bubbly. Add the lemon juice. Pour over apples in jar. Process 20 minutes in boiling water.

Esther Nisley (Bakery)

People don't care how much you know until they know how much you care.

BOLOGNA

50 lb. ground beef
1 3/4 lbs. Tender Quick
1 1/2 lb. brown sugar

1/2 oz. salt peter
1/2 t. garlic salt
1 1/2 t. black pepper

Mix above ingredients well. Let set for three days in a cold place, 40 degrees temperature. Add 7 1/2 lbs. cold water and 2 1/2 T. Liquid Smoke. Mix and put in jars for processing. Cook 2 hours or pressure 1 hour.

Millie Whetstone (Kitchen)

BEAN & BACON SOUP (CANNED)

4 lbs. dried navy beans,
soaked overnight
4 lbs. bacon
8 c. potatoes
2 t. pepper
2 bay leaves

4 qts. tomato juice
6 c. onions
4 c. carrots
6 c. celery
salt to taste

Combine all ingredients, except bacon and onion; cook until soft. Cut bacon into fine pieces and fry. Remove bacon and cook cut up onion in bacon grease until soft. Put all ingredients together and heat until it simmers. Remove bay leaves before putting in jars. Makes about 16 quarts. Cold pack 1 hour in 10 lb. pressure or 2 hours in canner.

Freda Yutzy (Waitress)

 If soup tastes very salty, a raw piece of potato placed in the pot will absorb the salt.

BREAD & BUTTER PICKLES

1 gal. pickles, sliced
2 peppers, sliced

8 small onions, sliced
1/2 c. salt

Mix the above ingredients and let set overnight in enough water to cover mixture. Drain pickles and put in quart jars. Make syrup and pour over the pickles.

Syrup

5 c. sugar
1 1/2 t. tumeric
1 t. celery seed

5 c. vinegar
1/2 t. ground cloves
2 T. mustard

Cold pack for 15 minutes.

Katie Miller (Bakery)
Carolyn Hershberger (Bakery)

CANNED APPLE PIE FILLING

5 c. water
7 - 8 c. sugar

12 rounded T. clear jel

Cook this mixture well. Slice about 7 1/2 quarts apples in a dish pan. Pour the cooked mixture over sliced apples and mix. Put in cans and cold pack for 20 minutes.

For pies:
Sprinkle with cinnamon and dot with butter. Add a top crust or add crumbs on top. For more tartness add lemon juice. Bake at 350 degrees until bubbling.

Crumbs
3/4 c. flour
1/2 c. sugar

1/3 c. butter

Mix well and put on top of pie.

Susanna Miller (Cook)

CANNING STEAK

2 gallon water   2 c. salt (scant)
2 c. brown sugar

Cook together and then cool. Put meat (thinly sliced), enough to fill a 13 quart mixing bowl, in canning jars and add 1 t. salt and 1 c. of above mixture to each quart. Cook in pressure cooker 1/2 hour (10 pounds pressure).

CHICKEN BOLOGNA

25 lbs. ground chicken   1 lb. tender quick

Mix and let stand for 12 or 24 hours. Add:

1 oz. black pepper   1/2 c. sugar
2 t. salt peter   3 T. liquid smoke
2 t. garlic salt

Mix well. Put in jars. Cold pack for 3 hours.

Freda Yutzy (Waitress)

CHILI SAUCE (CANNED)

1 gal.tomatoes(chopped & peeled) 2 c. chopped onion
2 c. chopped celery   3 T. salt
1 T. mustard seed   1 t. allspice
1 t. cinnamon   2 c. vinegar
2 c. sugar

Cook tomatoes 15 minutes. Pour off most of juice. Add all other ingredients. Cook 1/2 hour or until all ingredients are tender. Thicken with 4 to 6 T. cornstarch. Put in jars and can.

Walter Lehman (Essenhaus Foods)
Freda Yutzy (Waitress)

DILL PICKLES

1 qt. water
1/8 c. salt

1 c. vinegar
1 T. sugar

Combine ingredients. Decrease the amount of water used if cucumbers sliced or peeled. Soak pickles overnight in this mixture. Drain liquid off pickles and melt sugar in liquid. Pour over pickles in jars. Put dill on top. May add 1 garlic clove. In hot water bath, bring to a boil. Take off heat. Let set for 10 to 15 minutes. Remove from water. Cool jars.

Ronda Yoder (Waitress)

DILLY BEANS (CANNED)

Stuff pint jars with fresh green beans, lengthwise. Do not snap beans. In each jar put:

1/4 t. tabasco sauce or
cayenne pepper
1 clove garlic

1/2 t. mustard seed (optional)
1 dill head

Bring to boil:

5 c. vinegar
1/2 c. salt

5 c. water

Pour this mixture over beans. This will make 6 to 8 pints of beans. Process for 10 to 15 minutes.

Doreen Mast (Knot N Grain)

FREEZER CORN

4 qt. corn (cut off ear)
4 t. salt

1 c. sugar
1 qt. water

Boil 5 minutes. Stir to keep from sticking to kettle. Put kettle in sink of cold water to cool. Put cold corn in freezer boxes. Use juice to cover corn. Do not drain.

Joann Bontrager (Busser)

MINCE MEAT

2 lbs. cooked lean ground beef
1 1/2 t. cinnamon
2 t. salt
1/2 c. dark corn syrup

1 1/4 t. nutmeg
4 lbs. apples, ground
1 lb. raisins
4 c. brown sugar

Combine all ingredients and add water or cider to moisten until sloppy. Simmer until meats and fruits are tender and flavors are blended. Pack in jars and seal.

Walter Lehman (Essenhaus Foods)

MIXED PICKLES

2 to 3 qt. lima beans
1 qt. carrots, chunked
1 1/2 qt. celery, chunked

small amount of onions, chunked
3-5 heads cauliflower, chunked

Cook each ingredient separately in salt water. Mix all together. Add:

1 qt. raw mangos
3 1/2 qt. vinegar

2 qt. pickles
6 lb. sugar (granulated)

Add vinegar and sugar to ingredients. Heat and seal.

Marna Schlabach (Kitchen)

MOCK PINEAPPLE (CANNED)

1 gallon zucchini, peeled,
seeded & ground up
3 c. sugar

1 1/2 c. Realemon
1-46 oz. can pineapple juice

Bring to a boil. Simmer 20 minutes. Pack into pint jars. Cold pack for 30 minutes. Good for zucchini cake and bars.

Mary Lehman (Bakery)

PEACHES (FREEZING)

7 c. sugar
1 lg. can frozen Minute Maid
orange juice concentrate

17-20 lbs. peaches, sliced & peeled

Mix sugar and juice together. Add sliced peaches to the mixture. Put in containers and freeze.

Freda Yutzy (Waitress)

Patient: Doc, Am I getting any better?
Doctor: I don't know. Let me feel your purse.

PICKLED CABBAGE (CANNING)

7 qt. shredded cabbage
7 green peppers, diced thin

7 large green tomatoes, sliced
5 large onions, sliced thin

Make a solution containing:

4 c. vinegar
3 c. sugar
3 T. salt

4 1/2 t. tumeric
2 box mustard seed

Cook all vegetables and solution until very hot. Put in jars and seal.

Frances Blough (Waitress)

PICKLED OKRA

1 garlic clove or
1/2 t. garlic powder

1 t. dill seed
hot pepper, optional

Use each of the above ingredients per pint jar.

small sized okra
2 c. water

3 c. white vinegar
6 T. salt, canning

Place spices in each pint jar. Pack okra in the jar. Combine vinegar, water and the salt in a saucepan and bring to a boil. Simmer for 5 minutes. Pour over the okra. When bubbling stops, seal. Ready to eat in 2 weeks. Chill before serving.
Yield: 4 pints

Fannie Yoder (Van Driver)

PICKLES (TO CAN)

6 qt. sliced pickles

6 medium onions, sliced or chopped

Add 1/2 c. salt to ingredients and cover with water. Let set overnight. Drain and add the following:

3 c. vinegar
2 c. water
1 T. mustard seed

1 T. celery seed
3 c. brown sugar
3 c. white sugar

Bring to boil. Put in jars and seal.

Mary K. Schrock (Kitchen)

 Don't let your parents down. Remember, they brought you up.

PIZZA SAUCE (CANNED)

4 qts. tomato juice
8 t. basil
4 t. oregano
4 t. salt
1 chopped onion
3 slices Velveeta cheese

3 t. pepper
4 t. garlic salt
1/2 T. tabasco sauce
3/4 c. brown sugar
8 T. butter

Mix all ingredients and simmer until desired thickness. Pour into jars and process 20 - 25 minutes.

Doreen Mast (Knot N Grain)

PIZZA SAUCE

Dice and cook 3 pounds of onions and 1 1/2 T. crushed red pepper in a pint of vegetable oil. Add this to 11 quarts of tomato juice; add 4-12 oz. tomato paste, 1 T. sweet basil, 1 T. oregano, 1 1/2 c. sugar, and 1/3 c. salt. Boil for one hour and seal. Boil 2 or 3 garlic buds with tomato juice before putting through the sieve.

Freda Yutzy (Waitress)

PORK AND BEANS

Soak 10 pounds of dry beans over night in plenty of water. Drain water off and put beans in cans. Make cans a little over half full. Then mix the following liquid and pour over beans until cans are full.

8 qt. tomato juice
1 c. salt
4 c. white sugar
8 c. brown sugar

2 T. mustard
4 tsp. black pepper
1 c. cornstarch

Cold pack for 3 hours.

Walter Lehman (Essenhaus Foods)

Happiness makes up in height what it lacks in strength.

RED BEETS (TO CAN)

6 c. white sugar
3 t. celery seed
1 qt. vinegar

1 qt. water
3 t. mustard seed
1/4 c. salt

Mix ingredients. Bring to boiling point. Add 1 1/2 to 2 gallons red beets which have been cooked until tender, peeled, and cut to desired size. Bring to boiling point again. Put in jars and seal.

Ida Weaver (Waitress)

RED CINNAMON PICKLES

Peel, seed, and cut into chunks 2 gallons of large pickles. Soak in 8 1/2 quarts of warm water with 2 cups of lime for 24 hours. Drain and wash. Soak in cold water for 3 hours. Put into a large kettle and simmer for 2 hours in the following solution:

1 c. vinegar
1 T. alum

1 small bottle red food coloring
water to cover

Drain liquid. Make a syrup of the following:

6 c. vinegar
6 c. water
2 T. salt

20 c. sugar
16 cinnamon sticks
20 oz. red hots candy

Bring to a boil and pour over the cucumbers. Let stand overnight. Drain juice off pickles and re-heat the juice each day for three days. On the fourth day, heat juice and pack in jars.

Walter Lehman (Essenhaus Foods)

SALSA

8 c. diced tomatoes	2 c. green bell peppers, diced
1 c. diced hot peppers,	1 T. salt
jalapeno or chili	2 c. vinegar
2 c. diced onions	3 cloves garlic, grated

Bring the above ingredients to a boil. Lower heat and simmer for 2 hours. Add:

8 c. chopped tomatoes	1 c. chopped hot peppers
1 c. chopped green peppers	1 c. minced garlic
1 c. chopped onions	1 c. fresh chopped parsley

Continue cooking. While this cooks down, add 8 c. tomatoes and 1/2 c. vinegar. Cook down and add 8 c. chopped tomatoes, 1/2 c. vinegar. Cook down and add 8 c. chopped tomatoes, 1 c. chopped peppers, and 1 clove of minced garlic. I cook this for 7 hours total. Process in hot water bath for 10 minutes.

Dana Graber (Decorating Department)

SALSA

16-18 lb. tomatoes	10 cloves garlic or
6 sweet peppers	2 1/2 t. powder
4 chili peppers	8 jalapeno peppers
2 large onions	3 stalks celery

Chop all ingredients in a food processor or blender. Cook together for 10 to 15 minutes. Add:

3/4 c. white sugar	1 t. cumin
3/4 c. vinegar	1 1/2 c. clear jel
1/4 c. salt	1 T. oregano

Mix together. Add to the tomato mixture. Cook a bit. Cold pack for 20 minutes. Yield: 7 to 8 quarts

Option: You can cook the first 7 ingredients then put through a strainer.

Esther Nisley (Bakery)

SALSA

10-12 c. chopped tomatoes
2 c. green peppers
1/4 c. chopped hot peppers
4 1/2 c. chopped onions
3 c. chopped celery

1 T. salt
1 c. vinegar
2 T. parsley
2 t. oregano
1 or 2 garlic cloves

Mix all ingredients together and cook until vegetables are soft. Put into jars. Hot bath to seal. Serve with chips.

Laura Bontrager (Bakery)

SALSA

3 gallons tomato juice
2 T. oregano
1 T. paprika
hot peppers, w/seeds,
chopped fine

1 c. brown sugar
1 T. salt
1 T. black pepper
1 T. chili powder

Mix all ingredients and thicken with 2 c. clear jel. Add 10 green peppers and 10 onions, chopped fine or ground. Cold pack 10 to 20 minutes.

Lorene Schlabach (Cahsier/Dutch Country Gifts)

SPICE FOR TOMATO JUICE

1/2 c. celery salt
2 T. garlic salt
2 T. pepper

1/2 c. onion salt
3 T. sugar

Mix all ingredients together. Add 1 t. to a quart of juice. Add to juice before cold pack.

Rosanna Miller (Kitchen)

292

VEGETABLE JUICE (CANNED)

1 canner full of tomatoes   1/2 c. parsley
1 stalk celery   5 carrots
1/2 c. salt   1 c. brown sugar
3 onions   2 T. black pepper
2 peppers

Cook all ingredients together until vegetables are soft. Put through the strainer. Put into jars. Cold pack for 15 minutes.

Mary Lehman (Bakery)

VEGETABLE DRINK (CANNED)

2 qt. celery   4 onions
2 to 4 red beets   2 gal. tomato juice
6 carrots

Cook all ingedients, separately, until very soft. Mash vegetables. Strain and add 3 diced lemons, rinds and all. Add salt to taste. Cold pack for 10 minutes.

Irene Schrock (Kitchen)

VENISON BREAKFAST SAUSAGE

5 lb. ground venison,   5 t. tender quick curing salt
pork suet added   1 c. (8 oz.) beer or water
1 T. crushed sage leaves   1 T. coarse ground black pepper
1 T. crushed red (hot) peppers

After mixing ingredients, form patties or stuff in hog casings (use sheep casings for smaller links). Age in refrigerator for three days, then freeze for later use. Smoking (just a touch) is a worthwhile option.

David M. Lane (Material Handling)

APPLE BUTTER

3 gal. apple snitz,   10 lb. sugar
whole apples quartered,   1 qt. water
not peeled

Combine in 20 quart stockpot. Cover and boil slowly for 3 to 4 hours without removing cover. Remove from heat and put through sieve or food mill to remove apple peelings . Thoroughly mix.

Add:

1/2 c. vinegar   2 t. cinnamon
1/2 t. cloves   1 1/2 t. salt
1/2 t. allspice

Put in jars and seal. Cook in hot water for approximately 10 minutes.

Lena Miller (Meat Room)

DANDELION JELLY

Early in the morning, to avoid insects, pick 1 quart of dandelion blossoms, without stems. Boil blossoms in 1 quart water for 3 minutes. Drain and save the liquid. Use 3 c. dandelion liquid, 1 t. lemon or orange extract, 1 package powdered pectin, and 4 1/2 c. sugar. Cook jelly according to directions on Sure Jel box.

JoAnn Miller (Shop Supervisor)

GOOD APPLE BUTTER

10 lb. of uncooked apples   1/2 c. vinegar (scant)
or 5 qt. apple sauce   4 lbs. sugar

Mix in large roaster and boil in oven for 2 hours. Stir occasionally. Put in jars and seal.

Lori Miller (Waitress)

GREEN TOMATO JAM

5 c. green tomatoes 4 c. sugar
1 T. lemon

Cook 15 minutes. Add 1 box raspberry jello. Jam tastes like raspberry jam.

Katie Miller (Bakery)

PEACH MARMALADE

5 c. mashed peaches 7 c. sugar
1 small can crushed pineapple

Cook together 15 minutes. Add 2 small or 1 large box orange jello. Cook until jello is dissolved. Pour into jars and seal.

Erma Yoder (Maintenance)

PEACH PRESERVES JELLY

Cook peach stones and peelings (in enough water to cover) for 10 minutes. Drain. Use juice to make same as raspberry jelly using the recipe on the Sure Jel box. Must be sure to have enough juice from the peach stone water.

Clara Yoder (Kitchen)

PINEAPPLE JAM

7 c. sugar 5 c. crushed pineapple, unsweetened

Boil for 15 minutes. Add 1-6 oz. box of orange jello. Put in jars and seal.

Esther Nisley (Bakery)

RED BEET JELLY

6 c. red beet juice   2 boxes Sure Jel
8 c. sugar   2-6 oz. box raspberry jello
1/2 c. lemon juice

Follow "Grape Jelly" recipe on Sure Jel box.

Erma Yoder (Maintenance)

STRAWBERRY-RHUBARB JAM

5 c. rhubarb, diced   4 c. sugar

Mix and cook to a rolling boil, 10 minutes. Add 2 small boxes of strawberry Jello and mix well. Put in your jam jars and freeze.

Judy Beachy (Kitchen Supervisor)

CORN RELISH

9 ears corn   1/2 c. peppers
1 c. celery   1 c. onions
1/4 c. vinegar, a little less 1/2 c. oil
1/4 t. tumeric   1 t. dry mustard

Cook corn in boiling water about 5 minutes. Remove, cool and cut off the cob. Add remaining ingredients. Mix well and refrigerate overnight. Makes 3 - 4 c.

Becky Helmuth (Waitress)

Every time a jar is opened
For my family's repast,
I shall serve, as an extra,
Memories of the summer past.

CORN RELISH

4 T. flour, heaping
3 T. ground mustard
1 T. tumeric
1 gallon vinegar
6 T. salt
6 sweet peppers, diced

5 c. sugar
4 stalks celery, diced
22 pts. cabbage, shredded
22 pts. whole kernel corn, off the cob

Mix flour, mustard, tumeric. Add vinegar and mix well until forms a paste. Add the remaining ingredients and cook until vegetables are soft. Put into cans and hot bath to seal.

Sophia Helmuth, Becky Helmuth's Mother (Waitress)

LAZY HOUSEWIFE PICKLES

2 c. vinegar
1/4 c. mustard

1/4 c. salt
4 c. small fresh cucumbers

Mix together vinegar, mustard, and salt. Add the cucumbers. Let set for 2 days before eating. Do not heat!

Bertha Miller (Shop Supervisor)

CHEESE BALL

2-8 oz. cream cheese, soft
1 roll of bacon cheese
2 T. worcestershire sauce
sprinkle of garlic salt

sprinkle of Lawry's salt
2 T. diced onion
1 pkg. dried beef

Mix and form into ball. Refrigerate 1 hour, longer refrigeration is better.

Wanda Sue Bontrager (Grill Cook)

Never trouble another for what you can do yourself.

HOME MADE SWEETENED CONDENSED MILK

1/3 c. boiling water　　　　　1 c. instant dry milk
3 T. melted butter　　　　　　2/3 c. sugar

Combine all ingredients in blender and process until smooth. Pinch of salt may be added. Store in refrigerator. Keeps for several weeks.

Rosanna Miller (Cook)

PLAY DOUGH

1 c. flour　　　　　　　　　1 c. water
1/2 c. salt　　　　　　　　　2 T. vegetable oil
2 t. cream of tartar

Cook on medium heat until forms a ball (about 2 minutes). Place in baggy or in an airtight container. It will last for several months. It is ideal for young children.

Betty Troyer (Kitchen)

PLAY DOUGH

3 c. flour (or more)　　　　　4 T. alum powder
1 c. salt　　　　　　　　　　3 c. boiling water

Mix with spoon. Add 2 T. vegetable oil and food coloring.

Erma Yoder (Maintenance)

 People who fly into a rage always make a bad landing.

SCHOOL PASTE

1/2 c. flour	1/2 c. sugar
1/2 t. powdered alum	2 c. water

Cook on low heat, stirring constantly, until thick. Remove from heat. Add 15 drops of oil of cloves. Makes one pint. Will keep for several months.

Treva Yoder (Miller's Housekeeper)

HERMAN

Starter:

1/2 c. warm water	1 t. sugar
1 pkg. yeast	

Mix and let rise. It is now ready to feed.

Directions to feed:

Feed Herman on the first and fifth day (1/2 c. sugar, 1 c. flour, and 1 c. milk). On the tenth day, bake him. Keep Herman refrigerated in a glass or plastic bowl. Keep him covered, but not tightly. Stir Herman every day and he will stay happy.

HERMAN CAKE

2 c. Herman	1 c. sugar
2 c. flour	2 eggs
1/2 t. soda	2/3 c. oil
1/2 t. salt	1 c. raisins
1 1/2 t. cinnamon	1 c. nuts
2 T. baking powder	

Pour into 9 x 13 pan. Put a mixture of 1 c. brown sugar, 1 T. flour, 1 T. cinnamon, and 1/3 c. melted butter or oleo on top. Bake at 350 degrees for 35 to 40 minutes. Glaze with powdered sugar icing.

299

HERMAN CINNAMON ROLLS

2 c. Herman
2 c. flour
1/2 t. salt

1/2 t. soda
4 t. baking powder
1/2 c. oil

Mix and knead slightly on a floured board, until it is not sticky. Roll out dough to 1/4 " thick and spread with oleo. Sprinkle with cinnamon and sugar. Roll up as for jelly roll. Slice into 1/2" slices. Combine 1 stick of oleo, 1 c. brown sugar, and 1/2 c. nuts in the bottom of a 9 x 12 pan and place the slices of Herman on top. Bake at 350 degrees for 35 minutes.

HERMAN PANCAKES

1 c. Herman
1 c. flour
1/2 t. salt
1/2 t. soda

2 t. baking powder
1 c. milk
2 eggs, beaten

Combine dry ingredients. Blend with remaining ingredients. Mix until moistened. Use 1/4 c. batter for each pancake.

HERMAN BREAD

2 c. Herman
2 c. flour
1 1/2 t. soda
1/2 t. salt
1 c. sugar
1 1/2 t. cinnamon

2 eggs
2/3 c. oil
1 c. nuts, raisins, dates,
apples, or omit cinnamon
and use chocolate chips

Mix ingredients thoroughly and pour into greased pans. Bake at 350 degrees for 40 to 45 minutes.

Worry pulls tomorrow's clouds over today's sunshine.

HERMAN BISCUITS

1 c. Herman   1/4 t. salt
1 c. flour   1/3 c. oil
3/4 t. baking soda

Mix ingredients together. Drop by tablespoon on a baking sheet and
bake for 12 to 15 minutes at 350 degrees.

HERB MIXTURE (USE IN PLACE OF SALT)

1 t. pepper   2 t. basil, crushed fine
1 t. marjoram   6 t. paprika
1 t. cayenne   1 t. garlic powder
6 t. parsley, dried, crushed fine   6 t. onion powder

Mix all ingredients together and put in shaker with large holes. Can use
T. when mixing a larger batch.

Elma Miller (Waitress)

NOODLES

6 eggs   1/8 t. salt
1 to 2 T. water   4 c. flour

Combine and mix together eggs, small amount of yellow food coloring,
salt, and water. Add flour until well blended, but not sticky. Knead for 5
to 10 minutes. Cover & let rest for 30 minutes. Divide dough into
fourths and roll out thin on floured board. Let dry for 1/2 hour. Stack
sheets of dough on top of each other, sprinkling flour in between. Roll
up and cut into desired widths. Spread them out on a paper bag to dry
for at least one hour before cooking. If you do not intend to use right
away, place in zip-lock freezer bags and store (completely dry) in the
freezer until ready to use.

Wilma Weaver (Waitress)

NOODLES

2 c. egg yolks   1 1/2 c. hot water

Beat. Set scales at O. Put Fix Mix bowl on scales and fill to 4 lbs. with pastry flour. Let set with cover on for 15 minutes after mixing to egg mixture. Dough handles better when using hot water. Make a ball of dough and put through noodle cutter.

Mattie Marie Diener (Waitress)
Ida Weaver (Waitress)

NOODLES

2 qt. egg yolks   3 to 4 lbs. flour
1 c. water

Stir flour into the beaten egg yolk and water mixture. Roll dough out in thin sheets and let dry. Cut into noodles. Makes about 5 pounds.

Mary K. Schmucker (Kitchen)

SALT-FREE HOT "N" SPICY SEASONING BLEND

2 T. savory, crushed   1 1/4 t. ground pepper
1 T. powdered mustard   1 1/2 t. ground cumin
1 T. onion powder   1 t. garlic powder
1 t. curry powder

Combine all ingredients and mix well. Spoon into shaker with holes or stir in a small dish with plastic lid. Makes about 1/3 c. Use on meat, poultry, fish, vegetables, soups, or salads.

Elma Miller (Waitress)

Index

303